neil young and crazy horse

sleeps with angels

Transcribed by JOE DELORO

Special thanks to Joel Bernstein

editor: AARON STANG
transcription editors: COLGAN BRYAN and AARON STANG
digital photography: LARRY JOHNSON
design: ELAN SOLTES and JESSICA NARKUNSKI
    FX + DESIGN
book design: RICHARD CHIMELIS / THE POINT

© 1995 WARNER BROS. PUBLICATIONS INC.
All Rights Reserved

Any duplication, adaptation or arrangement of the compositions
contained in this collection requires the written consent of the Publisher.
No part of this book may be photocopied or reduced in any way without permission.
Unauthorized uses are an infringement of U.S. Copyright Act and are punishable by Law.

ISBN 0-89724-524-5

MY HEART
Down in the valley the shepherd sees
His flock is close at hand
And in the night sky a star is falling down
From someone's hand

Somewhere, somewhere
I've got to get somewhere
It's not too late, it's not too late
I've got to get somewhere

This time I will take the lead somehow
This time you won't have to show me how

When dreams come crashing down like trees
I don't know what love can do
When life is hanging in the breeze
I don't know what love can do

My heart, my heart
I've got to keep my heart
It's not too late, it's not too late
I've got to keep my heart

My love, I will give to you it's true
Although I'm not sure what love can do

Somewhere, somewhere
I've got to get somewhere
It's not too late, it's not too late
I've got to get somewhere

Somewhere someone has a dream come true
Somehow someone has a dream come true

PRIME OF LIFE
Shadows climb up the garden wall
Upon the green the first leaf falls
It's the prime of life and the king and queen
Step out into the sun (Oh yeah)

Are you feeling all right
Not feeling too bad myself
Are you feeling all right, my friend?

Footsteps run down the castle hall
To the rooms of the paper doll

It's the prime of life, where the spirit grows
And the mirror shows both ways (Oh yeah)

Are you feeling all right
Not feeling too bad myself
Are you feeling all right, my friend?

When I first saw your face
It took my breath away
When I first saw your face
It took my breath away

Shadows climb up the garden wall
Upon the green the first leaf falls
It's the prime of life and the king and queen
Step out into the sun (Oh yeah)

Are you feeling all right
Not feeling too bad myself
Are you feeling all right, my friend?

DRIVEBY

It's a random kind of thing
Came upon a delicate flower
I can't believe a machine gun sings
Driveby, driveby, driveby, driveby

Well he borrowed his girlfriend's car
Went out riding with the boys
Now she's gone like a shooting star
Driveby, driveby, driveby, driveby

Now she's gone like a shooting star
Trail of dreams Tragic trail of fire
Now she's gone like a shooting star
Driveby, driveby, driveby, driveby

Well you feel invincible
It's just a part of life
There's a feud going on and you don't know
Driveby, driveby, driveby, driveby

SLEEPS WITH ANGELS

She wasn't perfect
She had some trips of her own
He wasn't worried
At least he wasn't alone (Too late)
He sleeps with angels (Too soon)
He's always on someone's mind
He sleeps with angels (Too late)
He sleeps with angels (Too soon)

She was a teen queen
She saw the dark side of life
She made things happen
But when he did it that night
She ran up phone bills
She moved around from town to town (Too late)
He sleeps with angels (Too soon)
He's always on someone's mind
He sleeps with angels
He sleeps with angels

WESTERN HERO

Frontier town, home of the western hero
Frontier justice, dealt with the iron hand

He wore a long coat to the ground
He wore big boots that made a sound
He wore a six gun on his hip
But now he doesn't carry it

Sure enough, he was a western hero
On the deck, sighting an old Jap zero

And on the shores at Normandy
He fought for you, he fought for me
Across the land and on the sea
But now he's just a memory

And in the distance, the rocket's red glare
The bombs burst in the air
This time we're never going back

Through the years he changed somehow
He's different now
He's different now

Open Fire, here comes a western hero
Standing there, big money in his hand
Sure enough, he was a western hero, Sure enough

CHANGE YOUR MIND

When you get weak, and you need to test your will
When life's complete, but there's something missing still
Distracting you from this must be the one you love
Must be the one whose magic touch can change your mind
Don't let another day go by without the magic touch

Distracting you   (Change your mind)
Supporting you   (Change your mind)
Embracing you   (Change your mind)
Convincing you   (Change your mind)

When you're confused and the world has got you down
When you feel used and you just can't play the clown
Protecting you from this must be the one you love
Must be the one whose magic touch can change your mind
Don't let another day go by without the magic touch

Protecting you   (Change your mind)
Restoring you   (Change your mind)
Revealing you   (Change your mind)
Soothing you   (Change your mind)

You hear the sound, you wait around and get the word
You see the picture changing everything you've heard
Destroying you with this must be the one you love
Must be the one whose magic touch can change your mind
Don't let another day go by without the magic touch

Destroying you   (Change your mind)
Embracing you   (Change your mind)
Protecting you   (Change your mind)
Confining you   (Change your mind)
Distracting you   (Change your mind)
Supporting you   (Change your mind)
Distorting you   (Change your mind)
Controlling you   (Change your mind)
Change your mind   (Change your mind)
Change your mind, change your mind (Change your mind)
Change your mind

The morning comes there's an odor in the room
The scent of love, more than a million roses bloom
Embracing you with this must be the one you love
Must be the one whose magic touch can change your mind
Don't let another day go by without the magic touch

Embracing you   (Change your mind)
Concealing you   (Change your mind)
Protecting you   (Change your mind)
Revealing you   (Change your mind)
Change your mind, change your mind (Change your mind)
Change your mind   (Change your mind)
Change your mind, change your mind (Change your mind)
Change your mind   (Change your mind)
Change your mind, change your mind
Change your mind
Change your mind, change your mind
Change your mind
Change your mind, change your mind
Change your mind, change your mind

BLUE EDEN

Embracing, distorting, supporting, comforting
Convincing you, consoling you
Controlling you, destroying you
All over you

I know someday we'll meet again
We come and go that way my friend
It's part of me, it's part of you

You feel invincible, it's just a part of life
You feel invincible, it's just a part of life

SAFEWAY CART
Like a Safeway cart rolling down the street
Like a sandal mark on the Savior's feet
Just keep rolling on it's a ghetto dawn

Baby looks so bad with her TV eyes
Going, going, gone and the picture cries
It's a ghetto dawn

Baby looks so bad with her TV eyes
Going, going, gone and the picture cries
Baby looks so bad with her TV eyes

Like a Safeway cart rolling down the street
Past the Handy mart to the Savior's feet
Going, going, gone and the picture cries

Baby looks so sad
Baby looks so bad
It's a ghetto dawn

Like a Safeway cart rolling down the street
Like a sandal mark on the Savior's feet
Just keep rolling on to a ghetto dawn

TRAIN OF LOVE
Train of love
Racing from heart to heart
Running late
Still in the lonely part
This train will never run me down
But only take me where I'm bound
It's part of me and part of you
I'll always be a part of you

Sail along, Sail along silver moon
Don't be blue
Throw shadows in my room
I know in time we'll meet again
We come and go that way, my friend
It's part of me and part of you
I'll always be a part of you

"To love and honor 'til death do us part"
Repeat after me
This train is never going back
When the lonesome whistle blows
No one knows, No one knows

Train of love, Train of love
Train of love, Train of love
It's part of me, it's part of you
Train of love

TRANS AM
Trans Am
The wagons in the valley had pulled up for the night
Seth said "go get the plow out Merle, this place looks just right"
By then they were surrounded, by dawn they all were dead
I heard this from the old Trans Am, up the road ahead
That cowboy just kept talking, I thought I heard him say
He used to ride the Sante Fe before the tracks were laid
Trans Am

A nasty wind was blowing through the gates of Eden Park
One was swinging and one was hanging,
and the street lights all were dark
It crawled along the boulevard with two wheels on the grass
That old Trans Am was dying hard, but still had lots of gas
The golden gate was open wide, the sun came shining through
Where once the angels stood and cried everything was new
Trans Am

Global manufacturing, hands across the sea
The hotel filled with dealers, everything was free
Before the competition, ahead of all the rest
The product was presented, it clearly was the best
The power link was ruptured, the hotel shook and rolled
The old Trans Am just bounced around and took another road
Trans Am

An old friend showed up at the door
The mile posts flying by
He said come on, I said what for
He said I'll show you why
I got a call from north of here
They said some girl's broke down
There's good money in it for you and me
If we can get her back to town
She's somewhere north of Barstow
Lost on 66
An old Trans Am by the side of the road
That needs a headlight fixed
Trans Am

PIECE OF CRAP
Tried to save the trees
Bought a plastic bag
The bottom fell out
It was a piece of crap

Saw it on the tube
Bought it on the phone
Now you're home alone
It's a piece of crap

I tried to plug it in
I tried to turn it on
When I got it home
It was a piece of crap

Got it from a friend
On him you can depend
I found out in the end
It was a piece of crap

I'm trying to save the trees
I saw it on TV
They cut the forest down
To build a piece of crap

I went back to the store
They gave me four more
The guy told me at the door
It's a piece of crap

A DREAM THAT CAN LAST
I feel like I died and went to heaven
The cupboards are bare but the streets are paved with gold

I saw a young girl who didn't die
I saw a glimmer from in her eye
I saw the distance, I saw the past
And I know I won't awaken, it's a dream that can last

I feel like I died and went to heaven
The cupboards are bare but the streets are paved with gold

And all the lights were turned down low
And no one wondered or had to go
Out on the corner the angels say
There is a better life for me someday

I feel like I died and went to heaven
The cupboards are bare but the streets are paved wilh gold

Words and Music by Neil Young
except BLUE EDEN by Neil Young, Frank "Poncho"
Sampedro, Billy Talbot and Ralph Molina.
All songs ©1994 Silver Fiddle Music ASCAP
except TRAIN OF LOVE ©1993 Silver Fiddle Music ASCAP
and BLUE EDEN ©1994 Silver Fiddle Music ASCAP/
Falmouth Music BMI. Lyrics Reprinted by Permission.
All Rights Reserved.

contents

- A Dream That Can Last — 154
- Blue Eden — 91
- Change Your Mind — 55
- Driveby — 24
- My Heart — 6
- Piece Of Crap — 140
- Prime Of Life — 11
- Safeway Cart — 106
- Sleeps With Angels — 33
- Train Of Love — 112
- Trans Am — 123
- Western Hero — 46

PRIME OF LIFE

Words and Music by
NEIL YOUNG

* Gtr. 2 tuning: ⑥ = D.

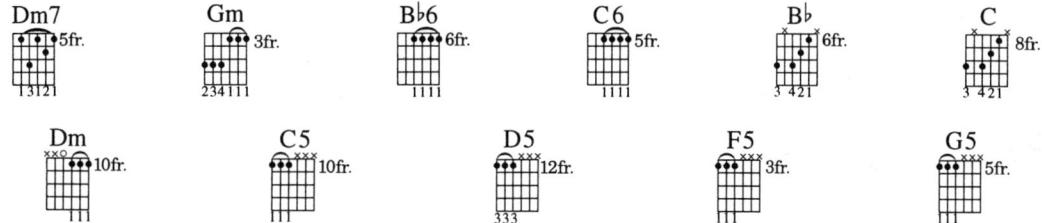

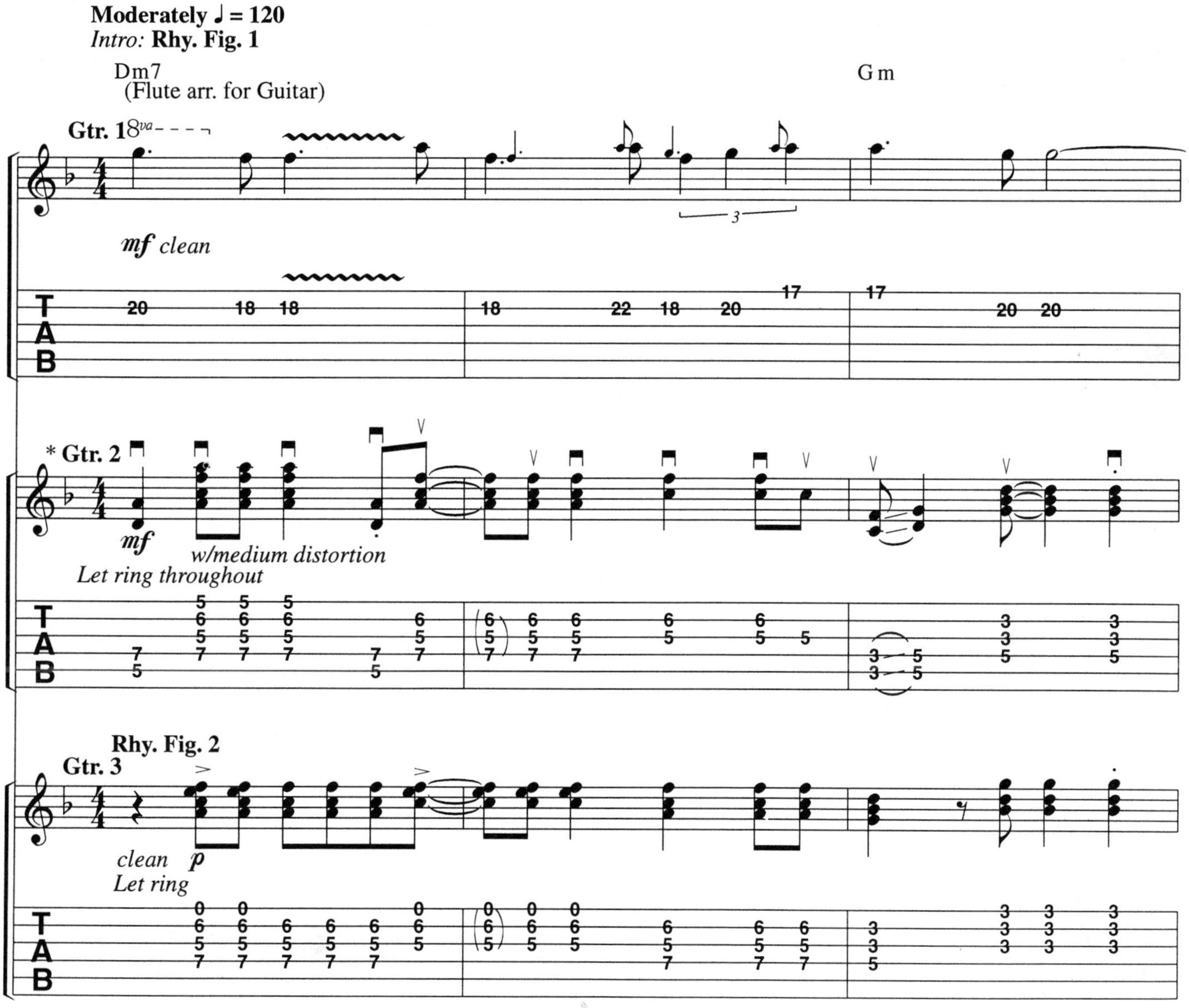

Verse:

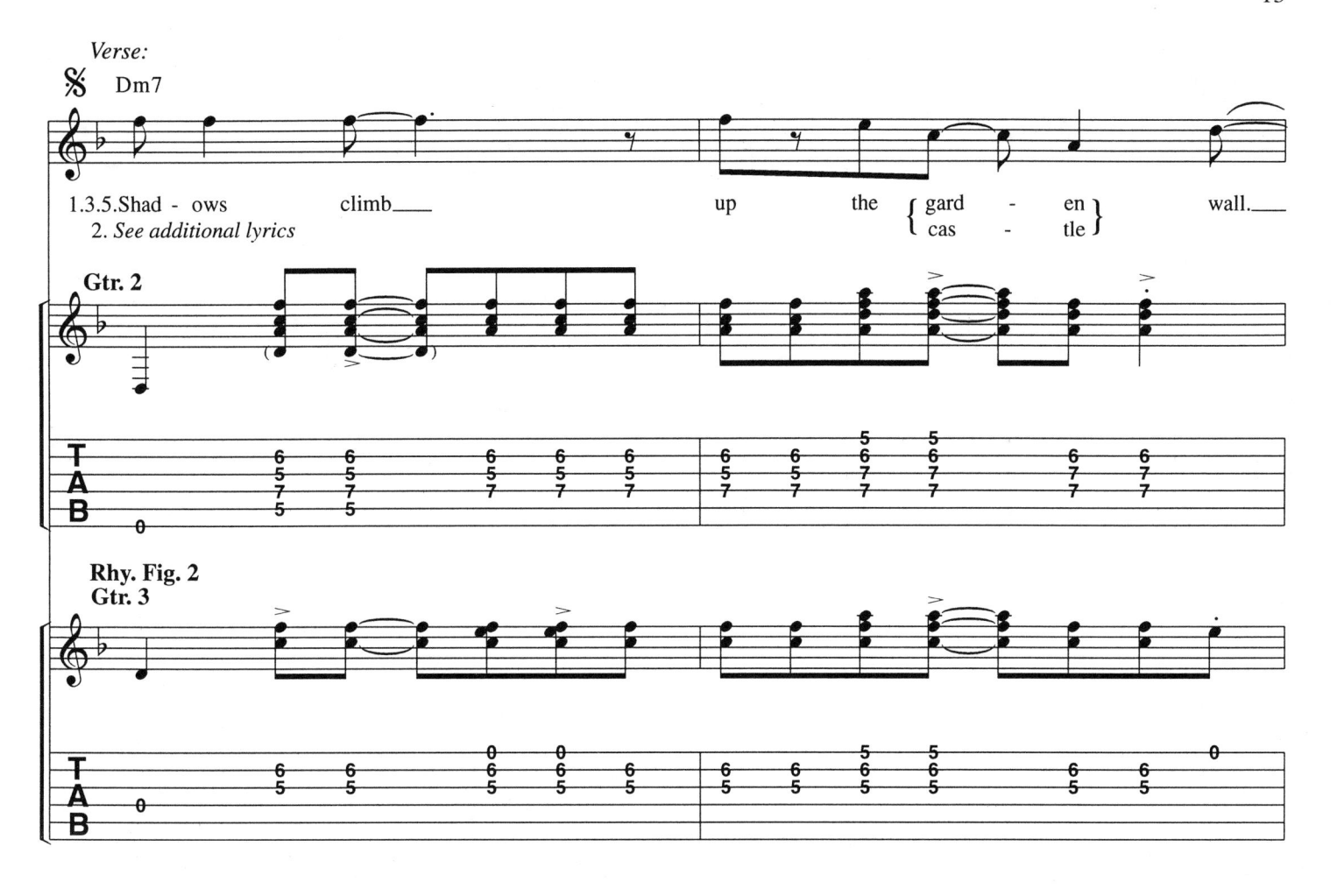

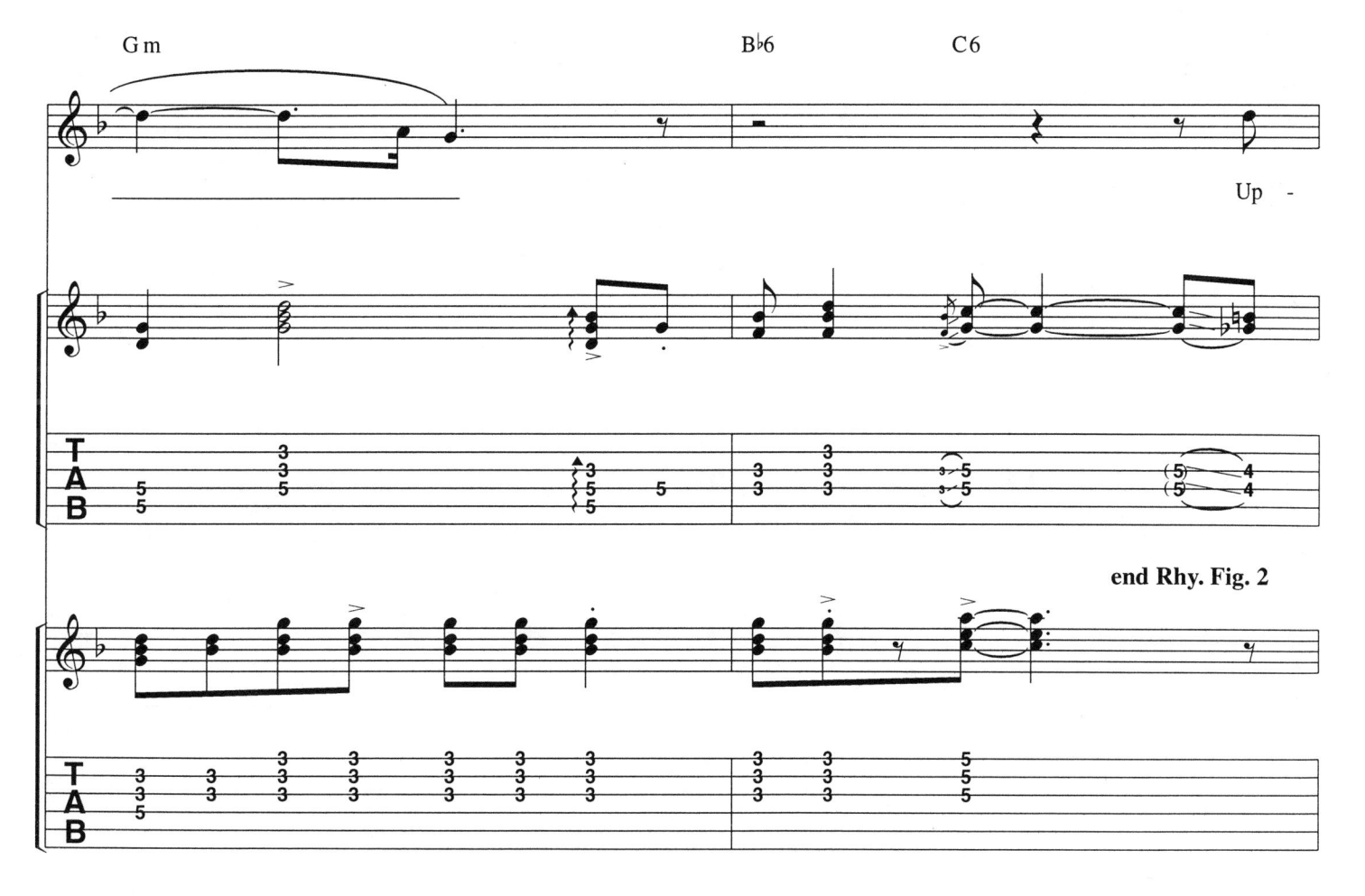

1.3.5. Shad - ows climb up the {garden / castle} wall.
2. *See additional lyrics*

Up -

w/Rhy. Fig. 2
To Coda
Dm7
Gm
B♭6
C6
on the green_ the first leaf falls.
Its the
Gtr. 2
Chorus:
Dm
Gm
Gm7
Dm
1. prime of life and the king and queen_ step out in - to the sun._
2. See additional lyrics
Background Vocals: Prime of life. It's the prime of life, prime of life. It's the
Gtr. 2
Light distortion
Gtr. 3

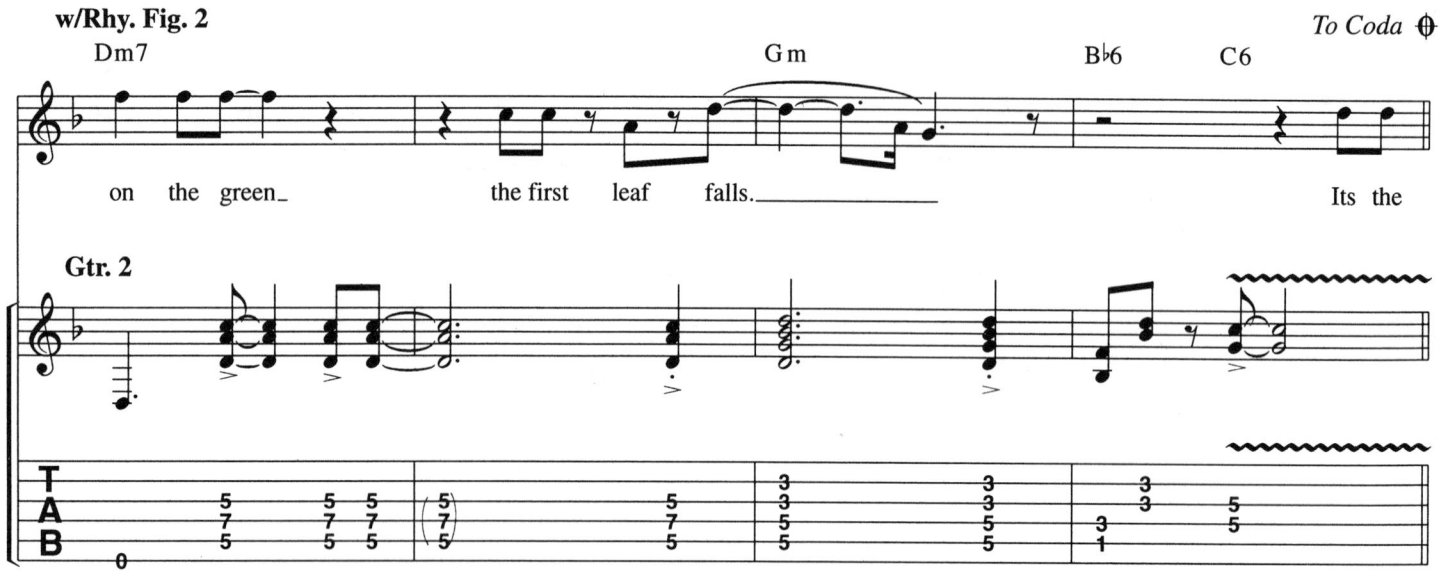

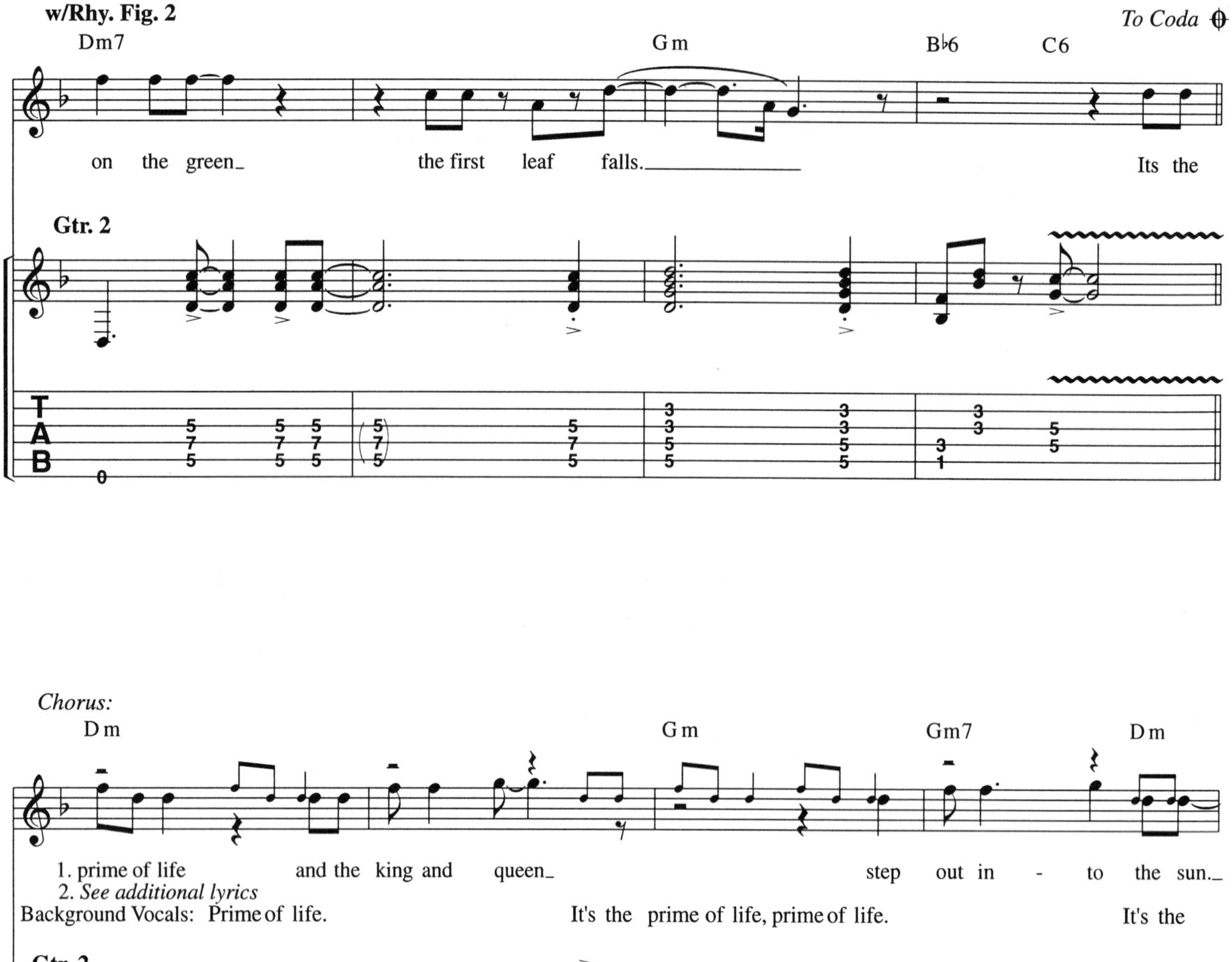

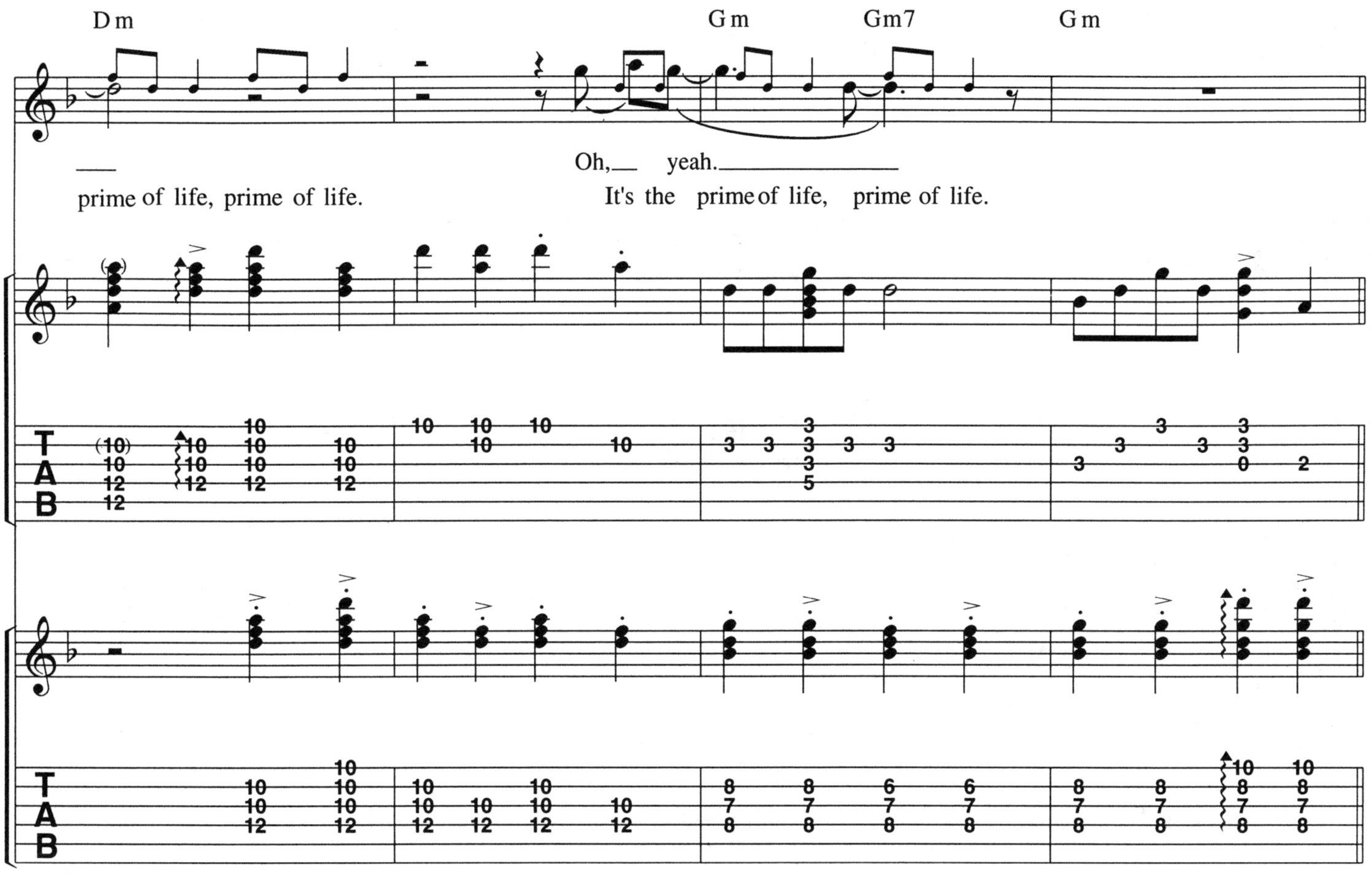
Dm
Gm
Gm7
Gm
Oh,
yeah.
prime of life, prime of life.
It's the prime of life, prime of life.
TAB
TAB

Interlude:

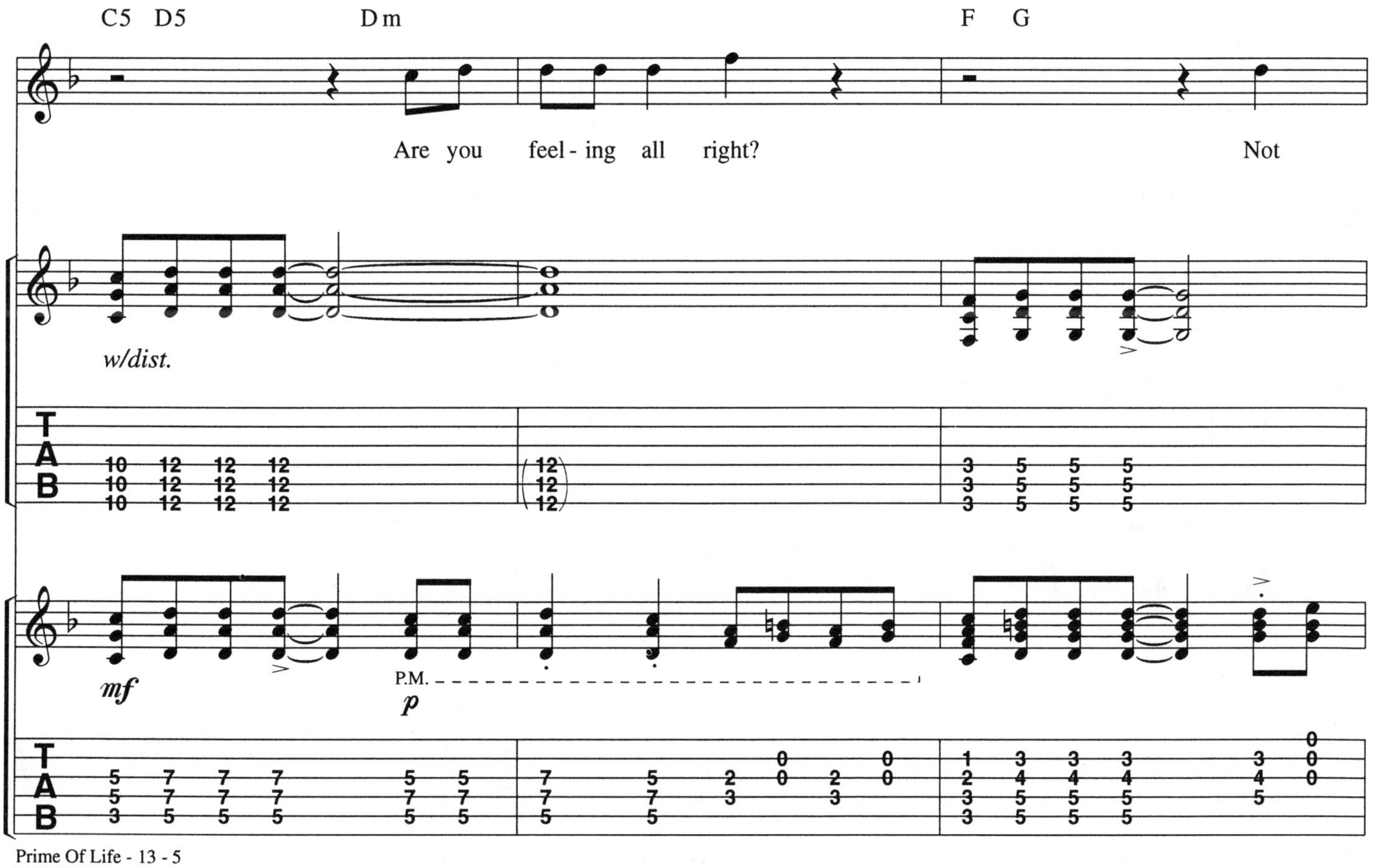
C5 D5
Dm
F G
Are you feel - ing all right?
Not
w/dist.
TAB
mf
P.M.
p
TAB

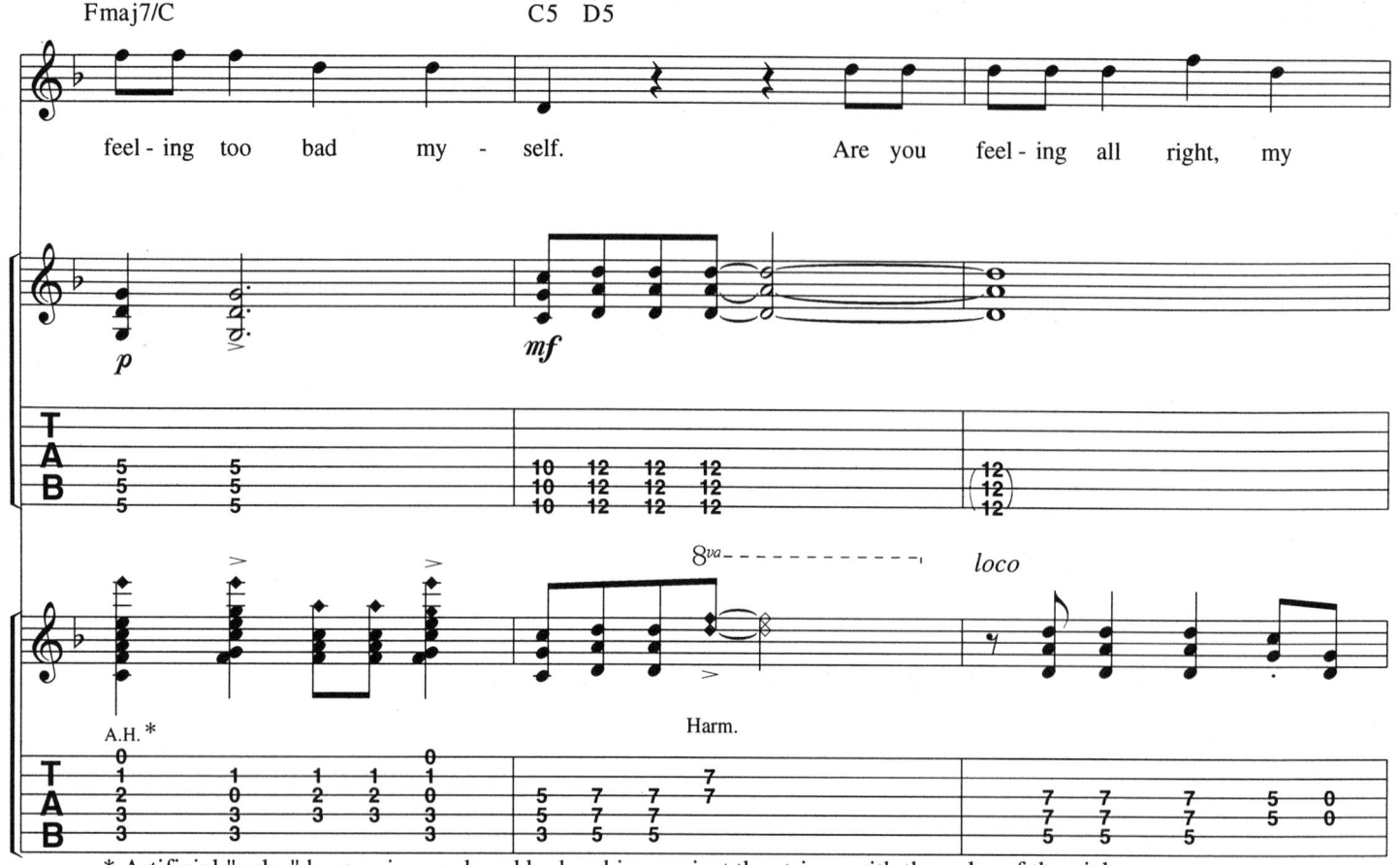

* Artificial "palm" harmonics produced by brushing against the strings with the palm of the pick hand simultaneously to strumming (pick @ XV, palm @ XXII approx.).

Bridge:
w/Flute

w/O.D.* O.D. only w/O.D. and standard signal

Gtr. 3

*Gtr. 2 is played through an octave divider (adding a note two octaves below), flanger, and delay (setting 3:2). Octave divider and flanger = left channel, standard signal and delay = right channel. The standard signal is occasionally out of the mix.

w/O.D. and standard signal

Prime Of Life - 13 - 7
PG9502

18

Prime Of Life - 13 - 8
PG9502

w/ Rhy. Figs. 1 and 2 (Gtrs. 1 & 3) w/ ad lib. variation.
B♭
G
Dm7
(Flute plays Intro figure)
O.D. and standard signal w/ delay
Gm
B♭6
C6
Gtr. 4
delay
delay

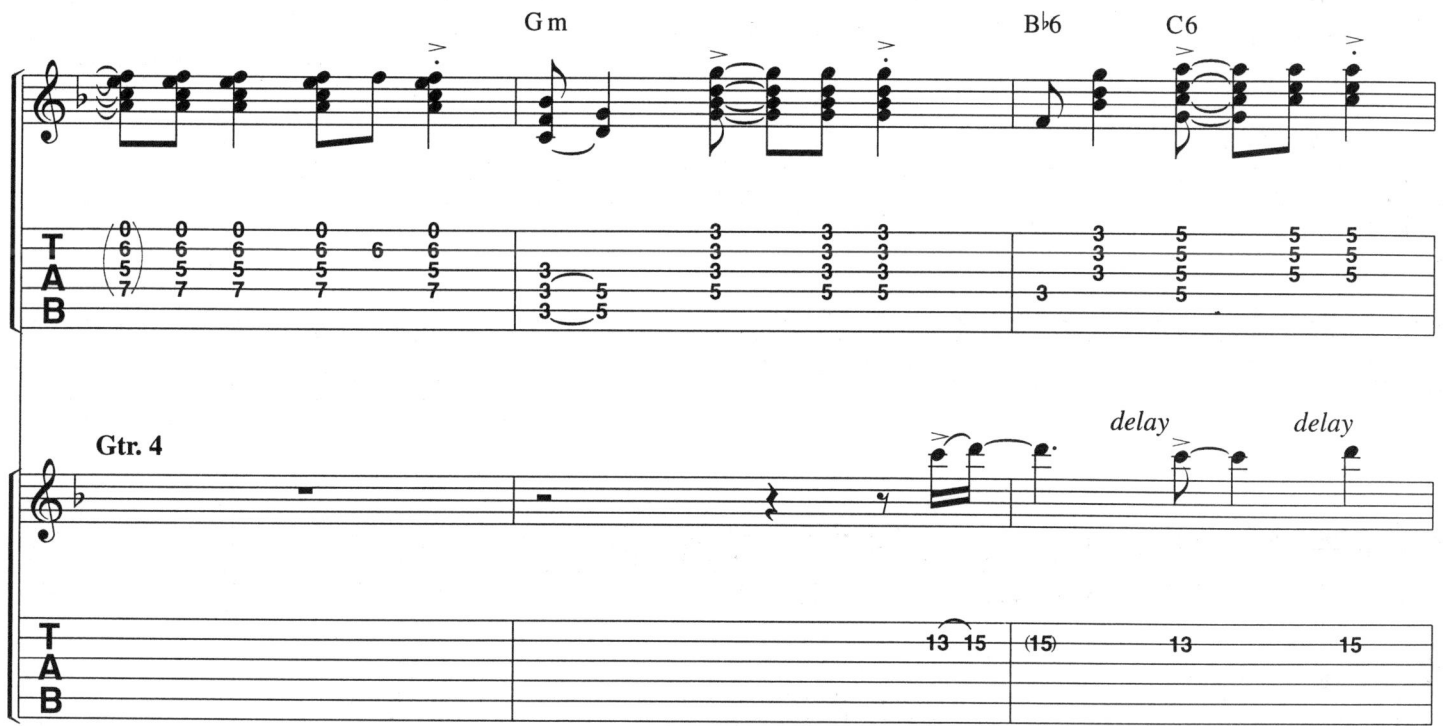

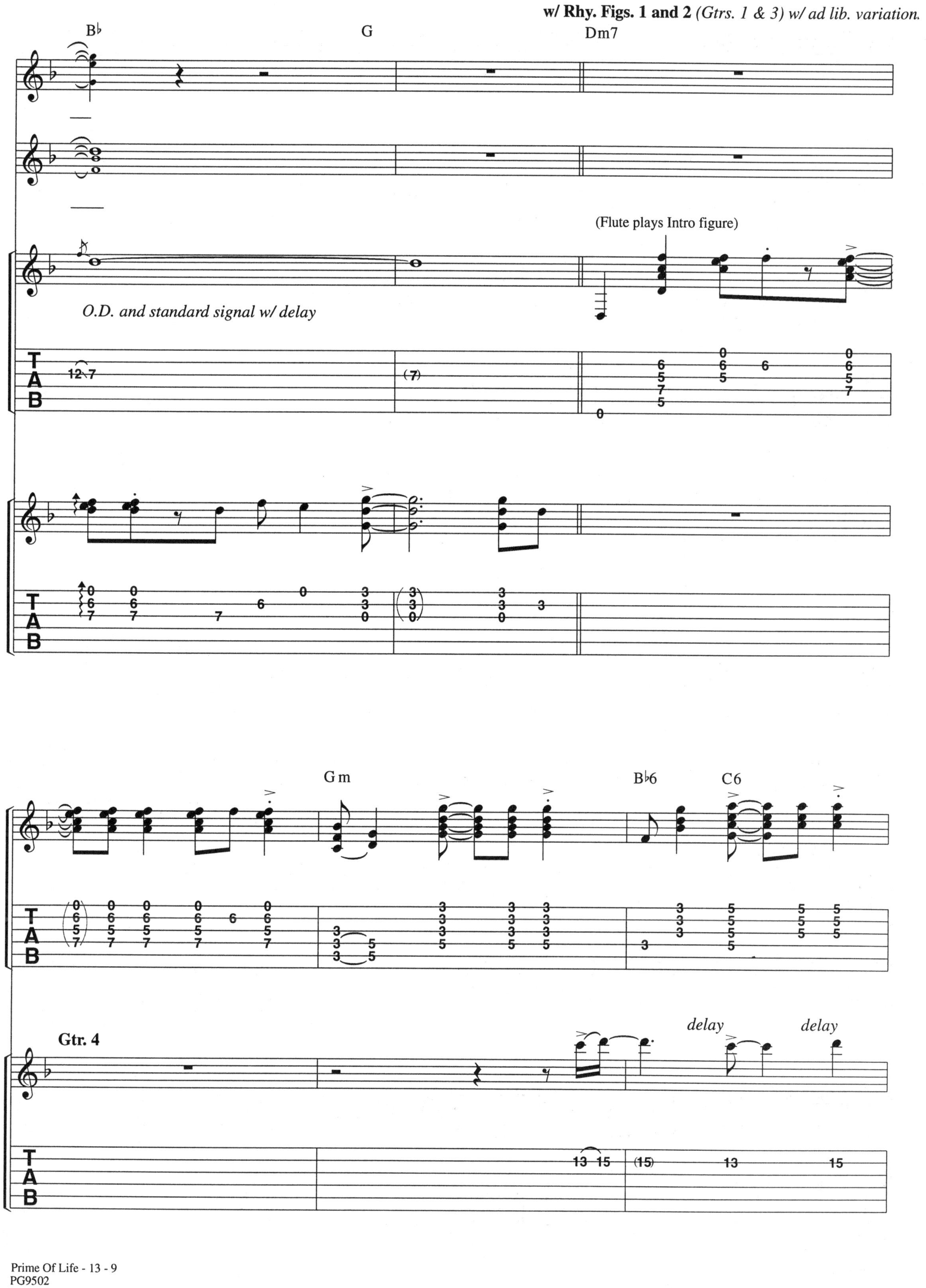

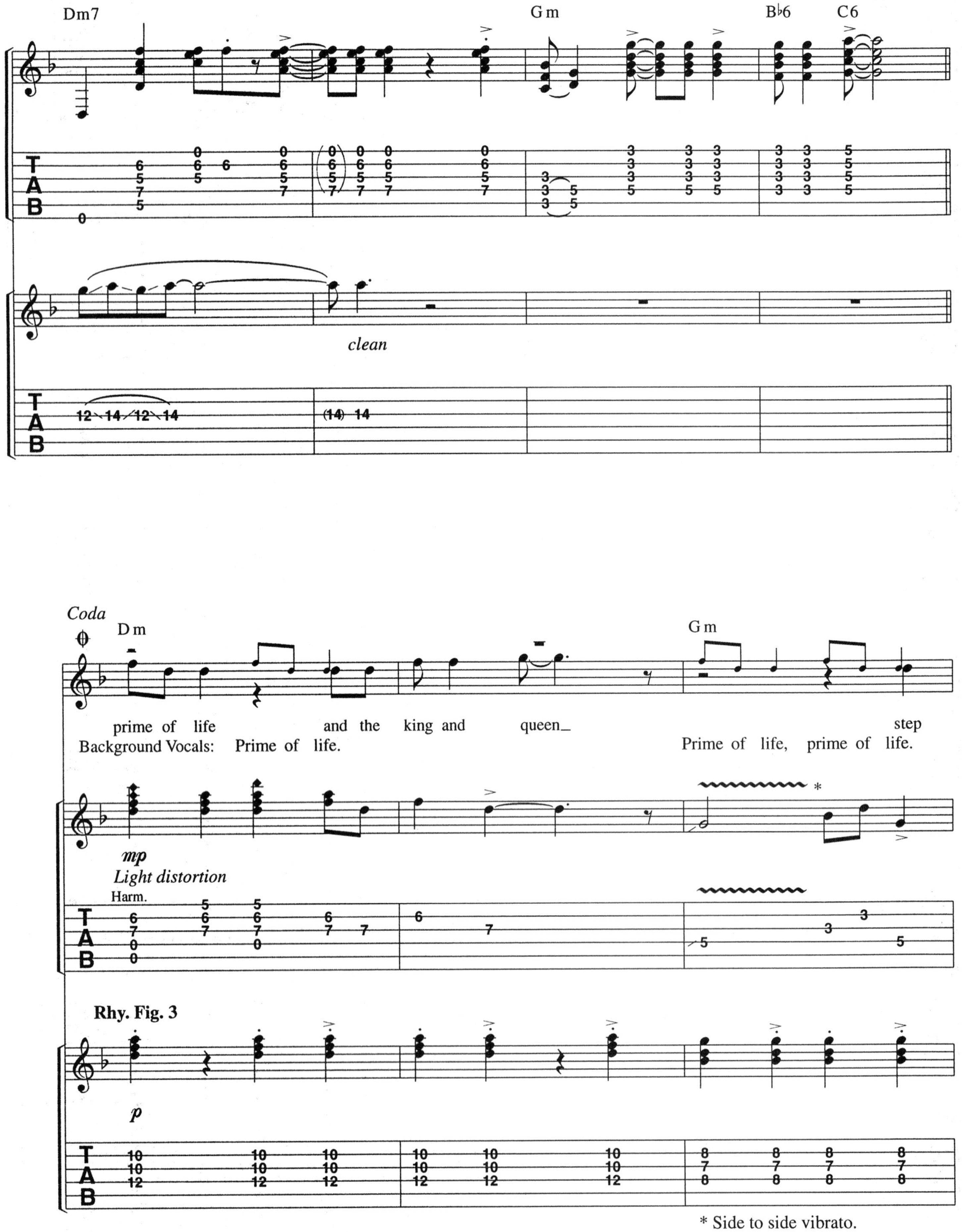

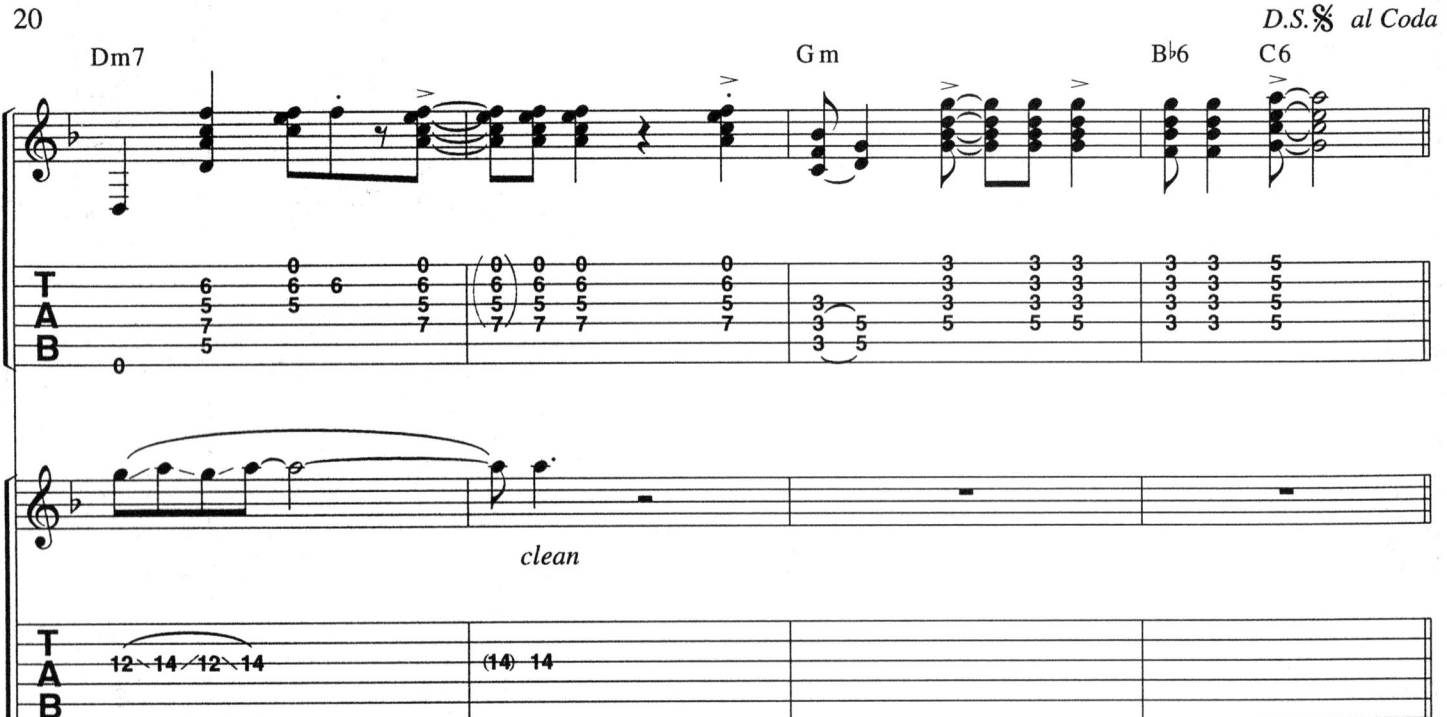

21

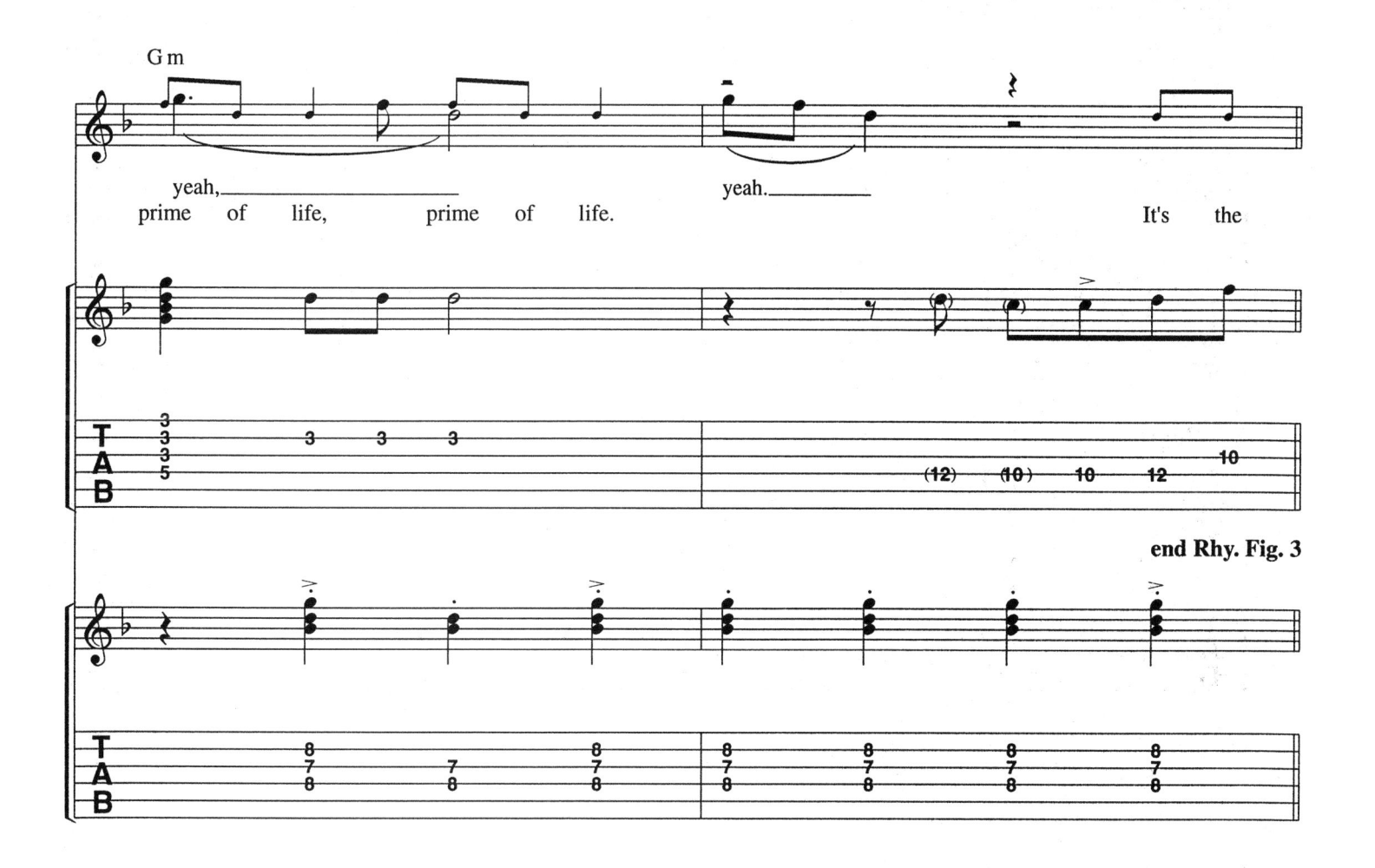

Gm7 ... **Dm**

out in - to the sun.___
It's the prime of life, prime of life.
Oh,___ It's the

Gm

yeah,___
prime of life, prime of life.
yeah.___
It's the

end Rhy. Fig. 3

Prime Of Life - 13 - 11
PG9502

22

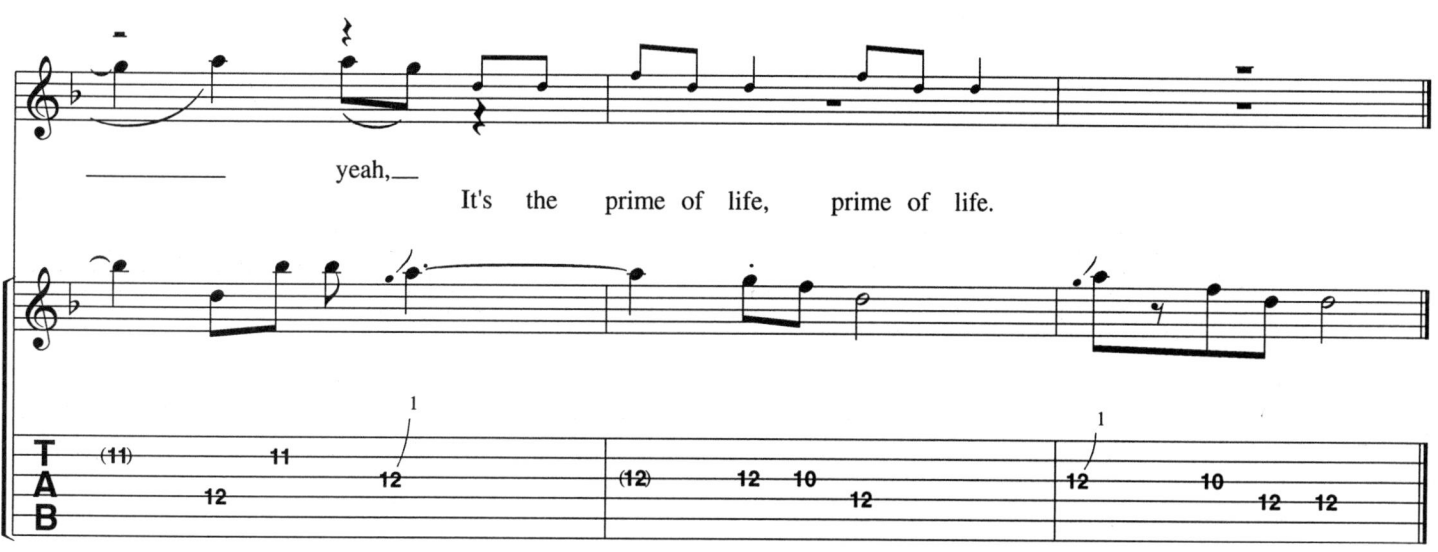

Verse 2:
Footsteps run down the castle hall
To the rooms of the paper doll.
(To Chorus 2:)

Chorus 2

It's the prime of life, where the spirit grows
And the mirror shows both ways. (Oh, yeah.)

DRIVEBY

Words and Music by
NEIL YOUNG

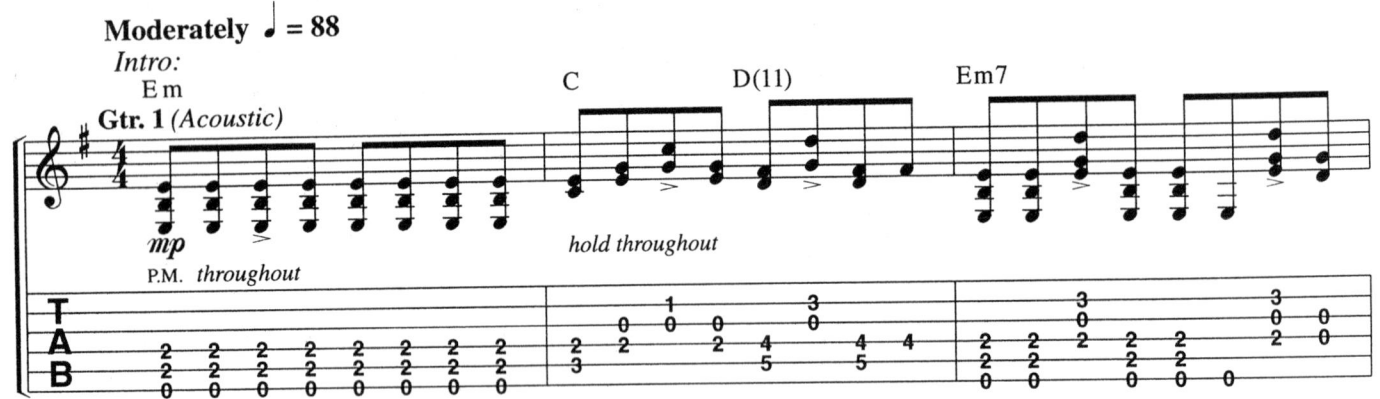

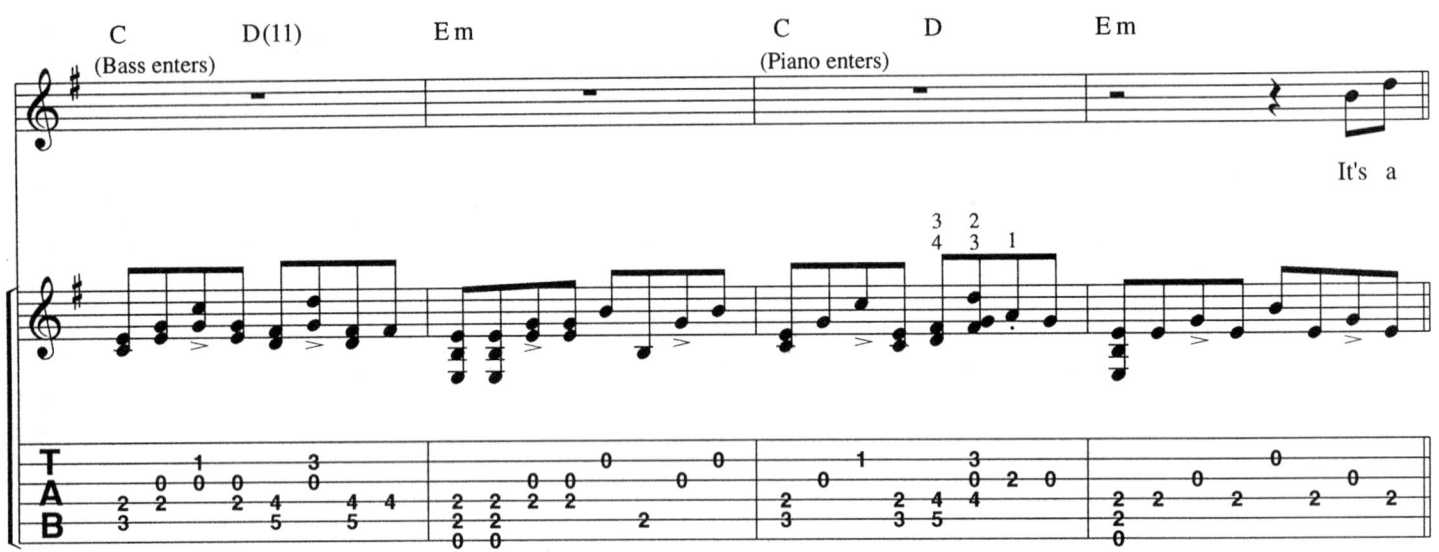

*Low string(s) with flatpick, high string(s) with fingers.

28

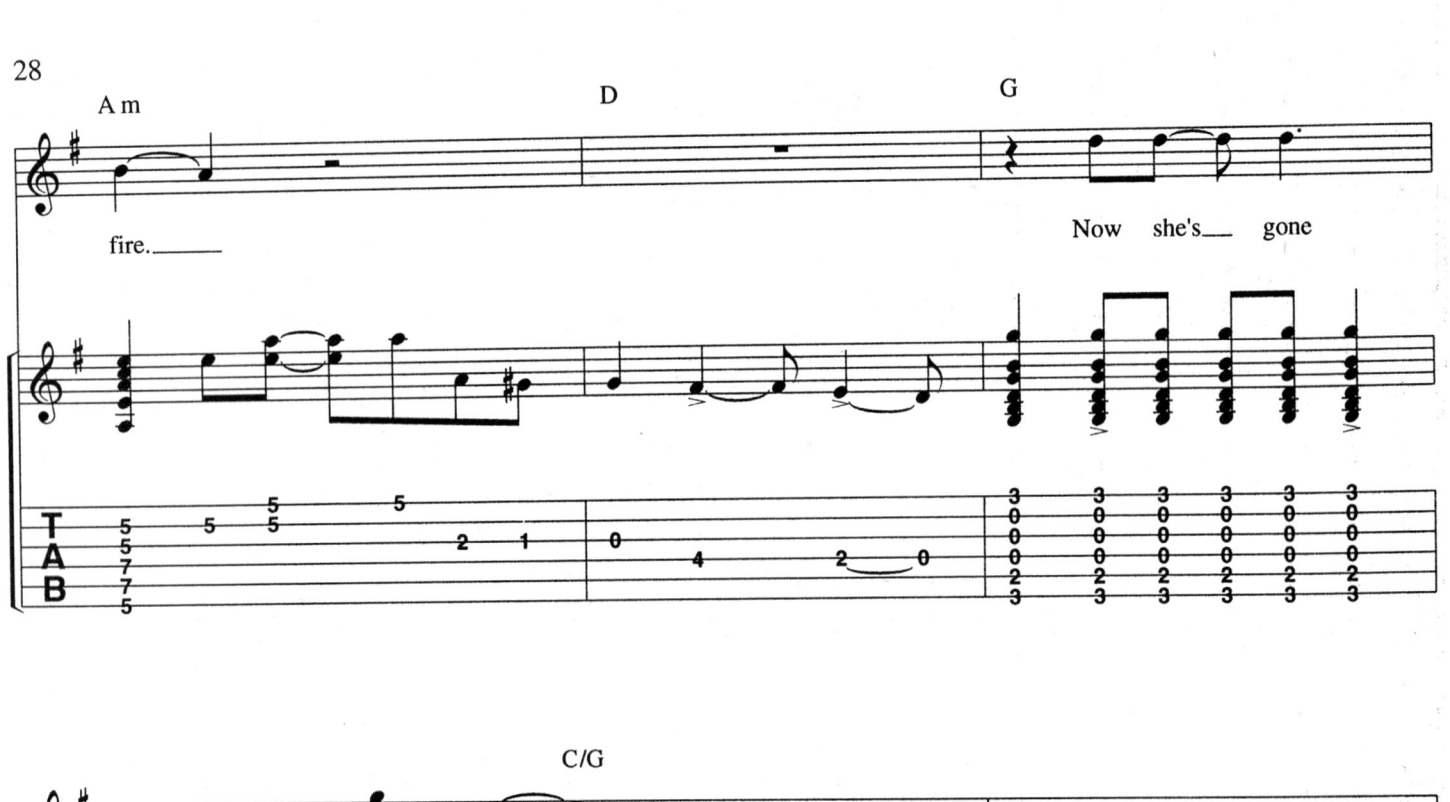

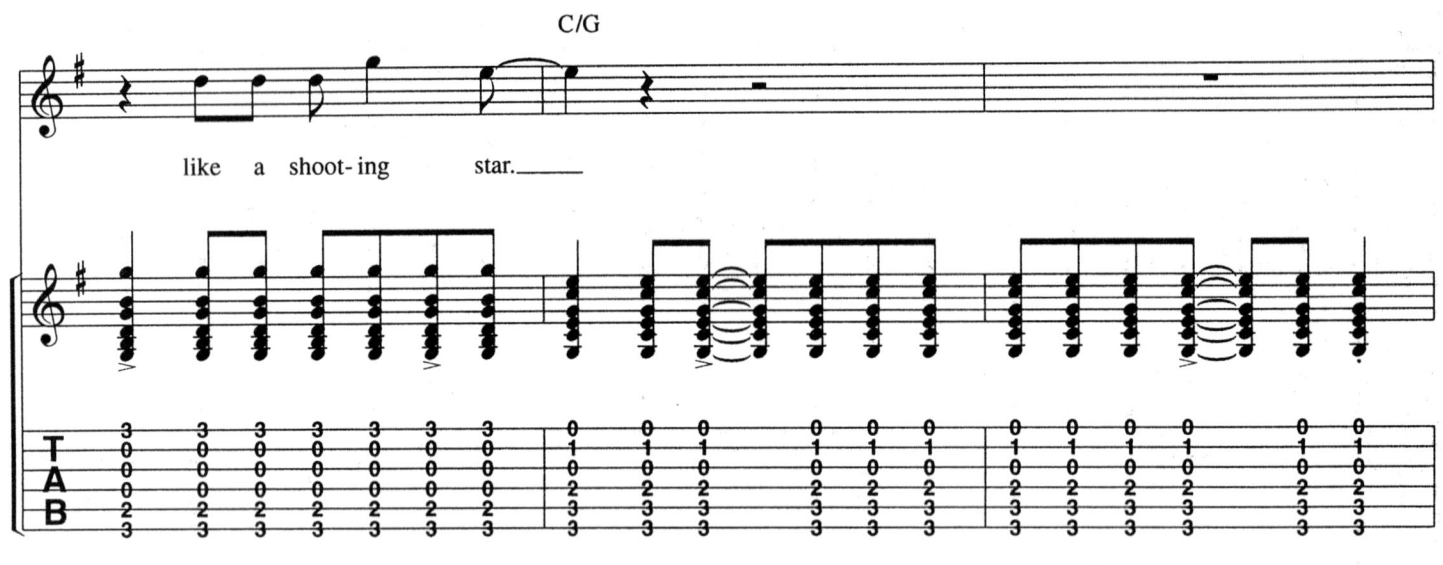

Driveby - 9 - 5
PG9502

30

Verse:

drive - by. Well you feel in - vin - ci - ble, it's just a part of life. There's a feud go - ing on and you don't know.

Chorus:

Drive - by, drive - by,

Driveby - 9 - 7
PG9502

32

Driveby - 9 - 9
PG9502

SLEEPS WITH ANGELS

Words and Music by
NEIL YOUNG

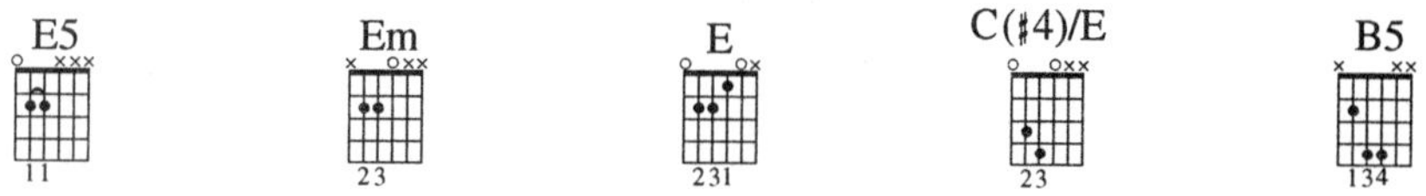

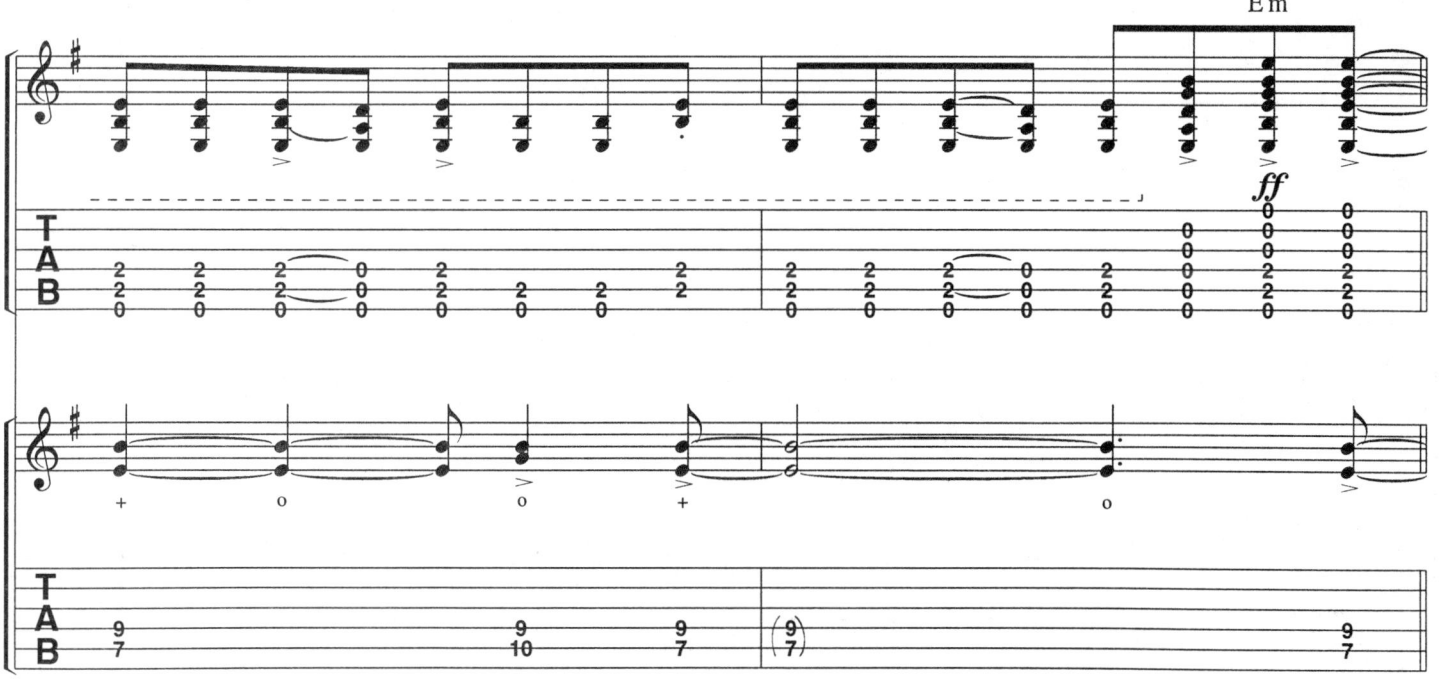

© 1994 SILVER FIDDLE MUSIC (ASCAP)
All rights reserved

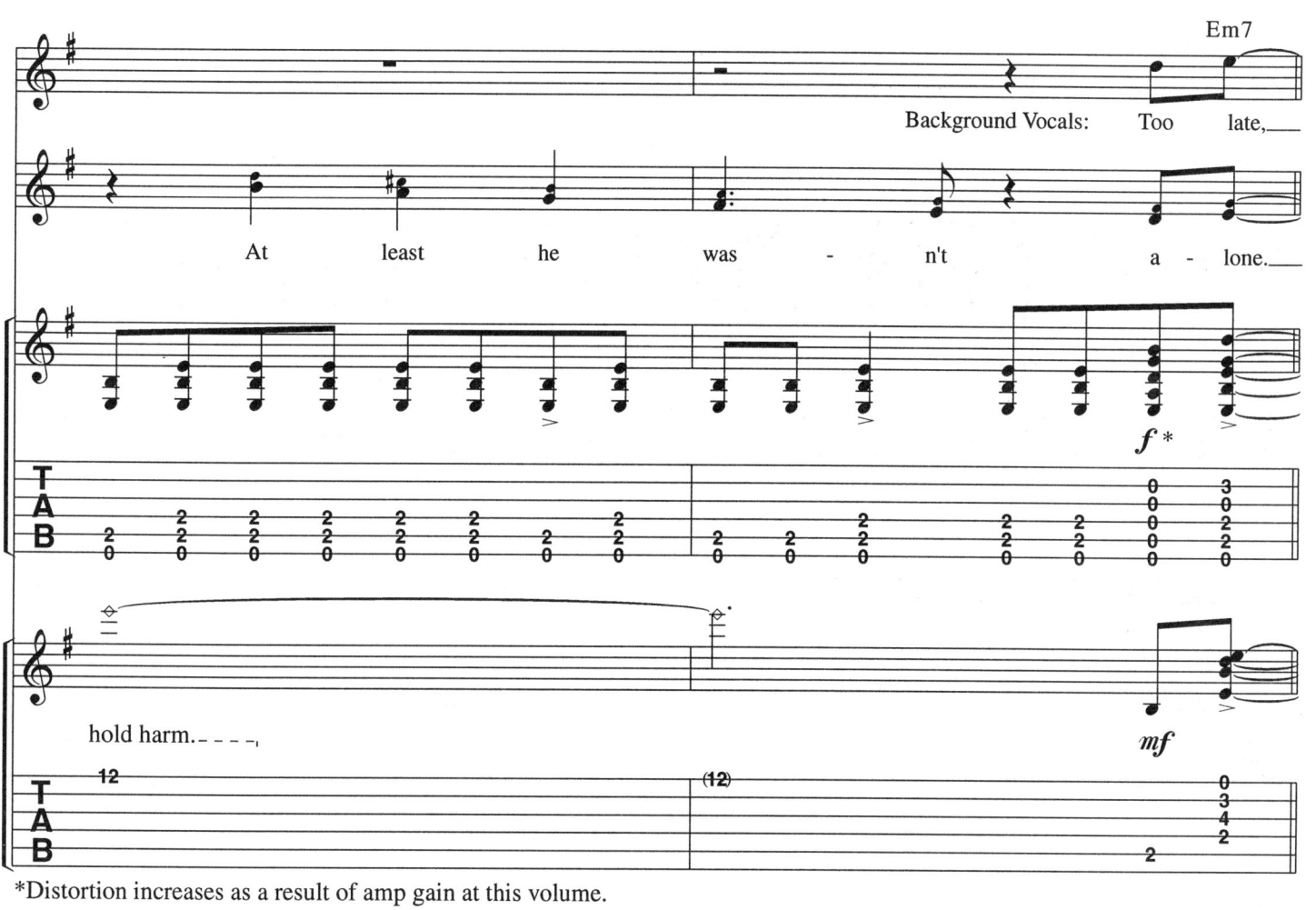

*Distortion increases as a result of amp gain at this volume.

Sleeps With Angels - 13 - 5

Em
C(♯4)/E
too late,
too soon,
on some - ones mind.
He sleeps with
rev. sustain
Em7(11) E
Em B5
too late,
too soon.
an - gels.
He sleeps with an - gels.
rev.sus.
tape echo

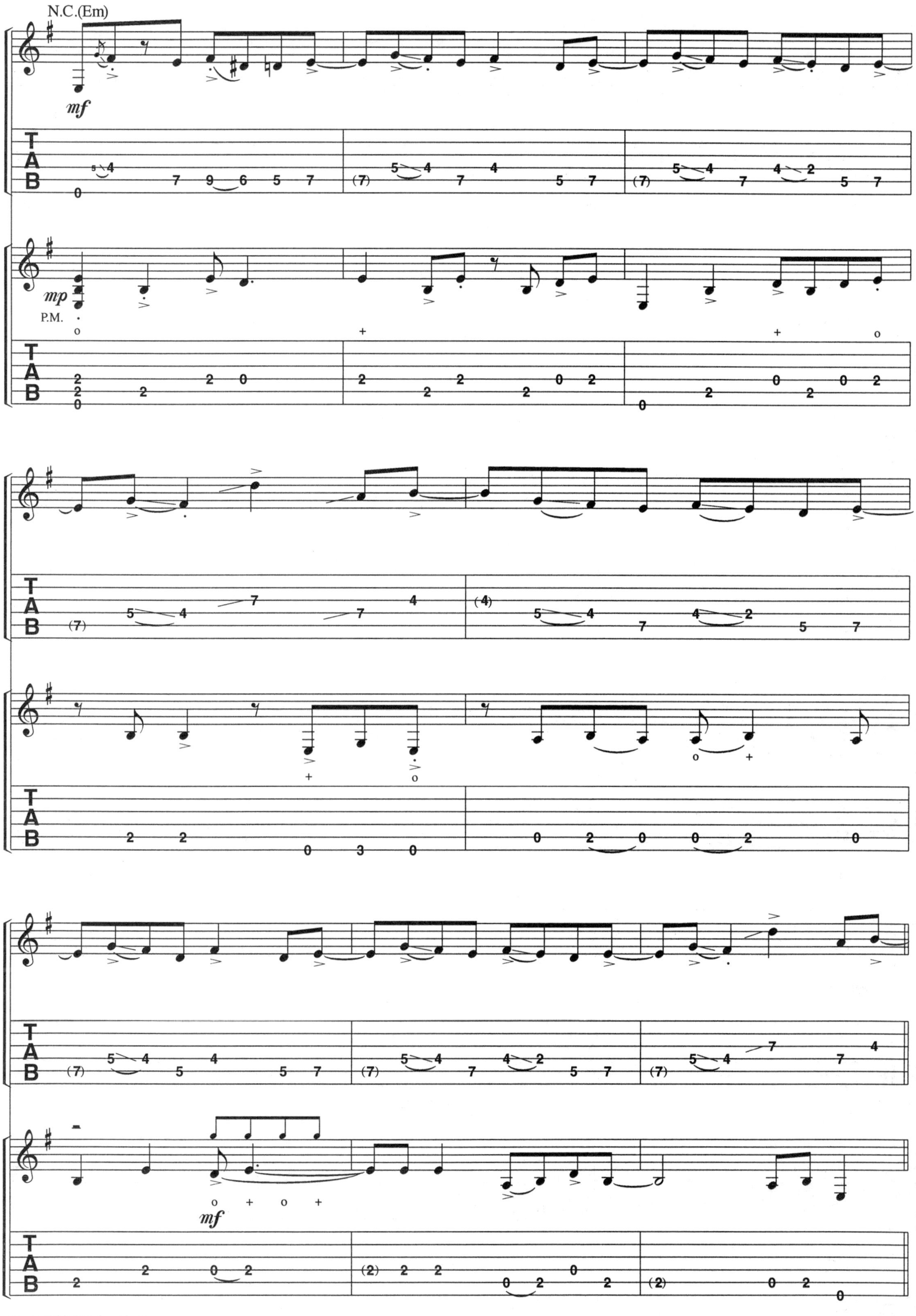
N.C.(Em)
mf
mp
P.M.
mf

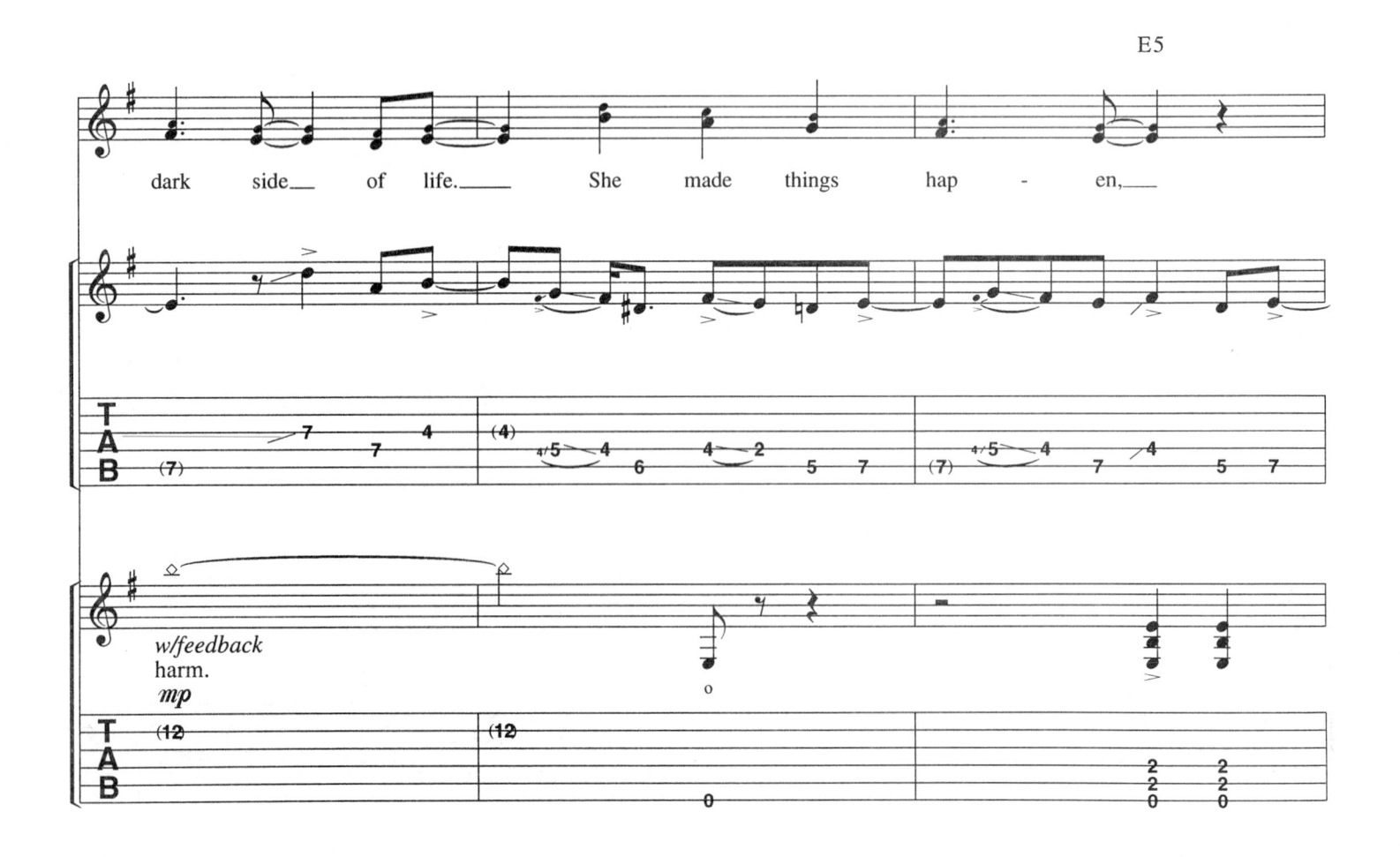

Verse 2:

She was a teen queen. She saw the dark side of life. She made things hap-pen, but when he did it__ that night,__ she ran up

w/o palm mute (till end)

phone bills.__ She moved a-round__ from town__ to town.__

flick toggle switch*

octave divider**

* Les Paul guitar: 3 position switch.
** Adds an octave below.

Sleeps With Angels - 13 - 9
PG9502

42

Bridge:

* Octave divider off.

Sleeps With Angels - 13 - 11
PG9502

44

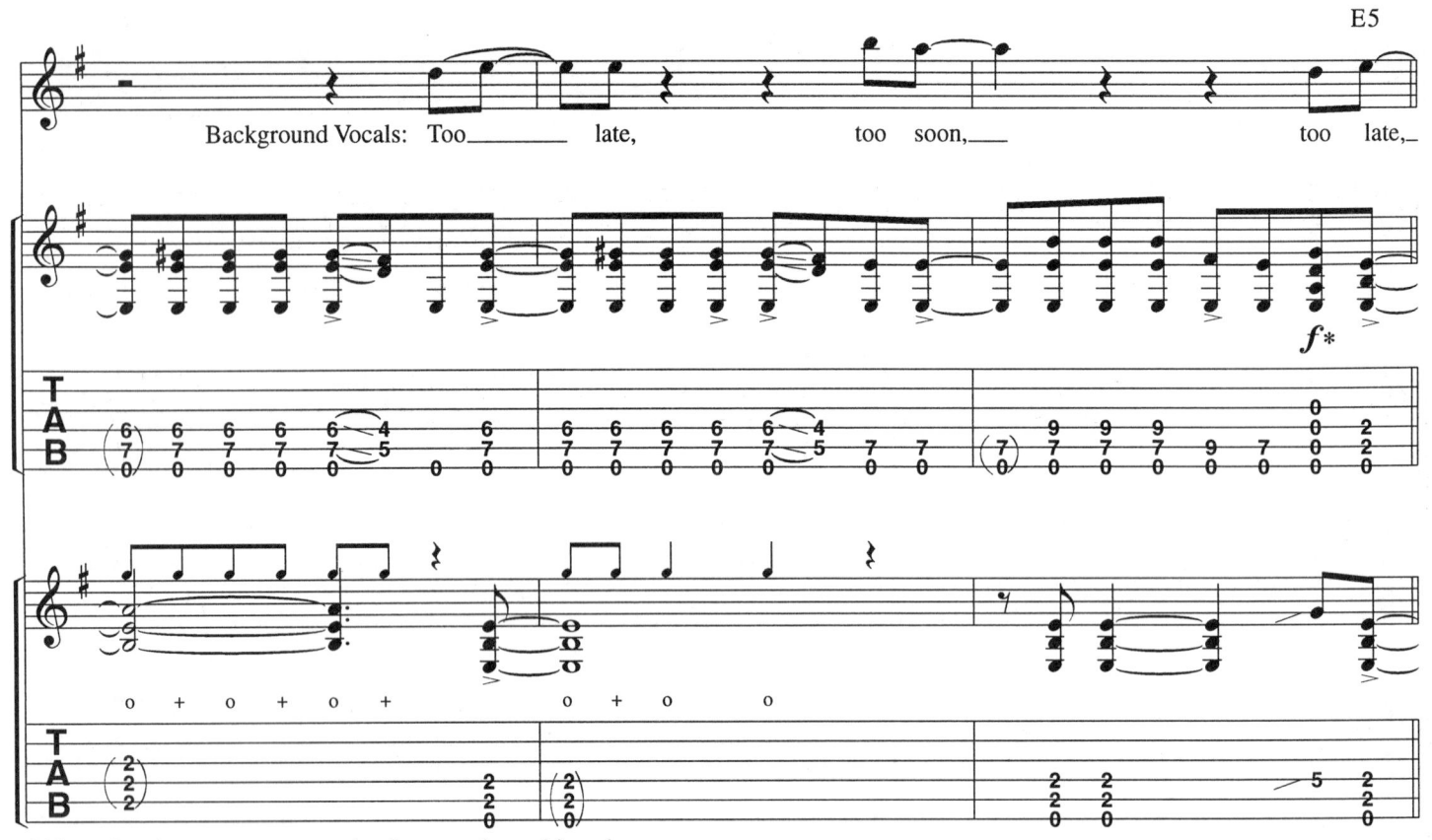

*Distortion increases as a result of amp gain at this volume.

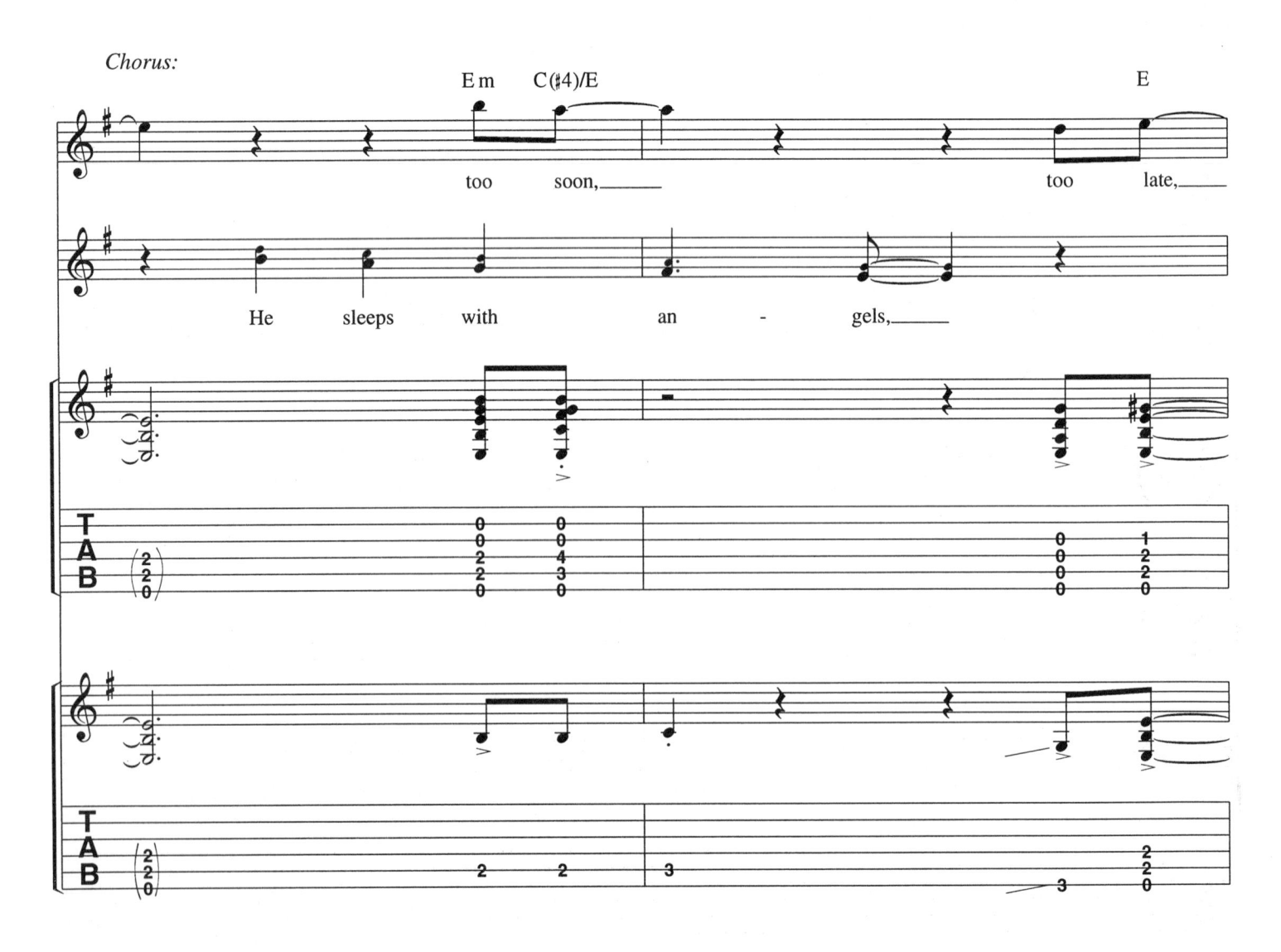

Chorus:

Sleeps With Angels - 13 - 13

WESTERN HERO

Words and Music by
NEIL YOUNG

© 1994 SILVER FIDDLE MUSIC (ASCAP)
All Rights Reserved

47

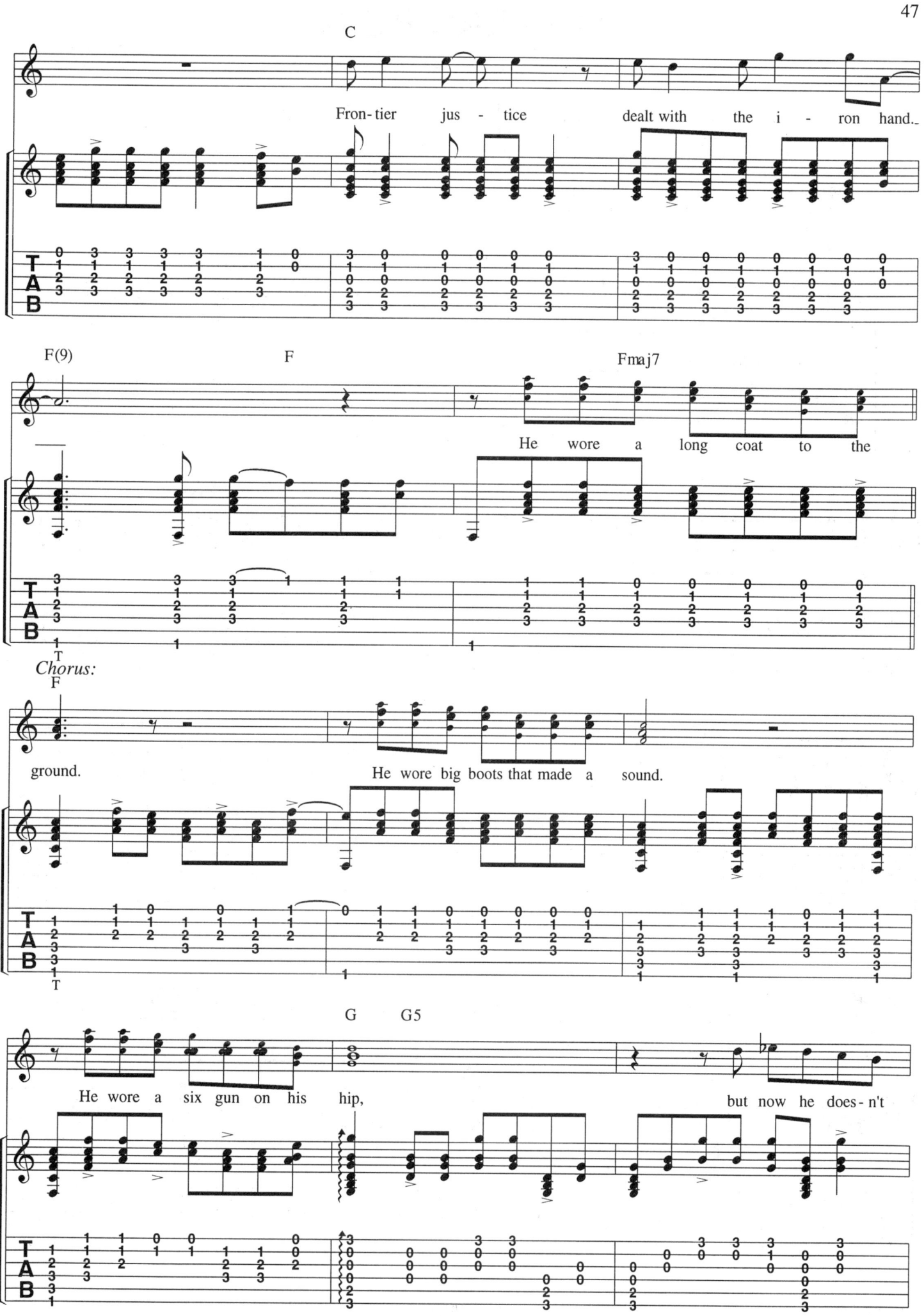

F
car - ry it.
Verse 1:
C
F(9)
Sure e-nough, he was a west - ern he - ro.
C
On the deck, sight-ing an old Jap
F
Fmaj7
ze - ro. And on the shores at Norm - an -
TAB

Chorus:

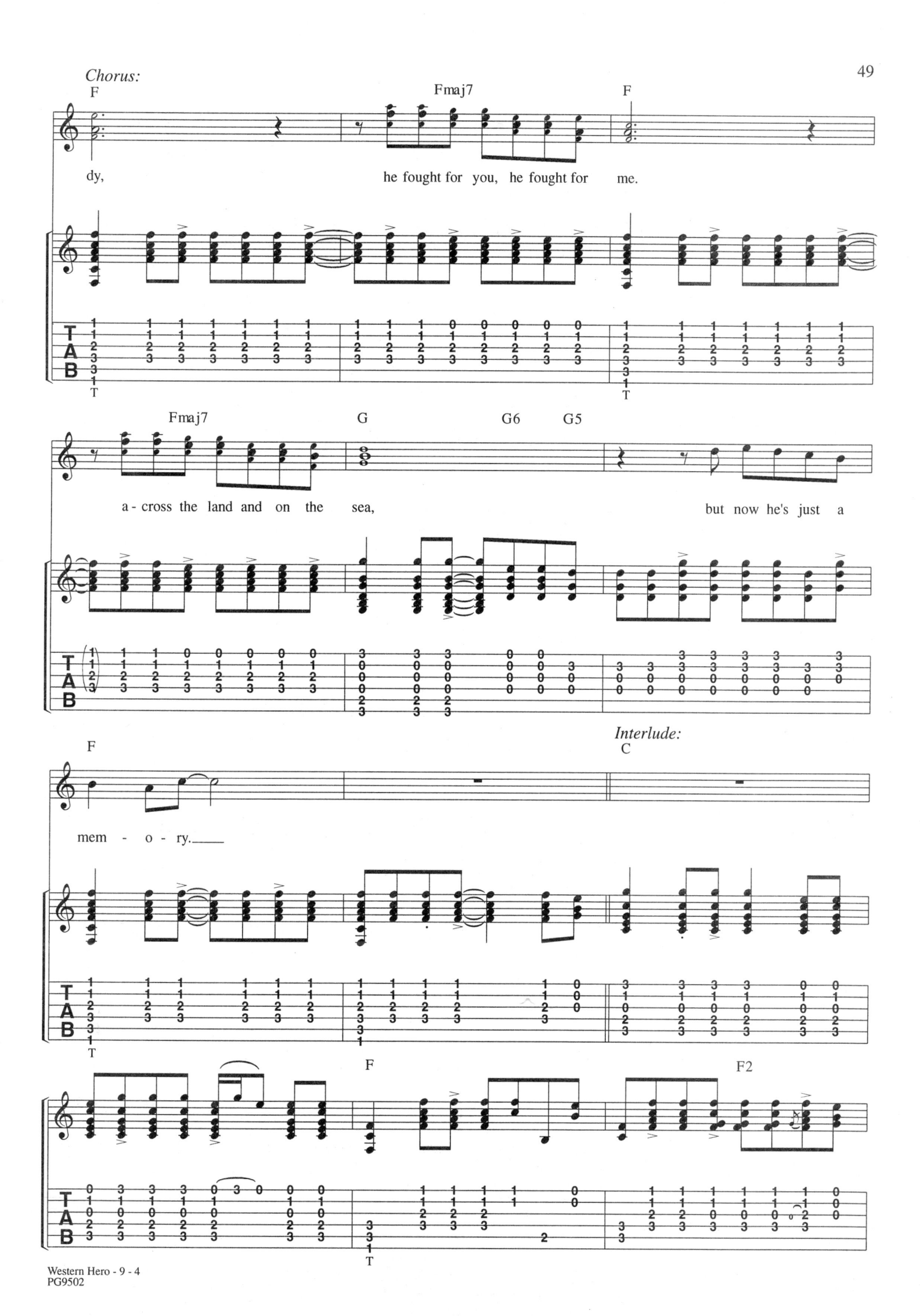

Lyrics: dy, he fought for you, he fought for me. a-cross the land and on the sea, but now he's just a mem - o - ry.

Interlude:

Chords: F, Fmaj7, F, Fmaj7, G, G6, G5, F, C, F, F2

Western Hero - 9 - 4

50

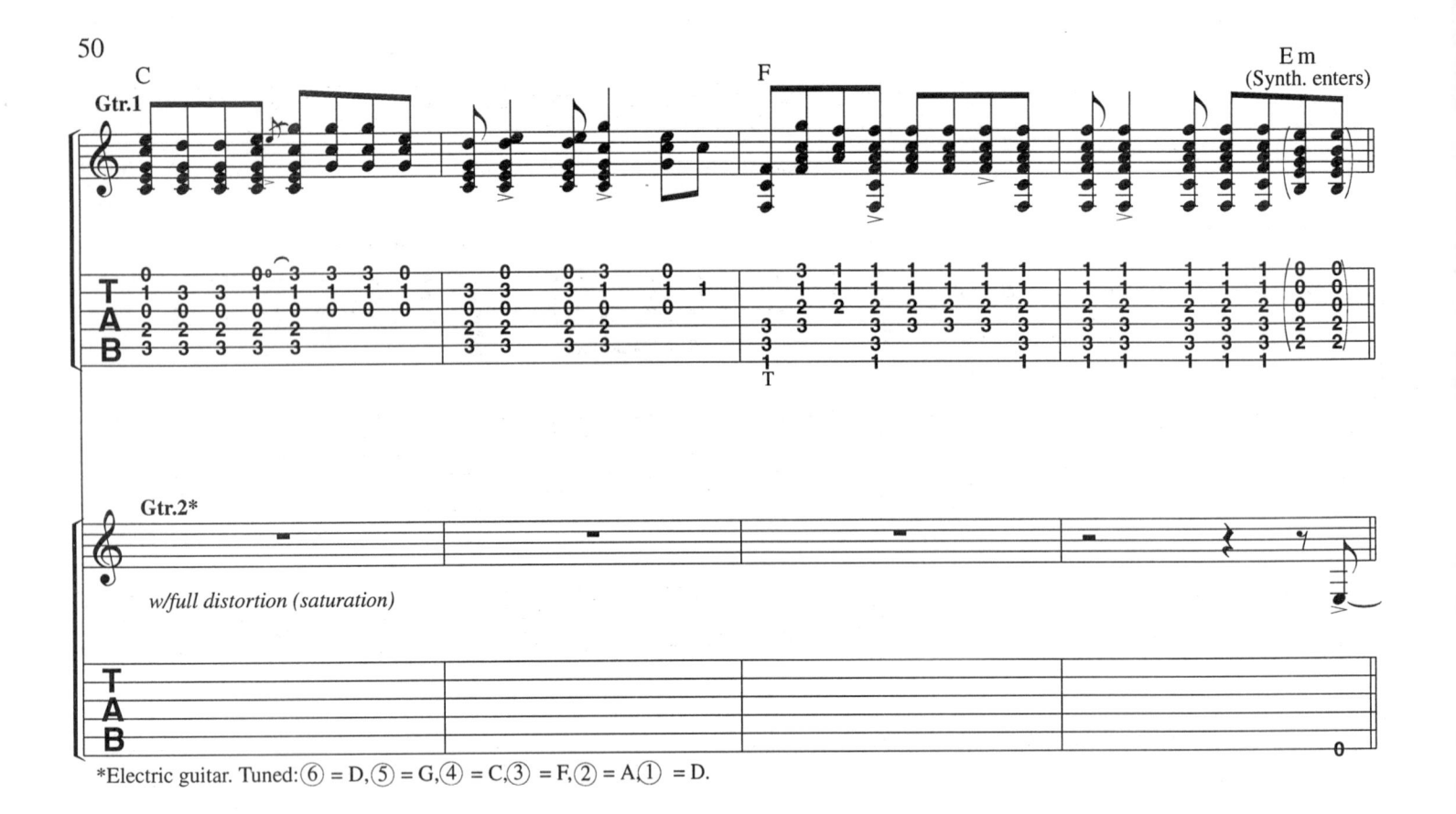

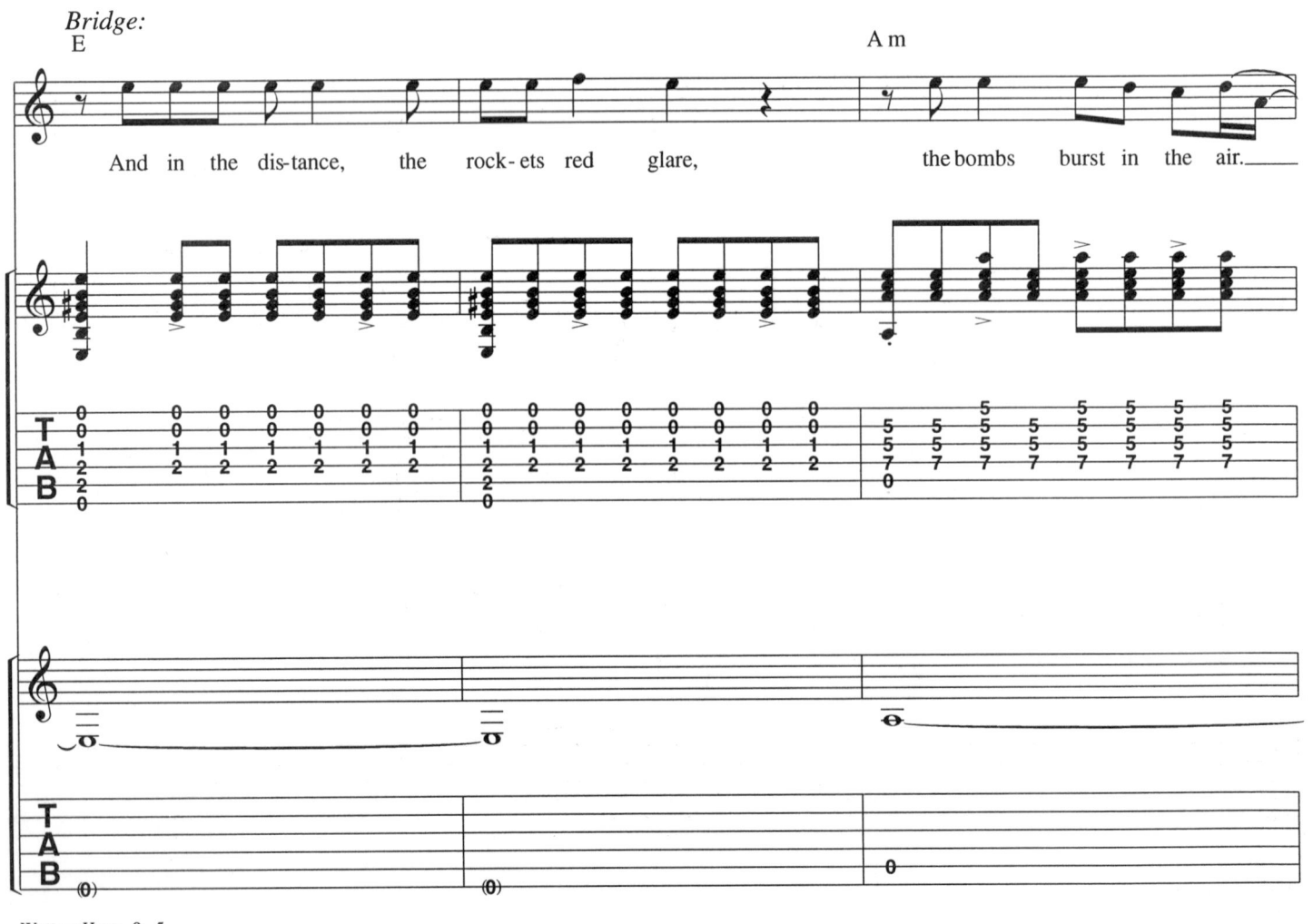

w/full distortion (saturation)

*Electric guitar. Tuned: ⑥ = D, ⑤ = G, ④ = C, ③ = F, ② = A, ① = D.

Bridge:

And in the dis-tance, the rock-ets red glare, the bombs burst in the air.

Western Hero - 9 - 5
PG9502

this time we're nev-er go-ing back.

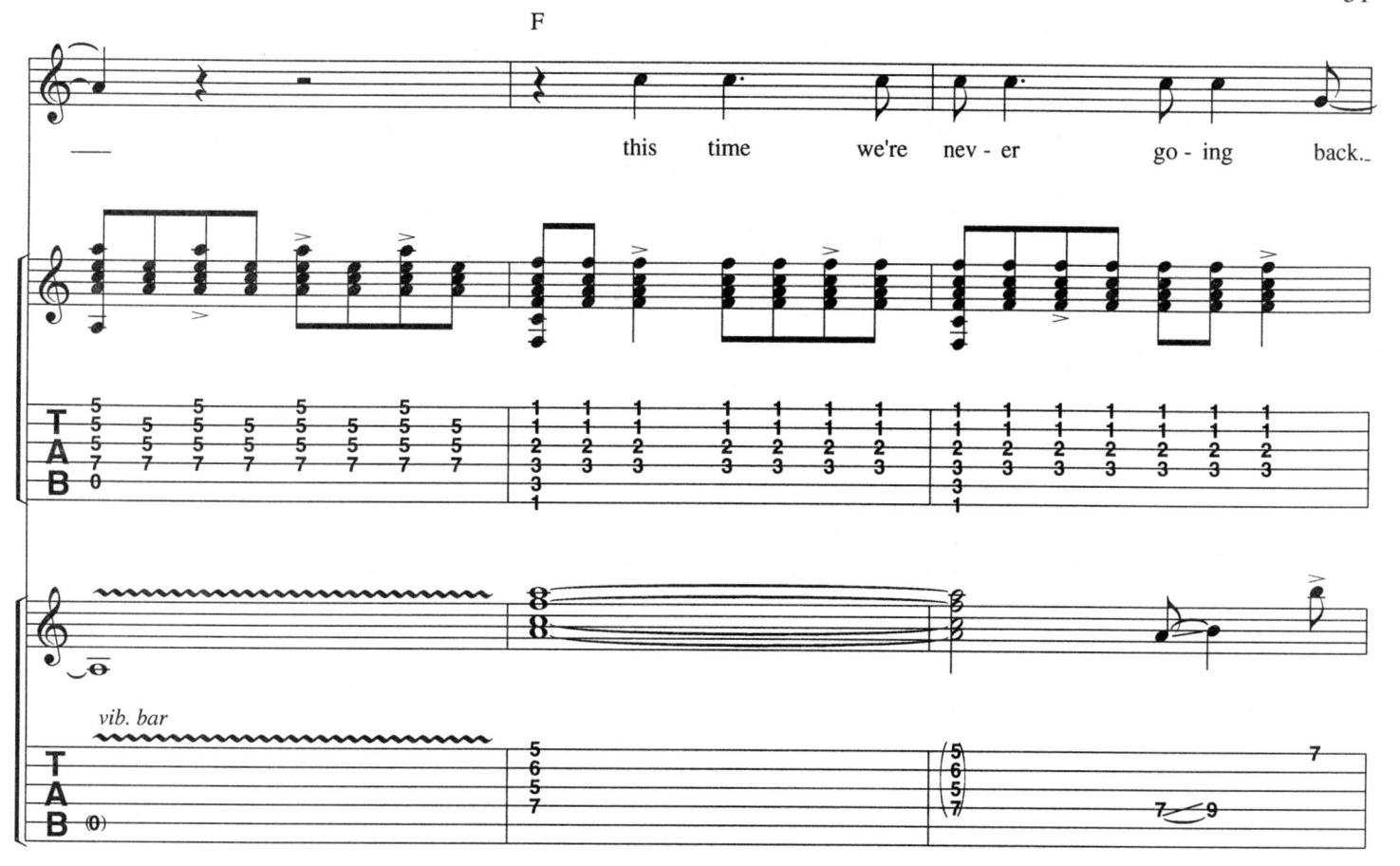

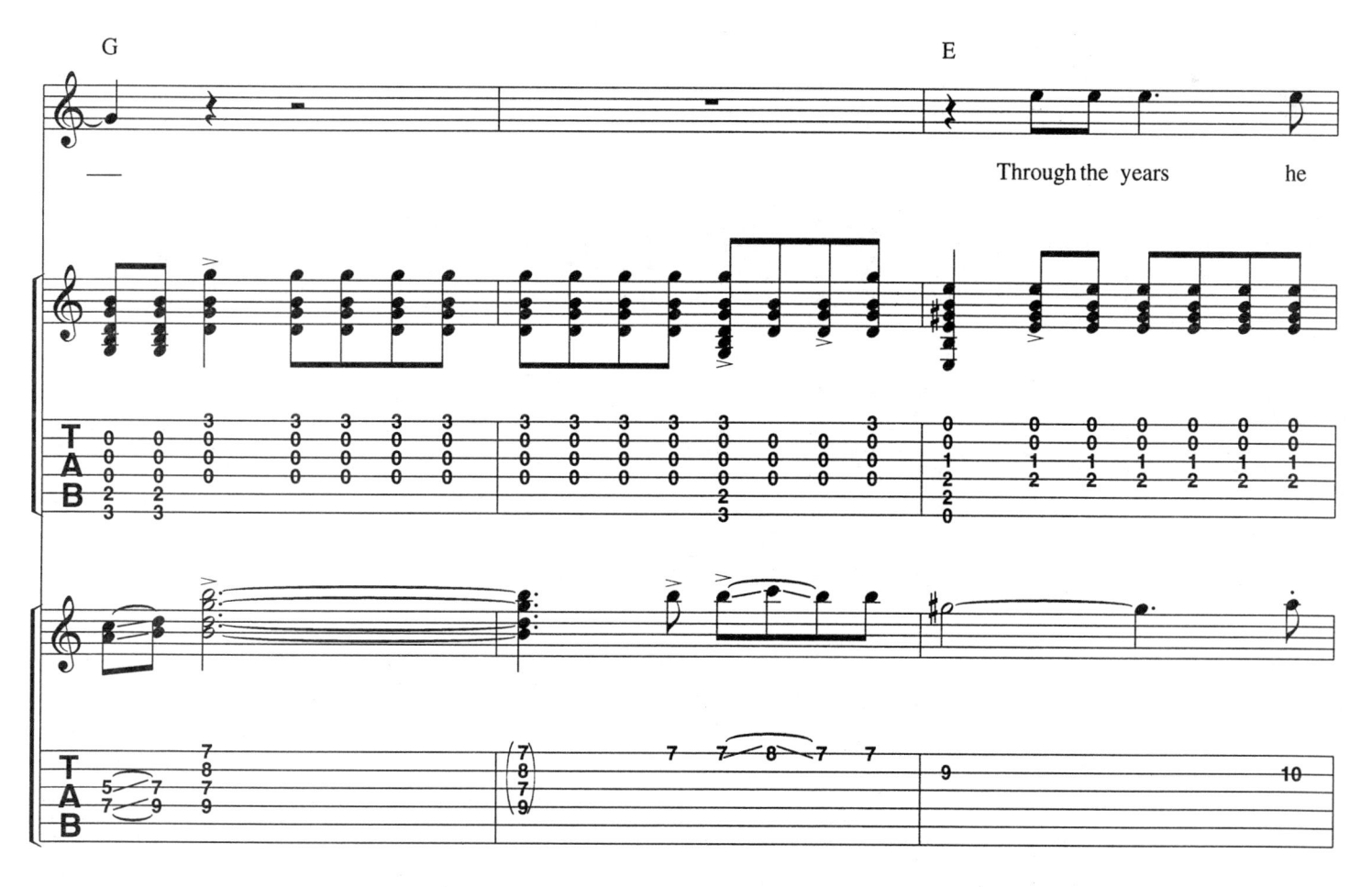

Through the years he

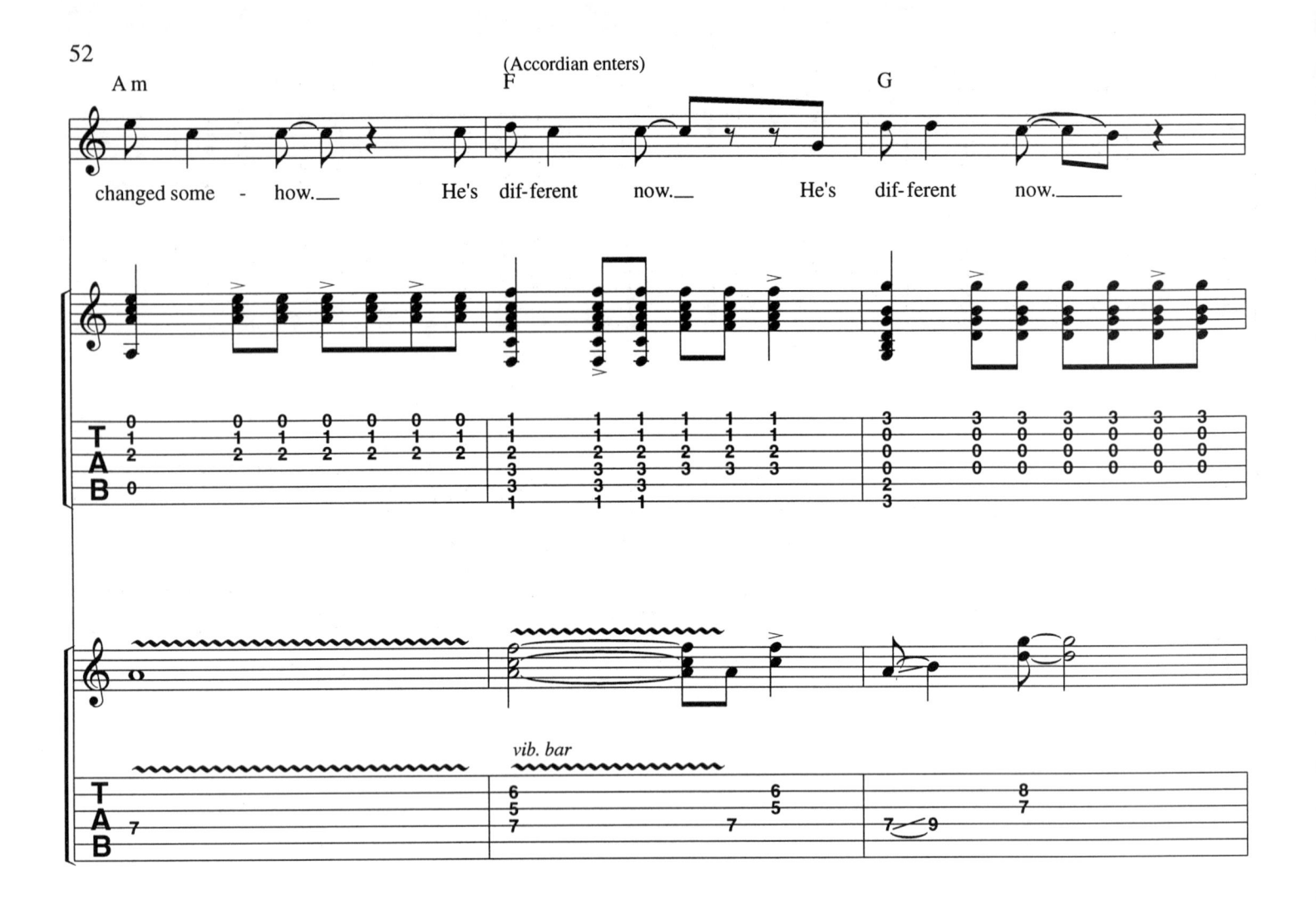

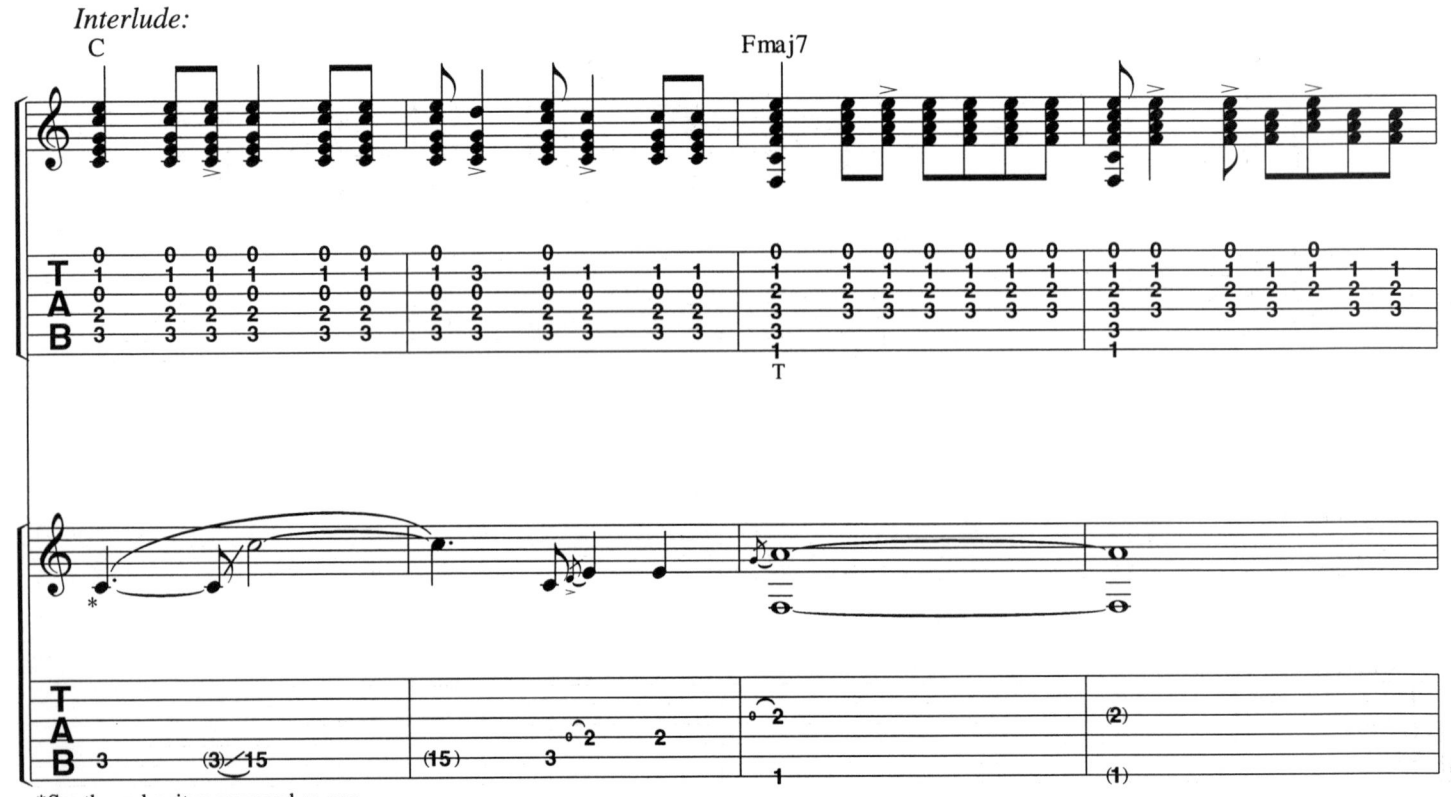

changed some-how.__ He's dif-ferent now.__ He's dif-ferent now.__

*Synth. and guitar arranged as one.

Verse 2:

O-pen fire, here comes a west-ern he-ro,

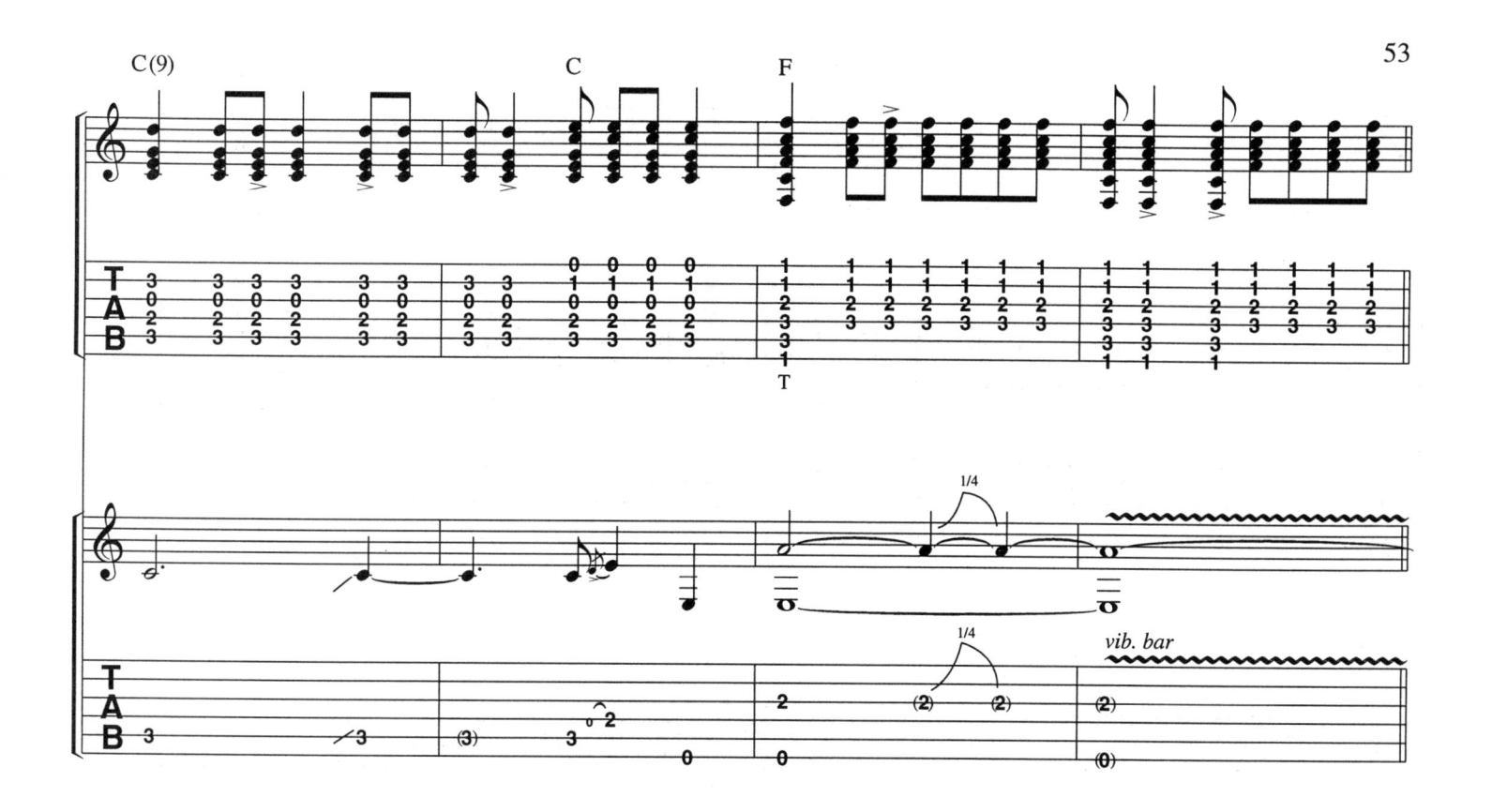

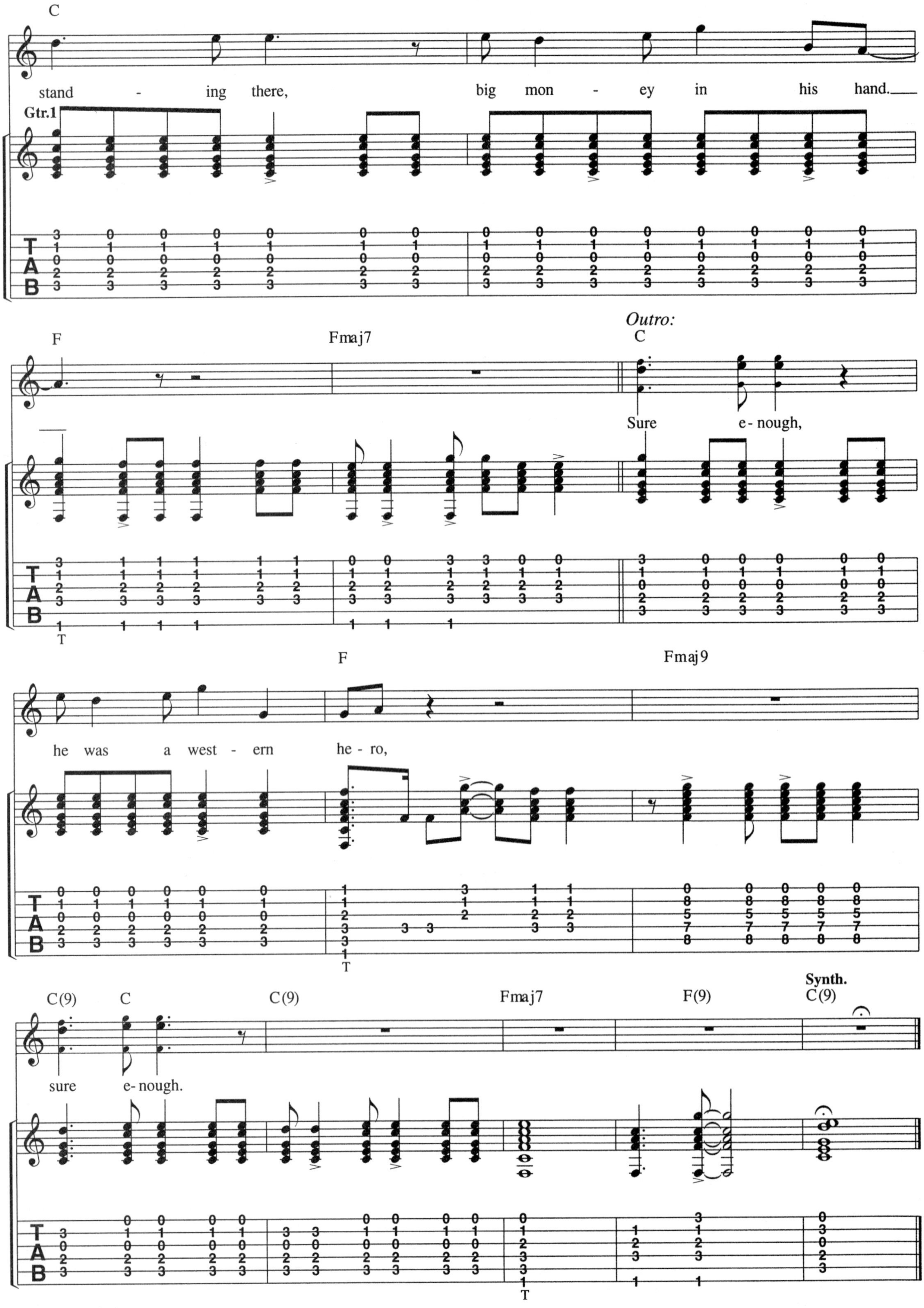
C
stand - ing there, big mon - ey in his hand.
Gtr.1
F
Fmaj7
Outro:
C
Sure e-nough,
F
Fmaj9
he was a west - ern he-ro,
C(9)
C
C(9)
Fmaj7
F(9)
Synth.
C(9)
sure e-nough.

CHANGE YOUR MIND

Words and Music by
NEIL YOUNG

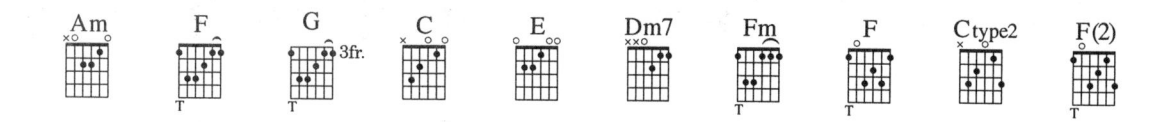

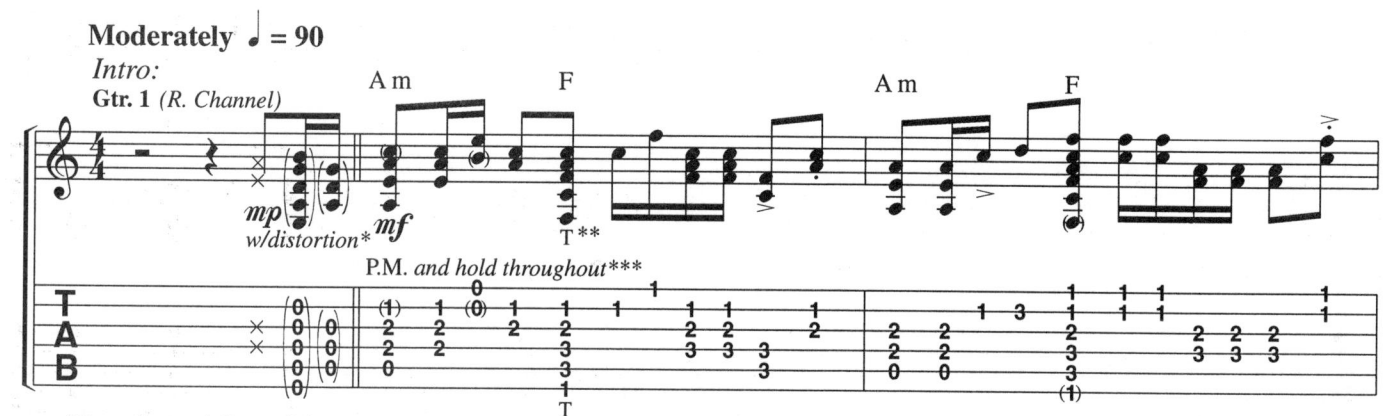

*Overall sound from mixing amps (each with different amounts of distortion). No distortion effects used, just the amp(s).
**Thumb (used on this chord throughout).
***Palm mute strings ⑥-③ primarily.

© 1994 SILVER FIDDLE MUSIC (ASCAP)
All Rights Reserved

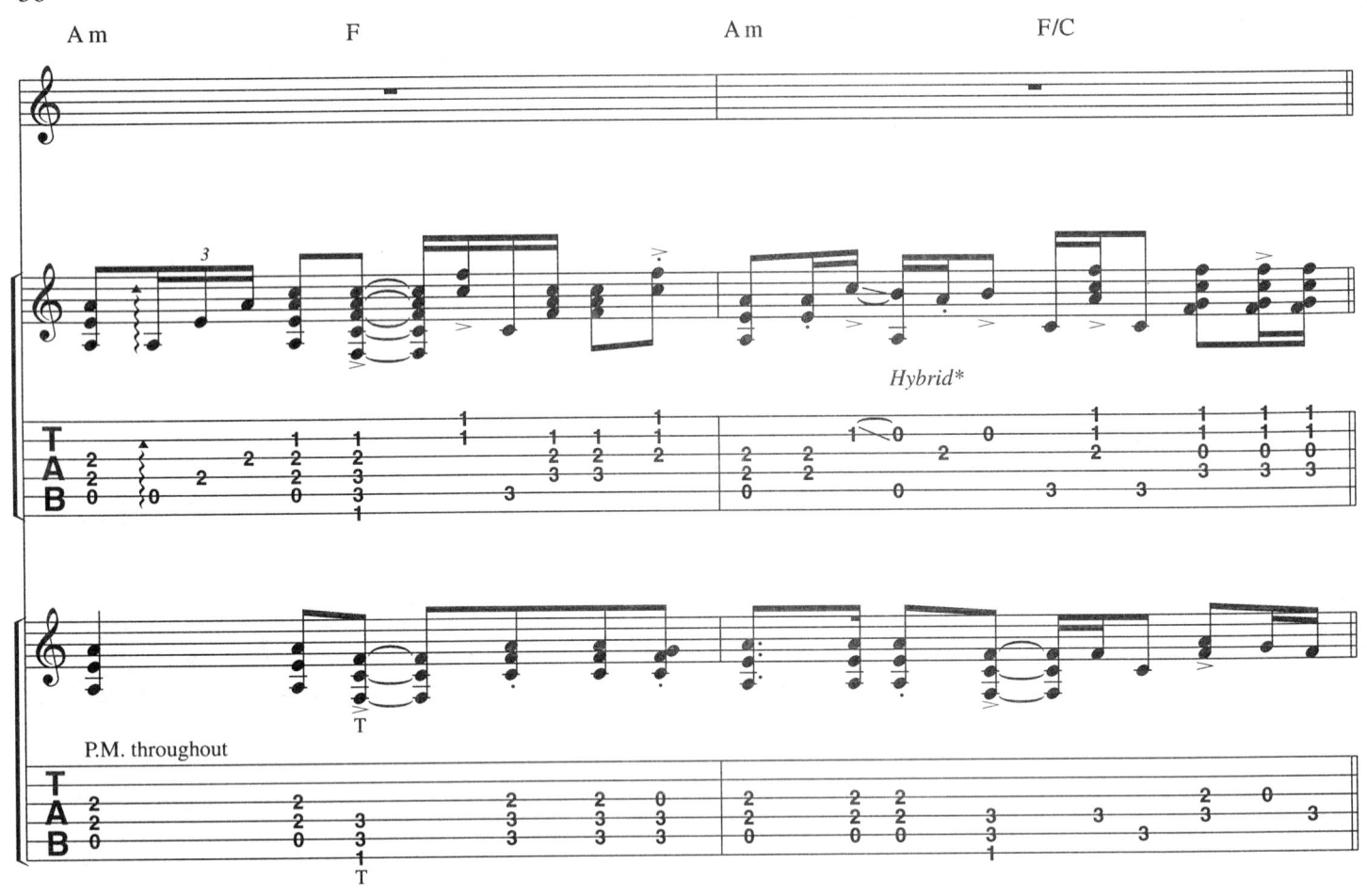

1. When you get weak, and you need to test your
2. *See additional lyrics*

*Low strings flatpicked, upper strings fingerpicked.
**Choked with pick hand palm rather than strummed.

57

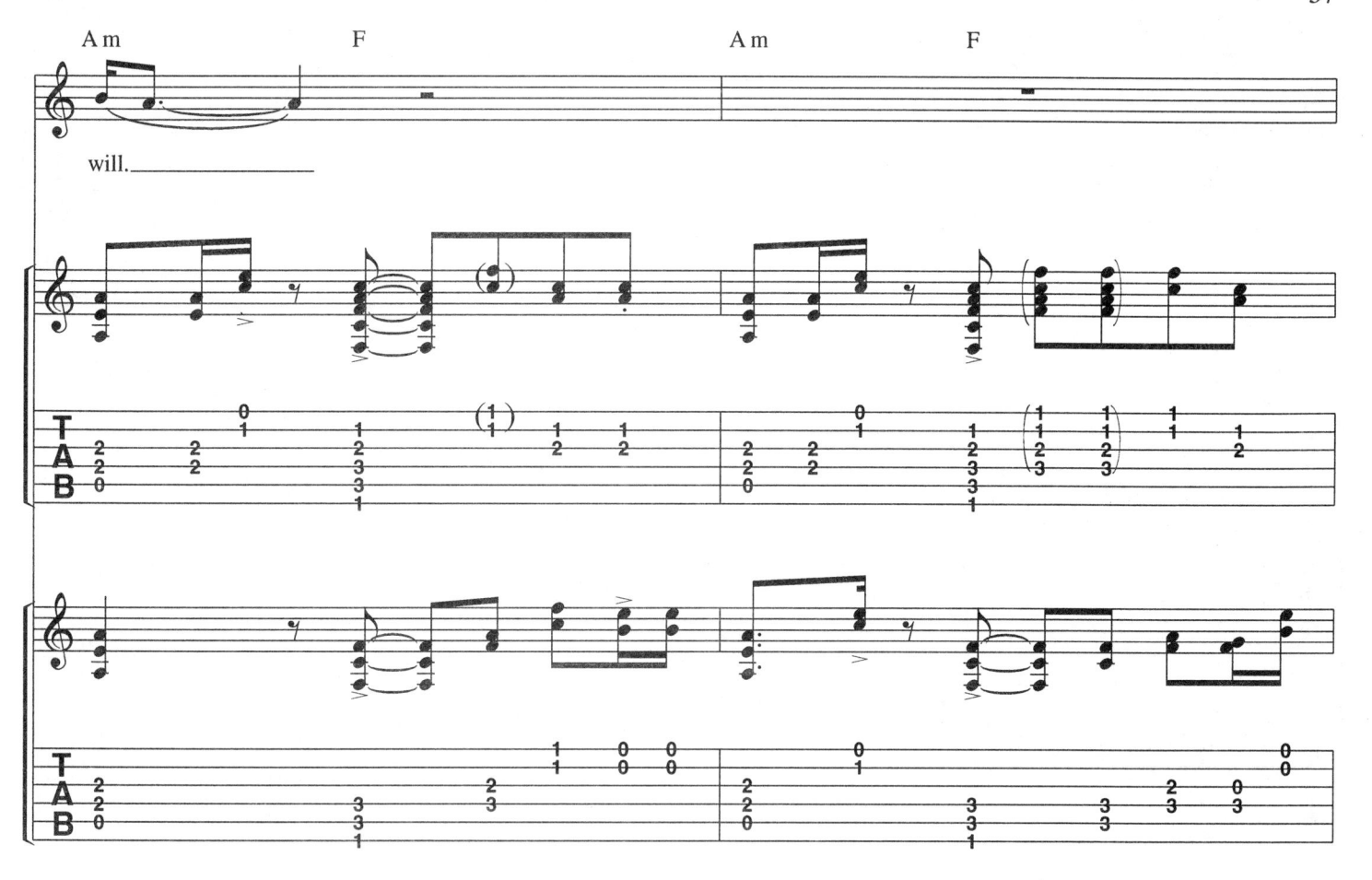

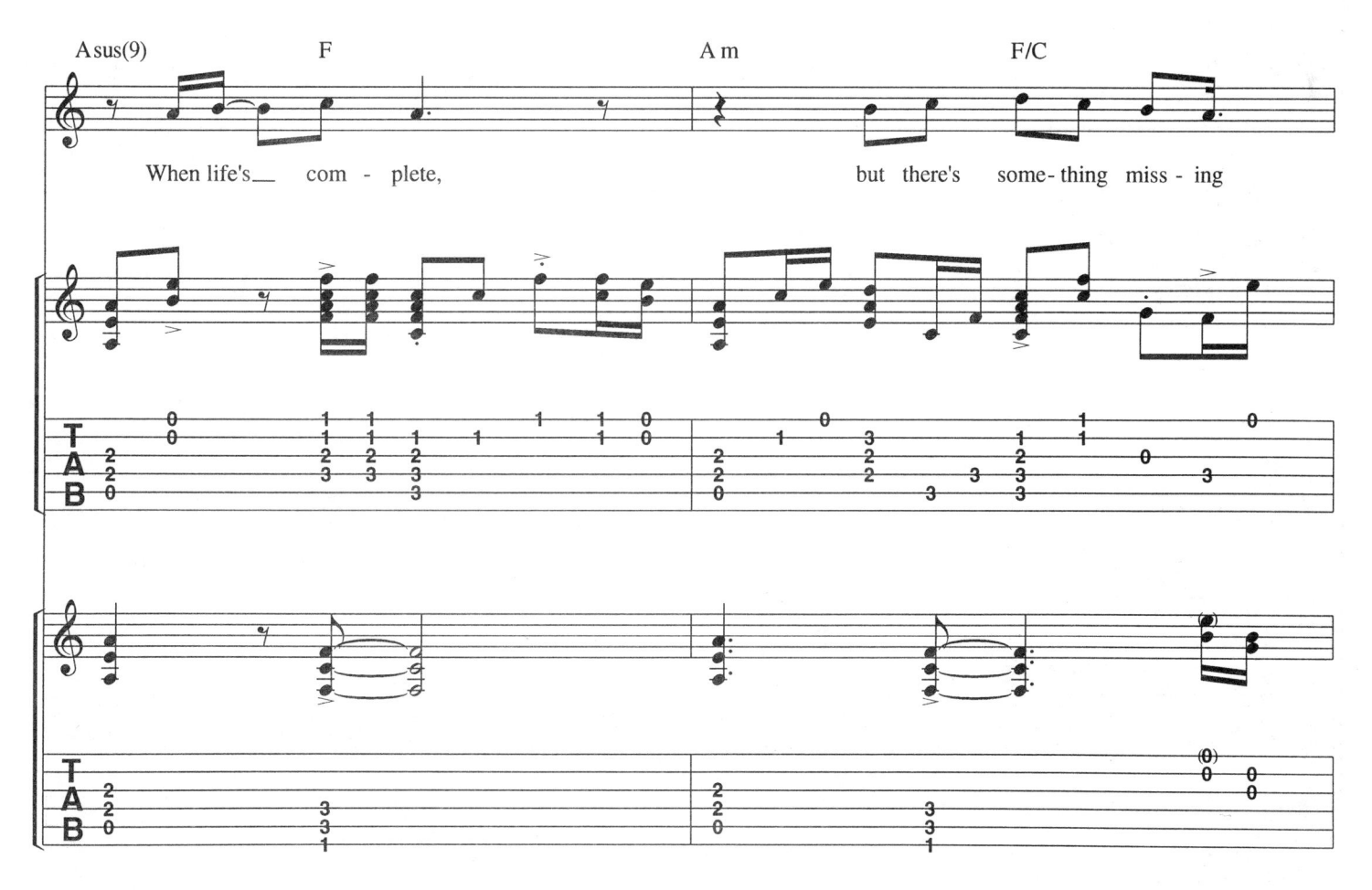

will._____

When life's__ com - plete,   but there's some-thing miss-ing

Change Your Mind - 36 - 3
PG9502

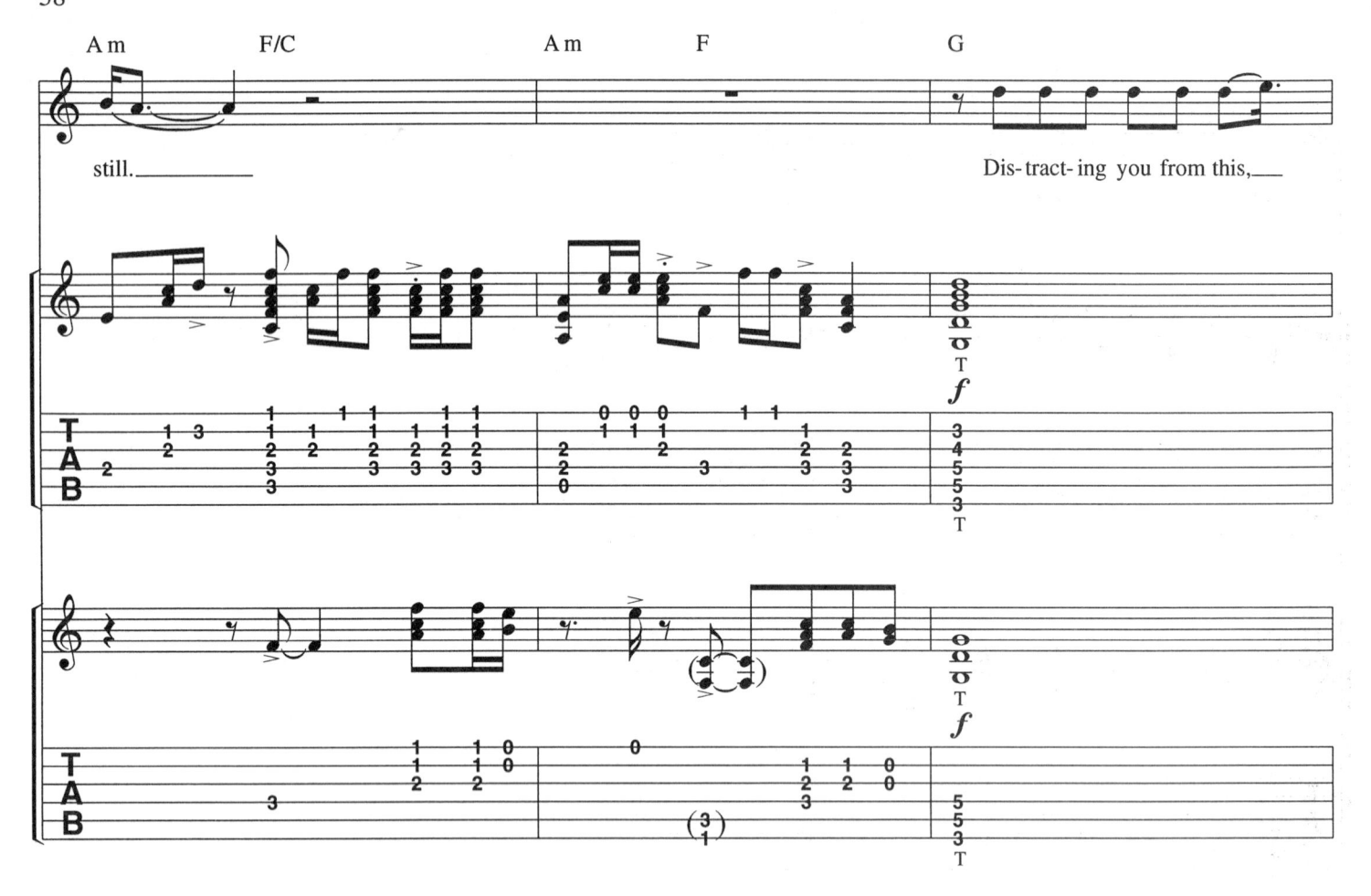

still. Dis-tract-ing you from this,___ must be the one___ you love,___ must be the one___ whose mag-ic touch can change your

harm.   harm.

Change Your Mind - 36 - 4

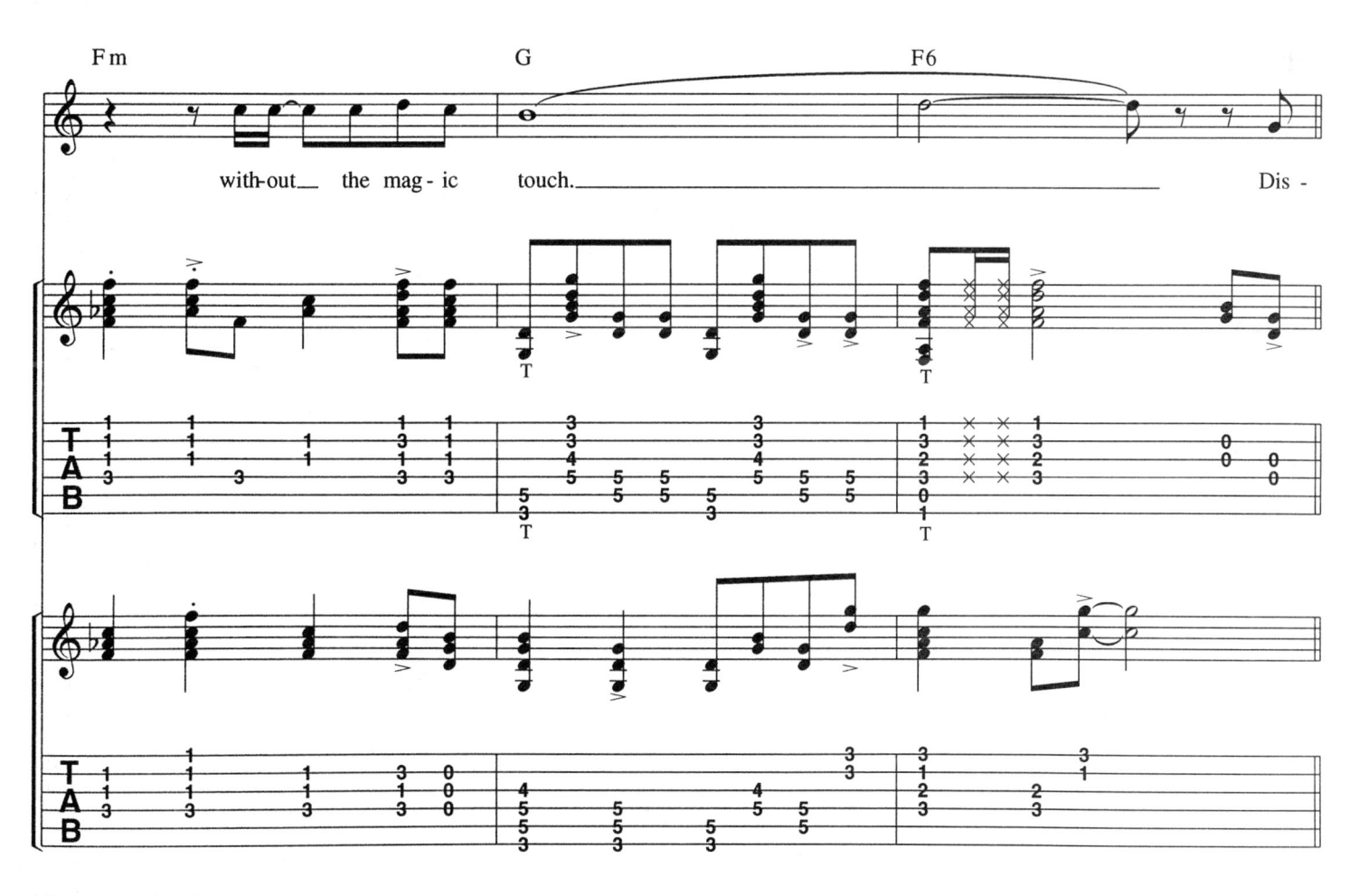

mind, don't let a-nother day go by

with-out the mag-ic touch. Dis-

Chorus:

| C | C5 | F(9) | Fmaj7 | F |

1. tract - ing you,
2. *See additional lyrics*

sup -

Background vocals: change your mind,___

| C | | F | |

port - ing you,

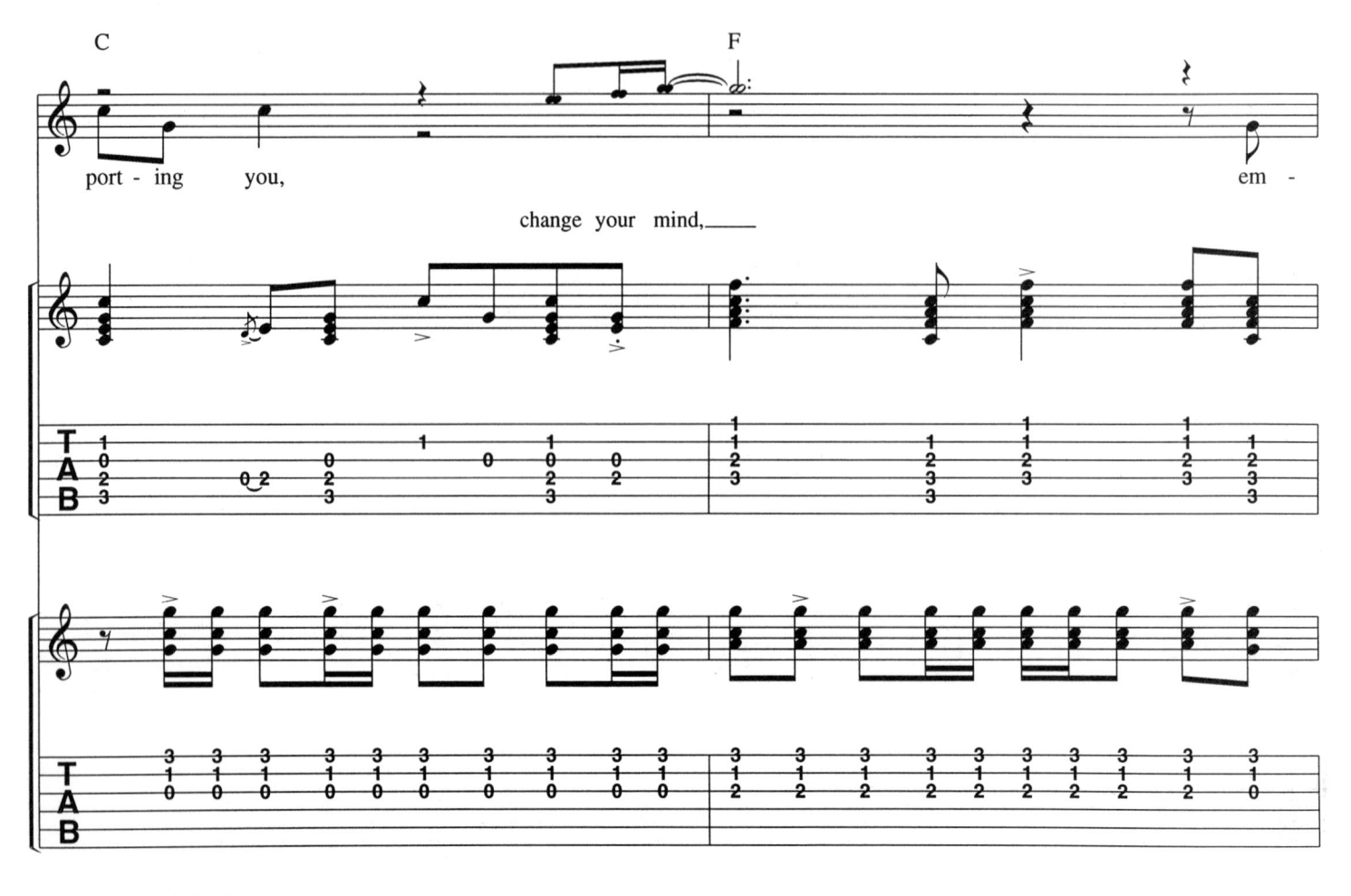

em -

change your mind,___

Change Your Mind - 36 - 6
PG9502

61

brac- ing you, con-

change your mind,

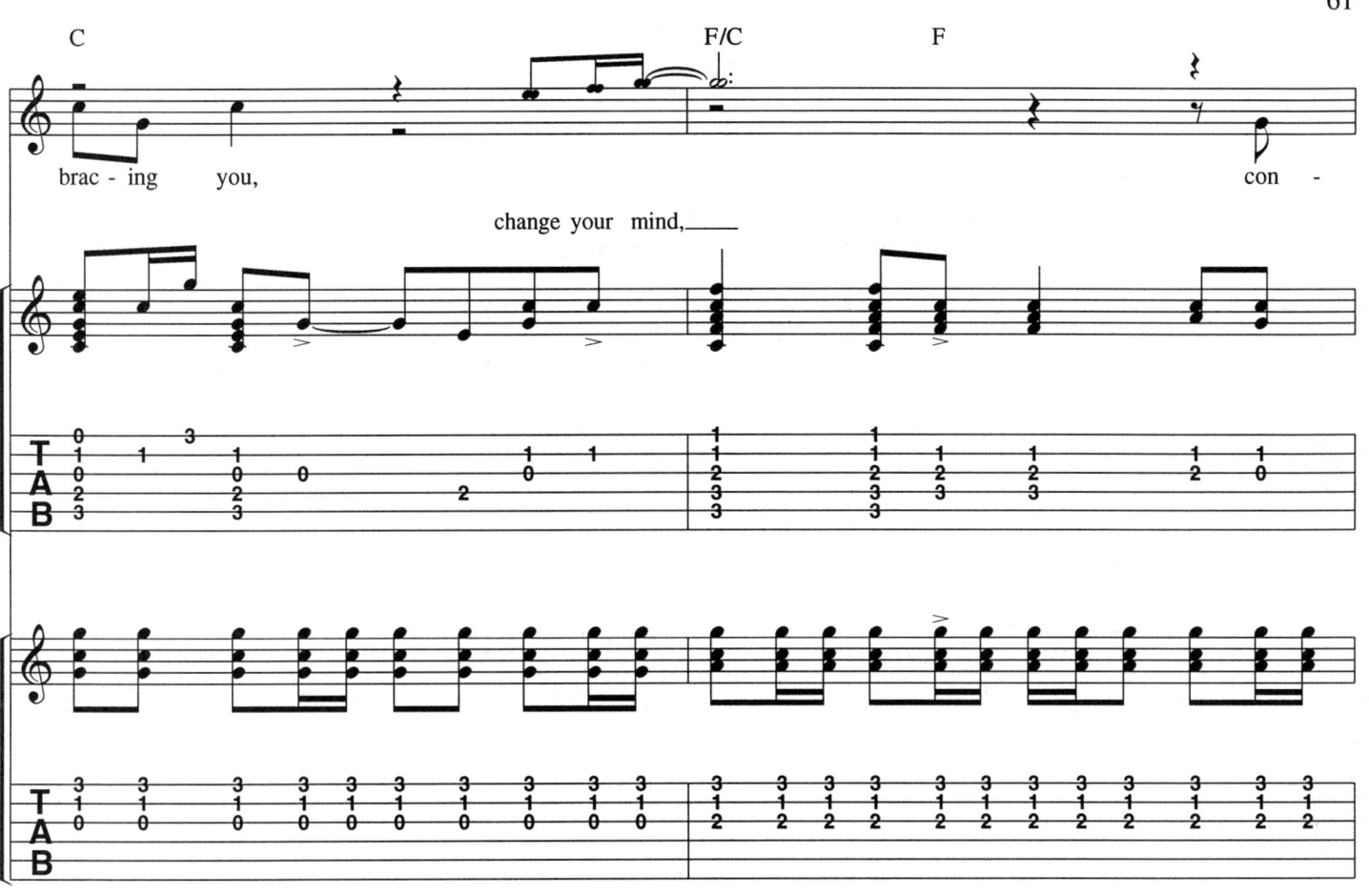

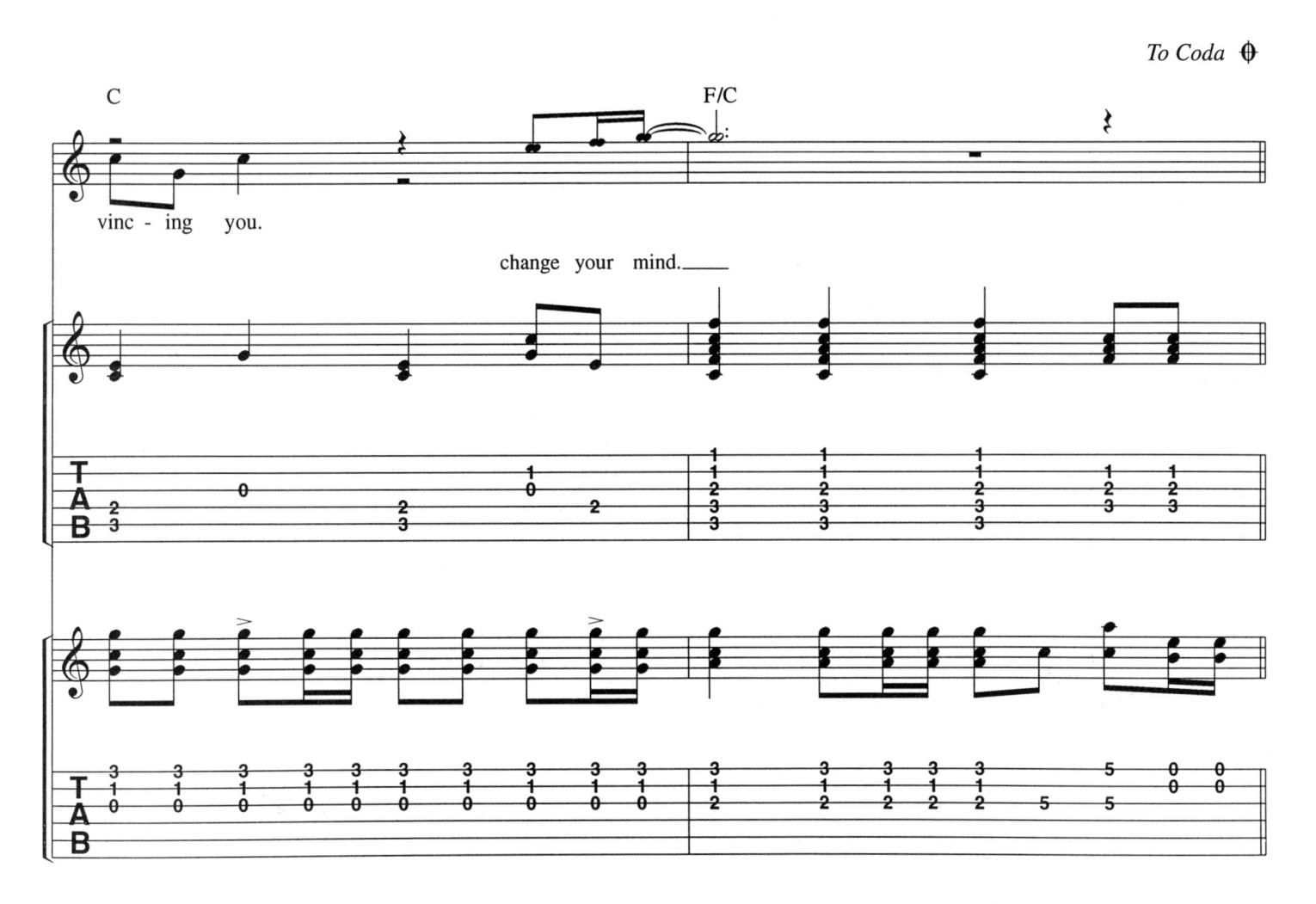

vinc- ing you.

change your mind.

To Coda ⊕

Change Your Mind - 36 - 7
PG9502

*As string ③ is pulled-off at XIV, strings ③ -① ring open for one beat.

*Cue-sized notes are from another track. They are played through an active divider (sounding 2 octaves lower) with the lower sound mixed louder.

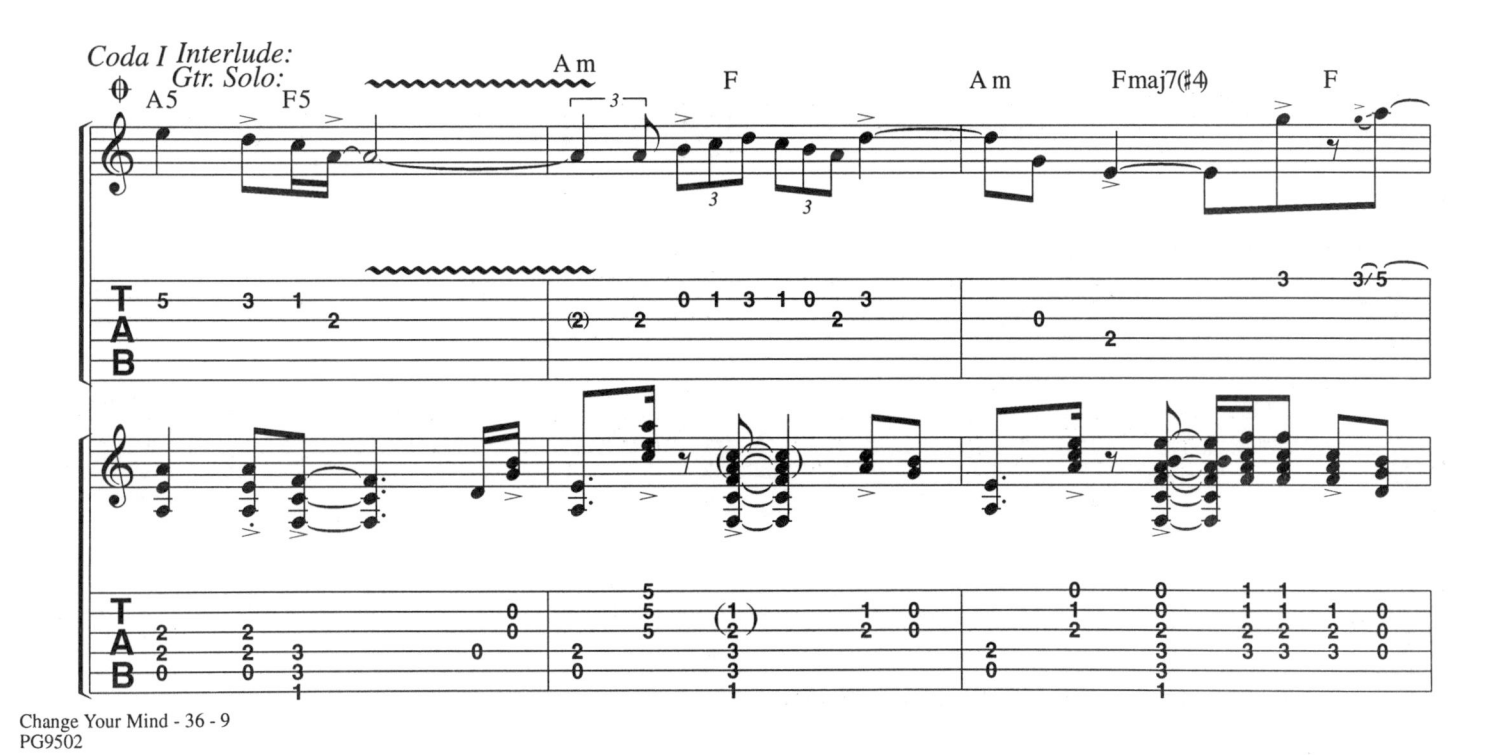

*This chord holds for rest of measure.

Coda I Interlude:
Gtr. Solo:

Change Your Mind - 36 - 9
PG9502

Gtr.2 continues simile
Am Fmaj7 Asus2 F Am F
f
mf
Am F Am F Am
Gtr. 1
toggle pick-up selector
neck pick-up
play behind beat
reverb effect
A.H.
A.H.
Am F Am F Am F Am F
f

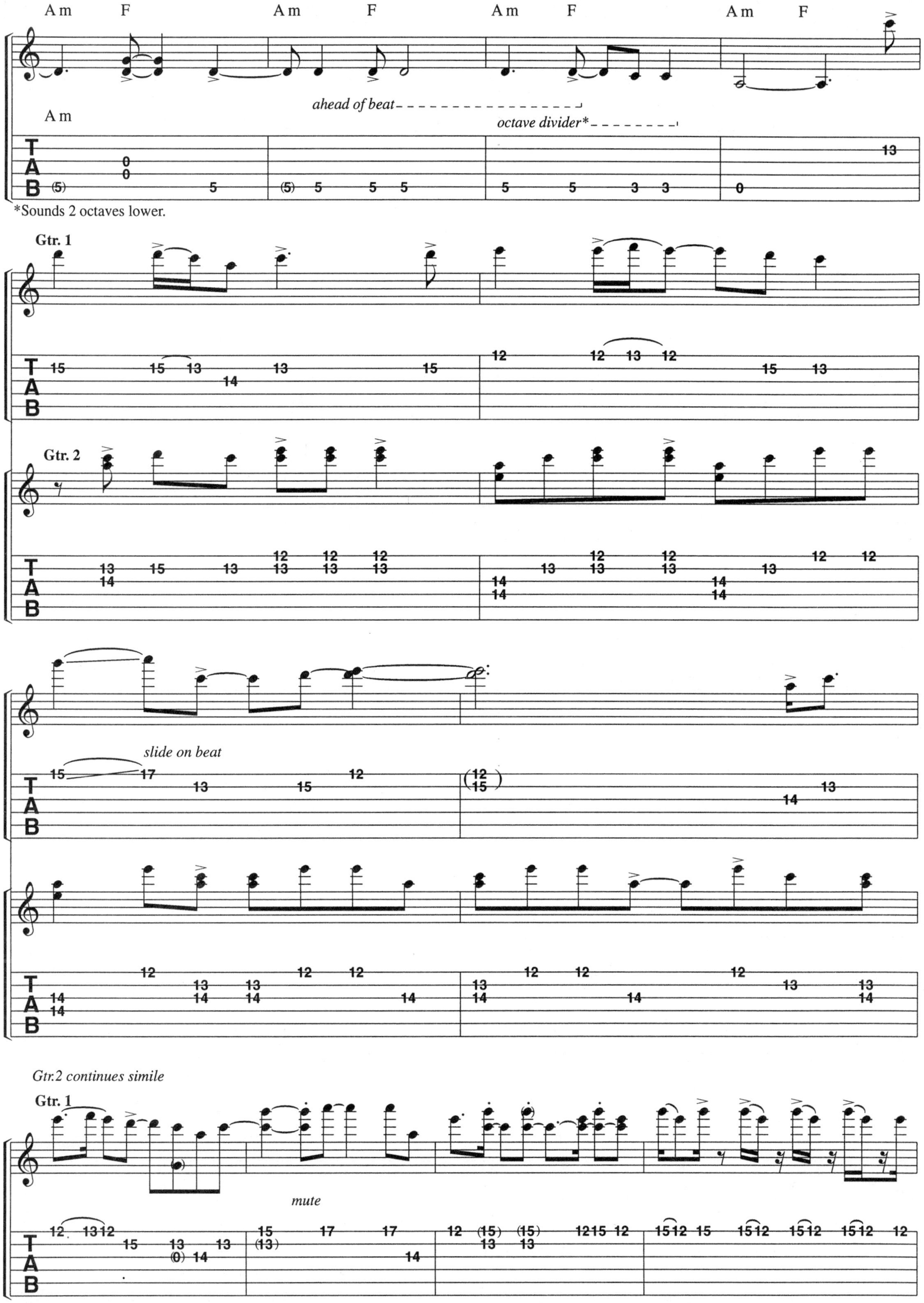
Am F Am F Am F Am F
Am
ahead of beat
octave divider*
*Sounds 2 octaves lower.
Gtr. 1
Gtr. 2
slide on beat
Gtr.2 continues simile
Gtr. 1
mute

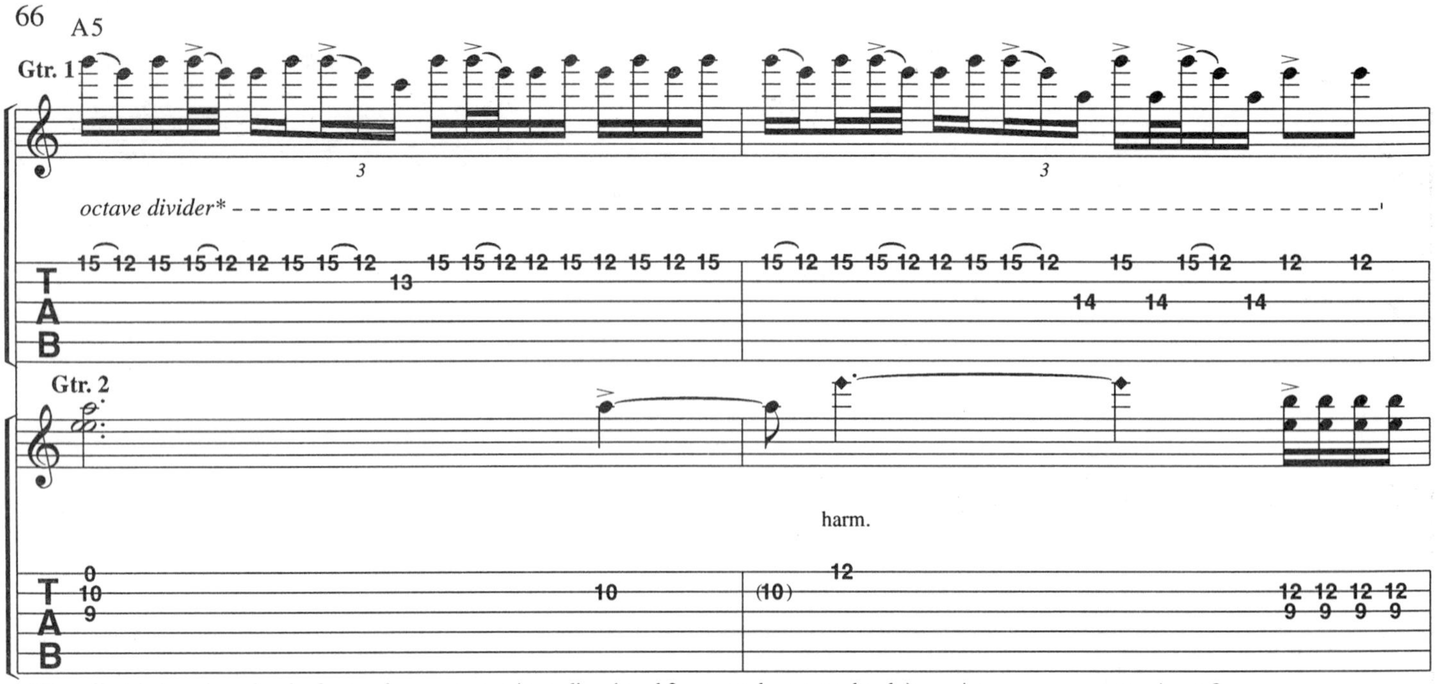

*The effect is heard randomly due to slow response (sounding 1 and 2 octaves lower randomly).

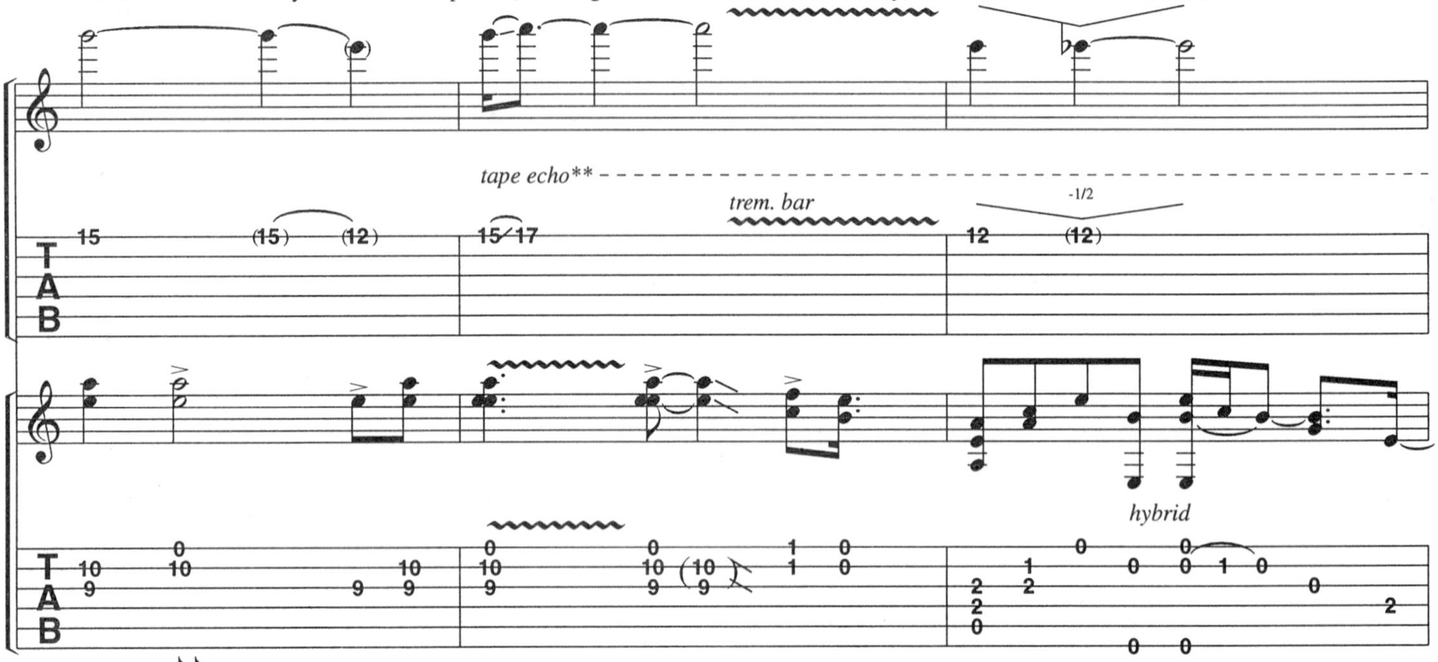

**Echo set at ♪♪ rate with 2 repeats (echo notes are'nt notated).
***With side to side (violin) hand vibrato

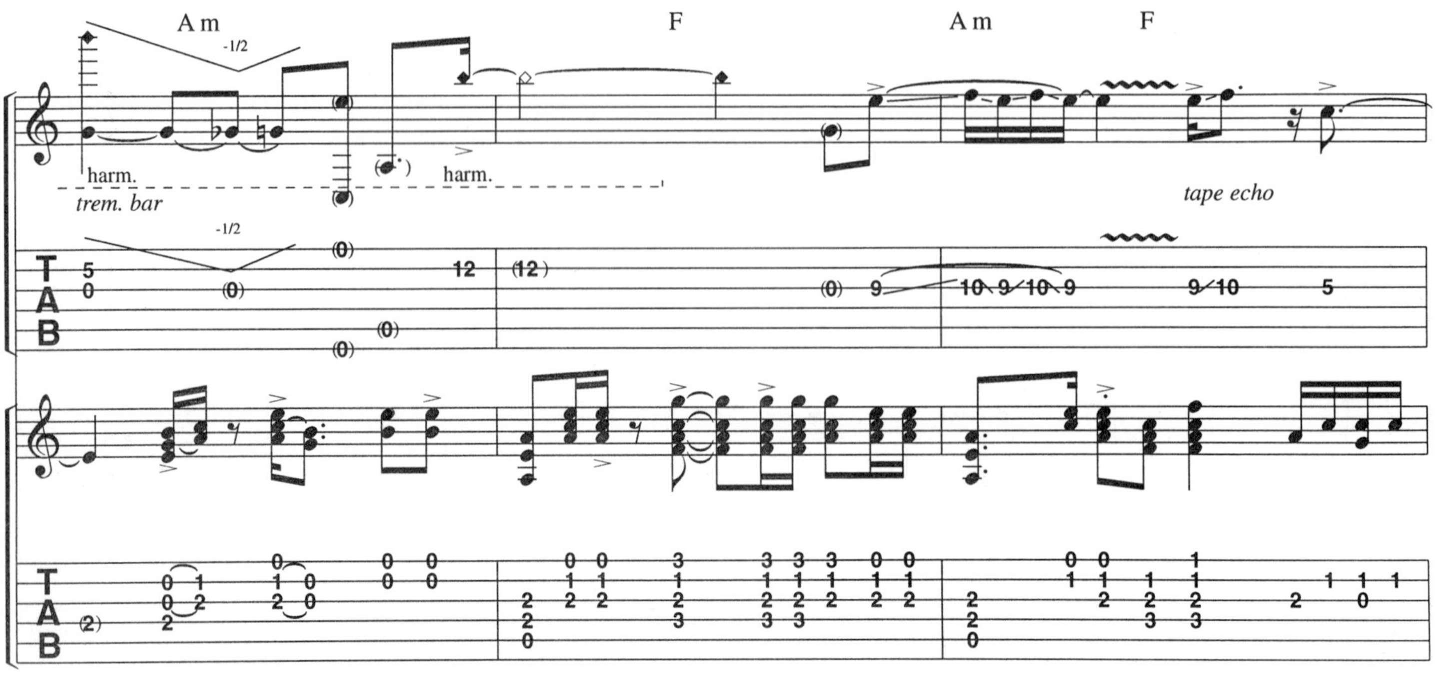

Change Your Mind - 36 - 13

Verse:

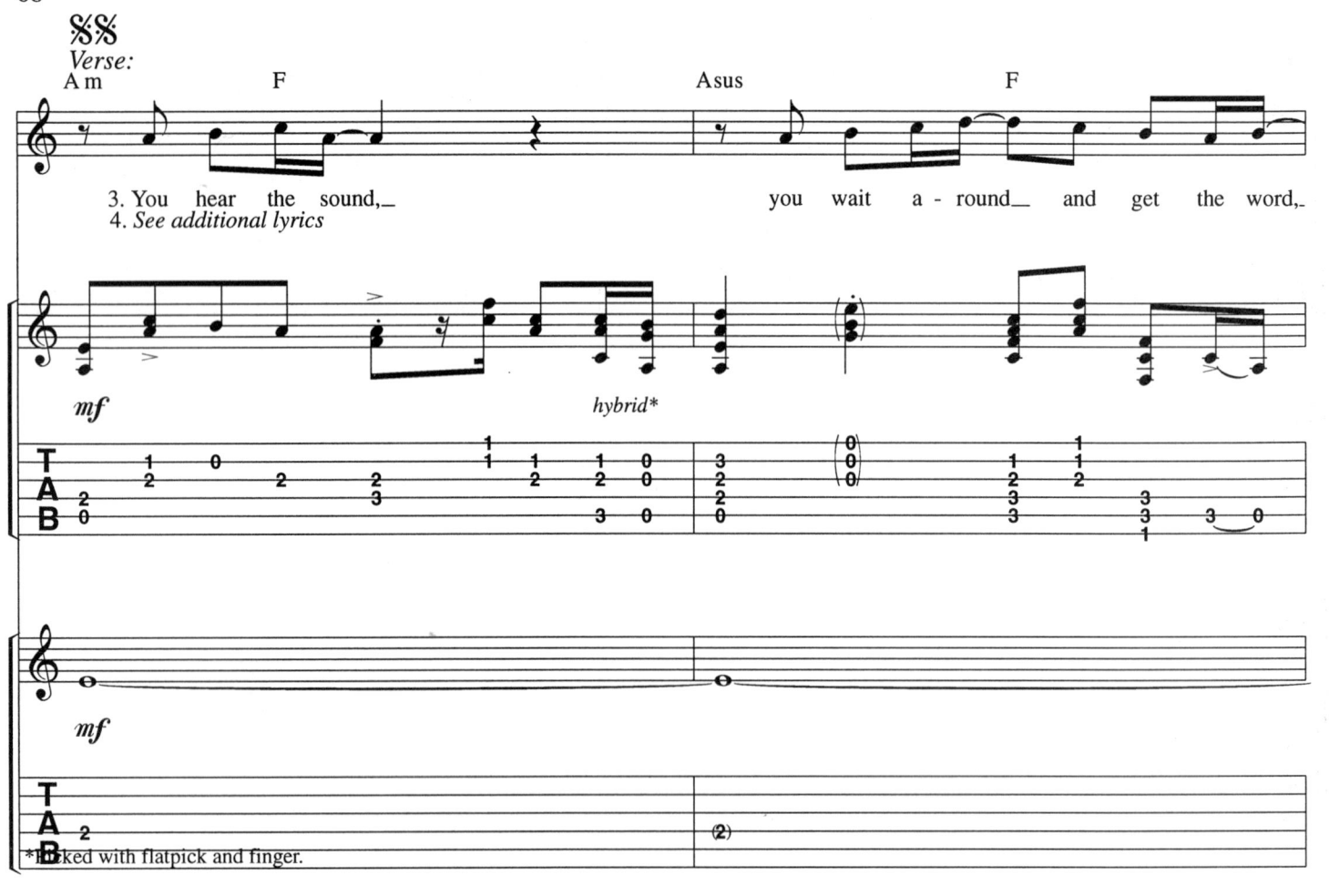

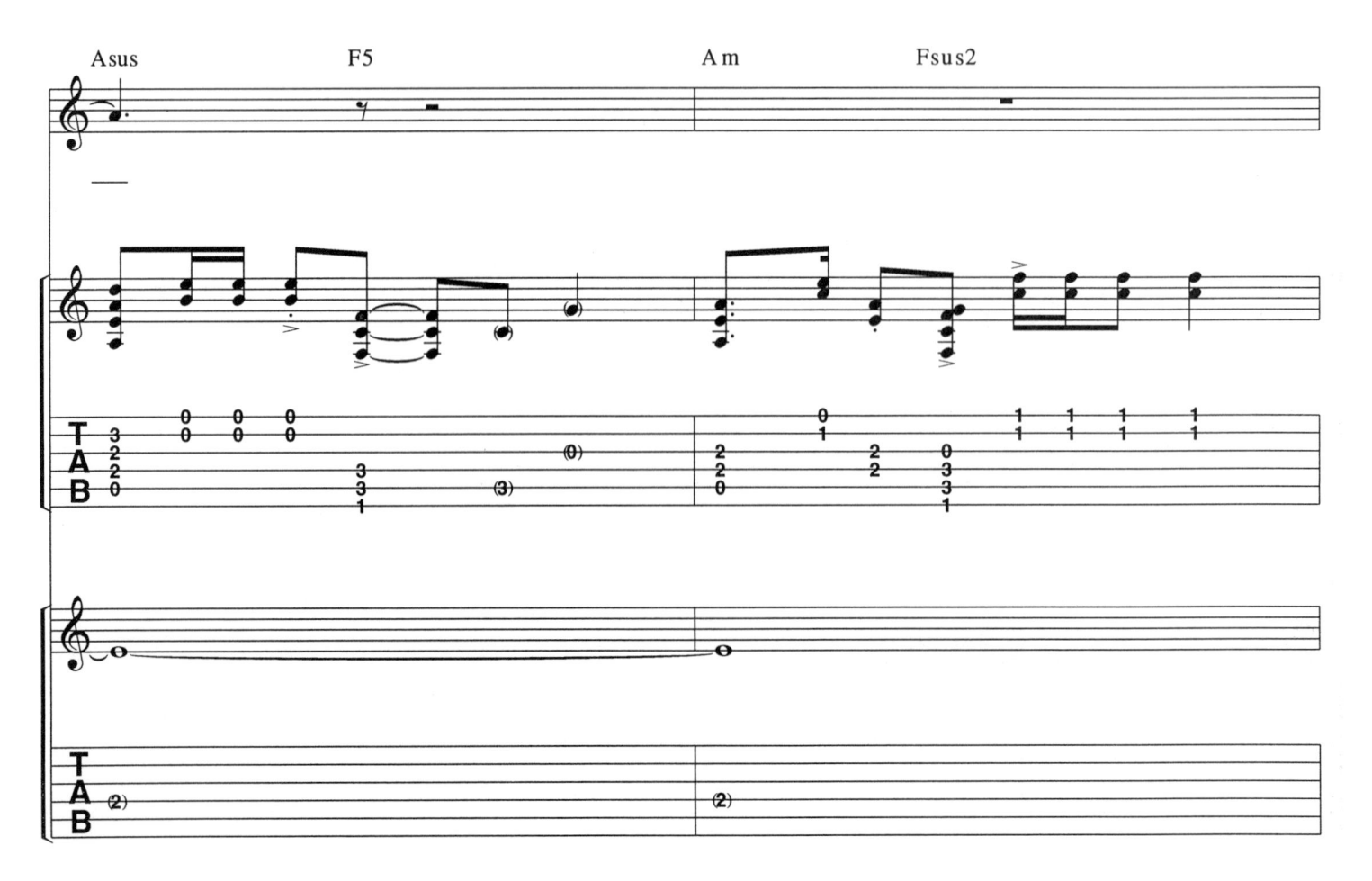

3. You hear the sound,__ you wait a-round__ and get the word,__
4. *See additional lyrics*

*Picked with flatpick and finger.

Change Your Mind - 36 - 14

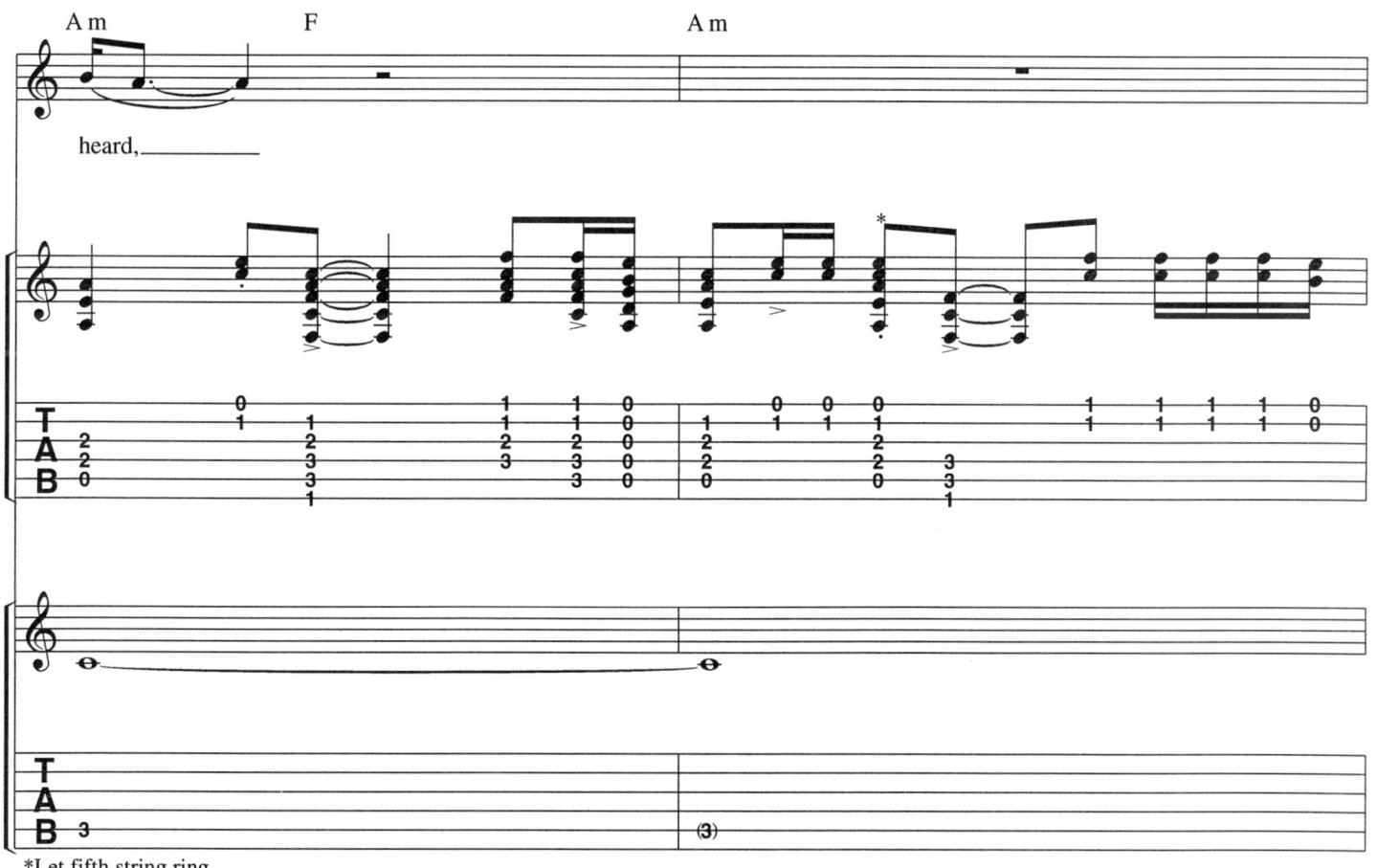

*Let fifth string ring.

Change Your Mind - 36 - 15
PG9502

70

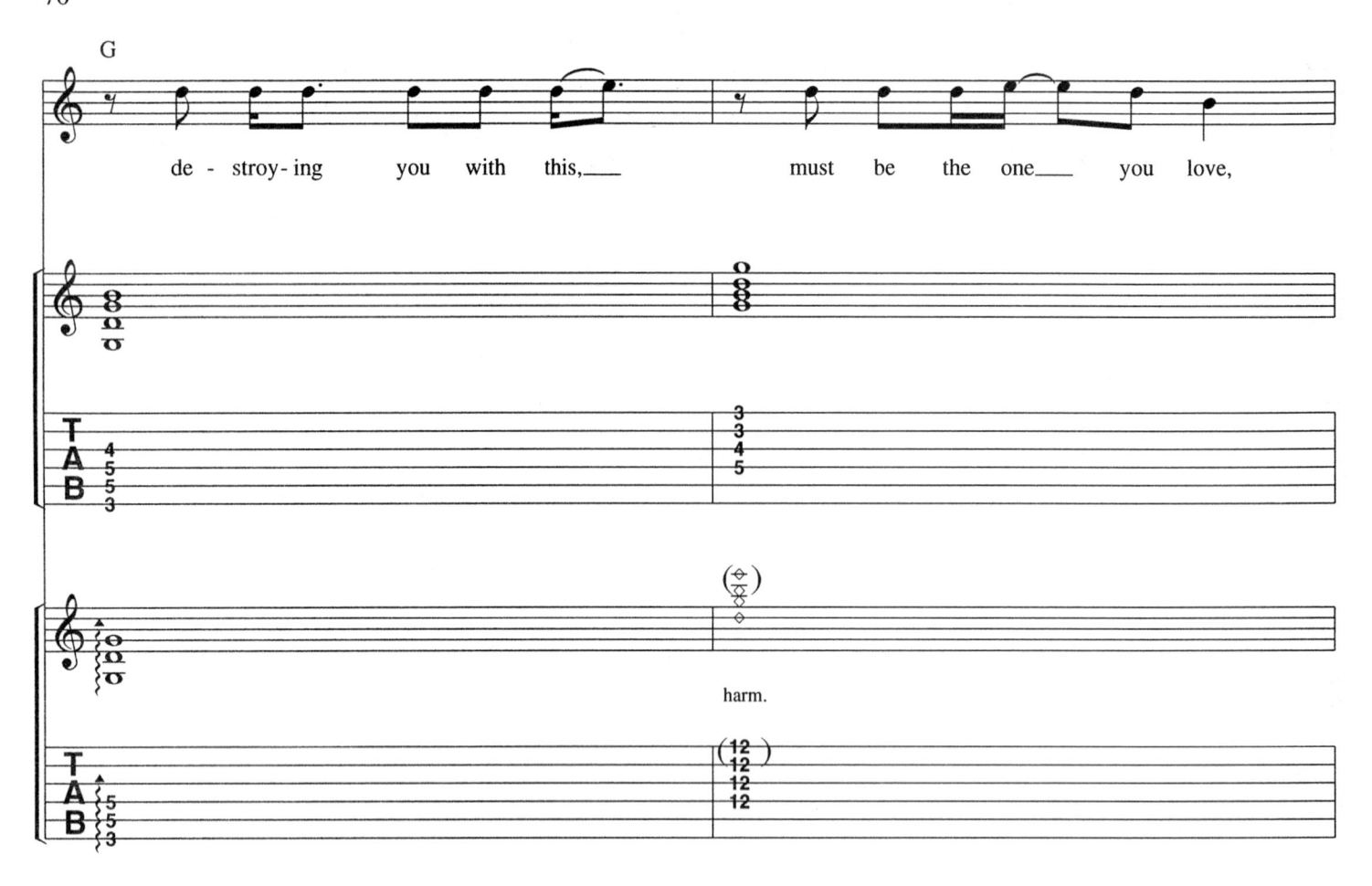

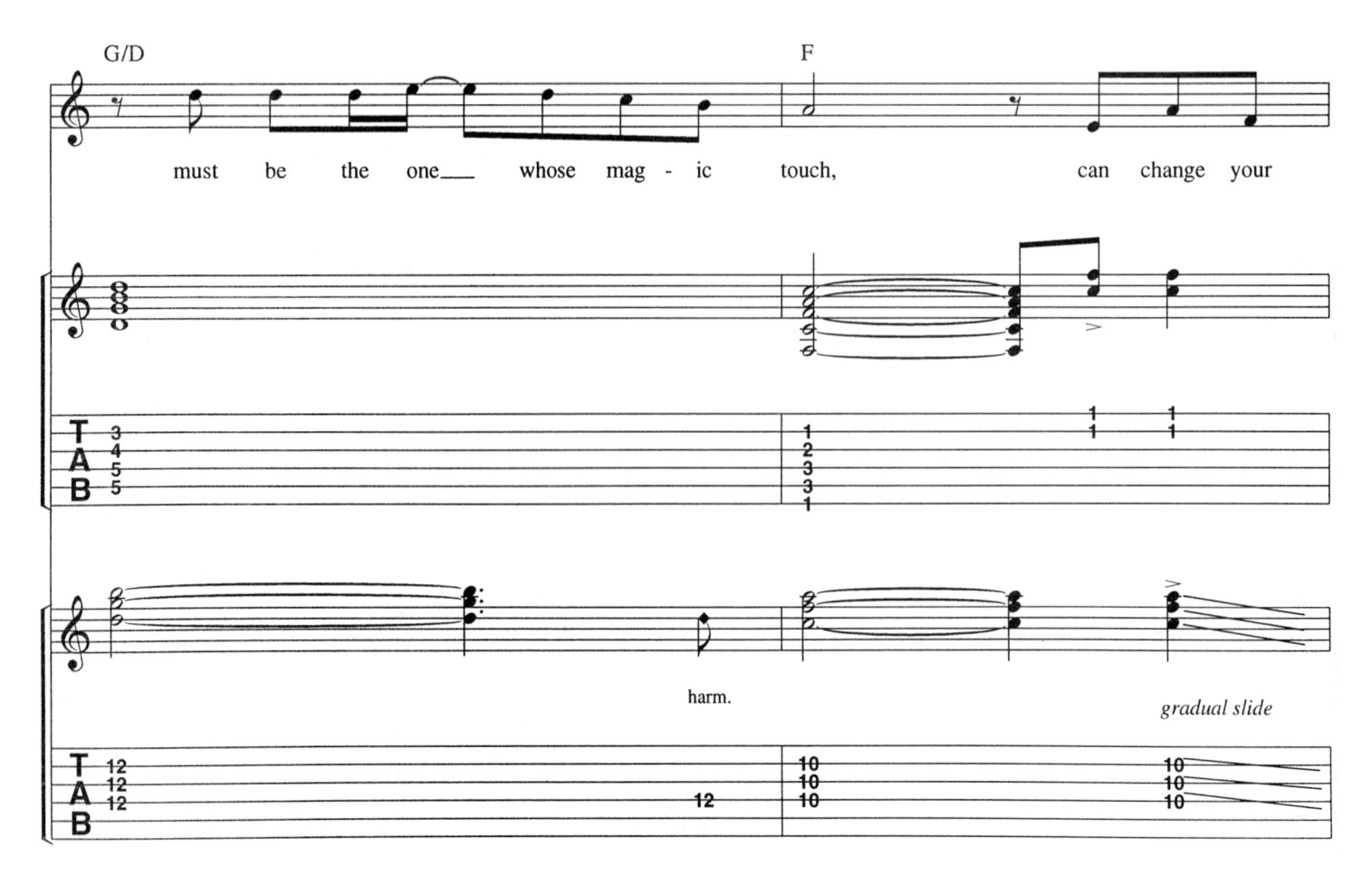

C/G
E
mind, don't let a - noth - er day go
hybrid
Dm7
Fm Fm6 Fm7 Fm6 Fm
by with - out the mag - ic

touch.___ De-

Chorus 3 & 4:

3. stroy - ing you
4. *See additional lyrics*

Background vocals: Change your mind,___

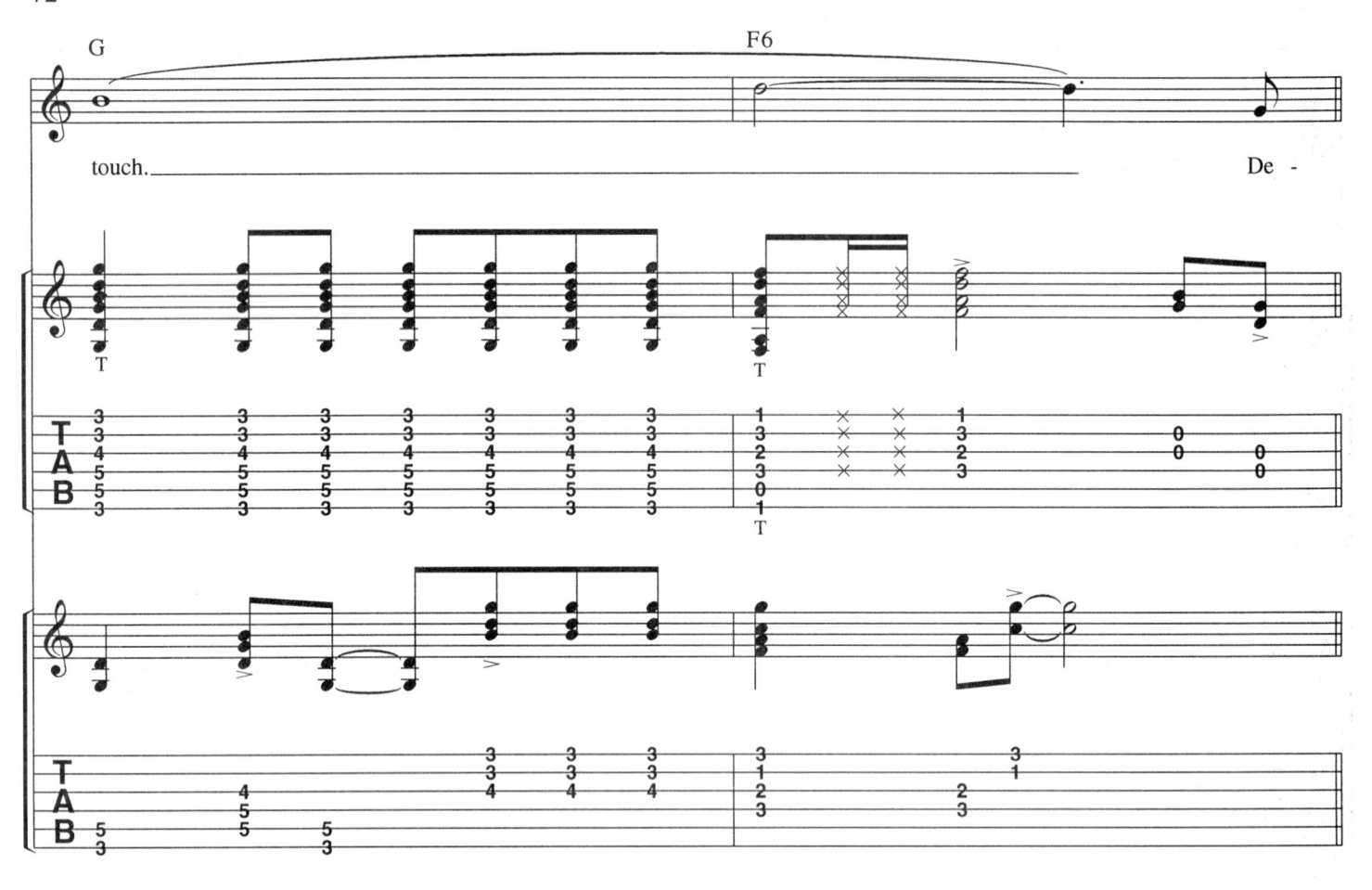

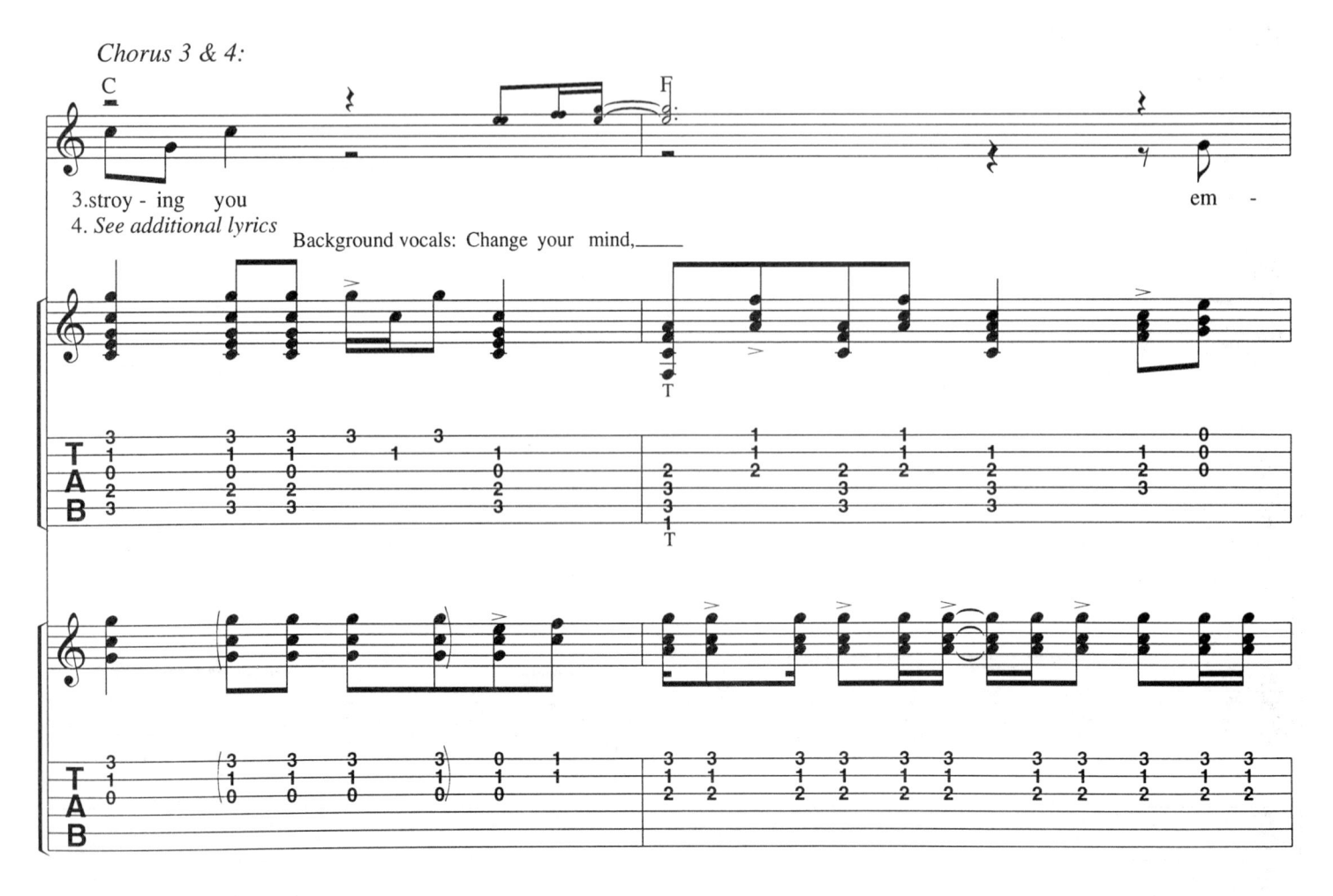

em-

Sheet music: "Change Your Mind"

Lyrics:
brac-ing you, change your mind, pro-
tect-ing you, change your mind, con-fin-ing you, Change your mind, dis-
tract-ing you, change your mind, sup-port-ing you, change your mind, dis-
tort-ing you, change your mind, con-troll-ing you, change your mind, change your mind,
change your mind, change your mind, change your mind, change your mind.

74

Guitar Solo:

ahead of the beat

Change Your Mind - 36 - 20

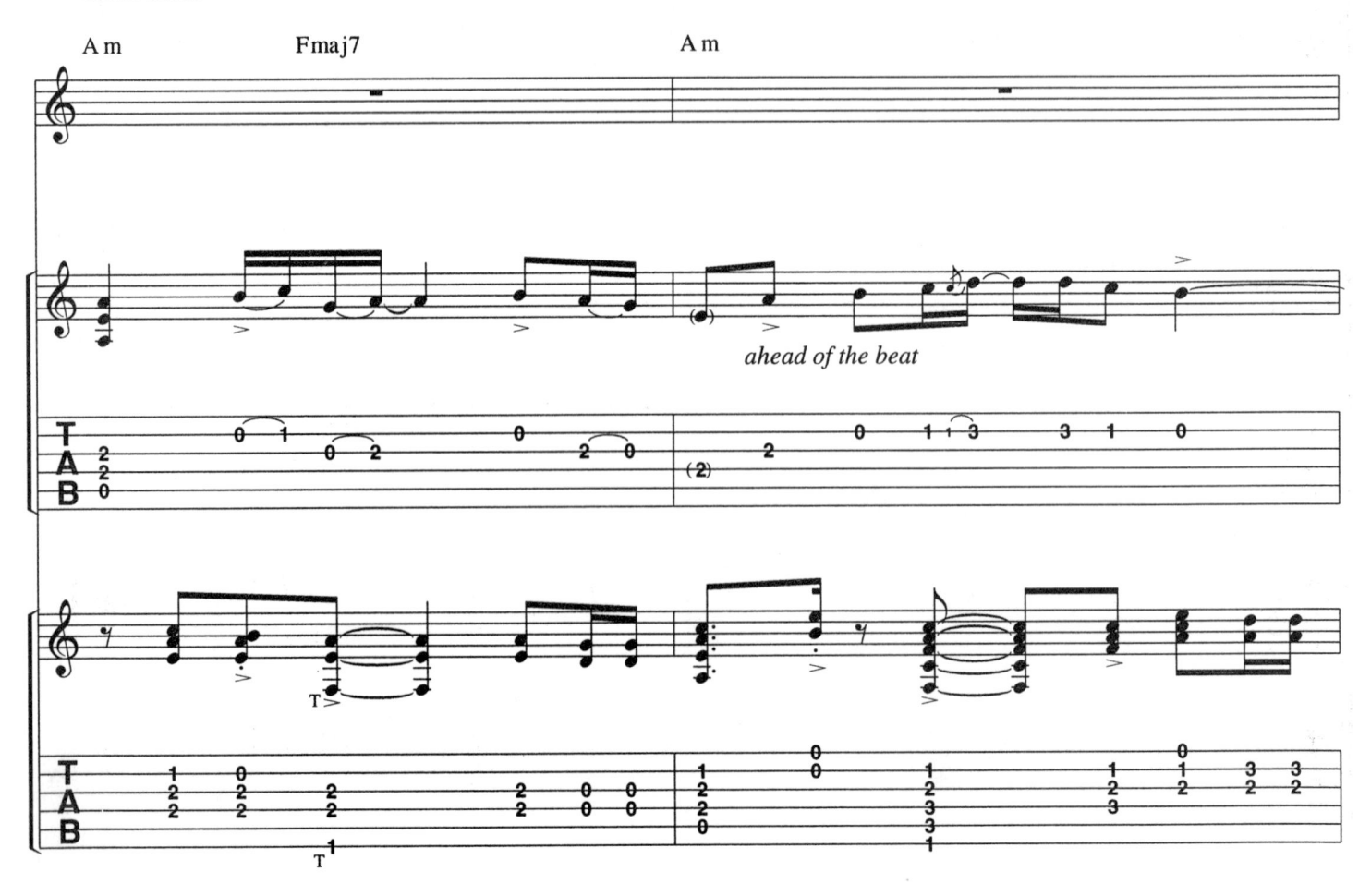

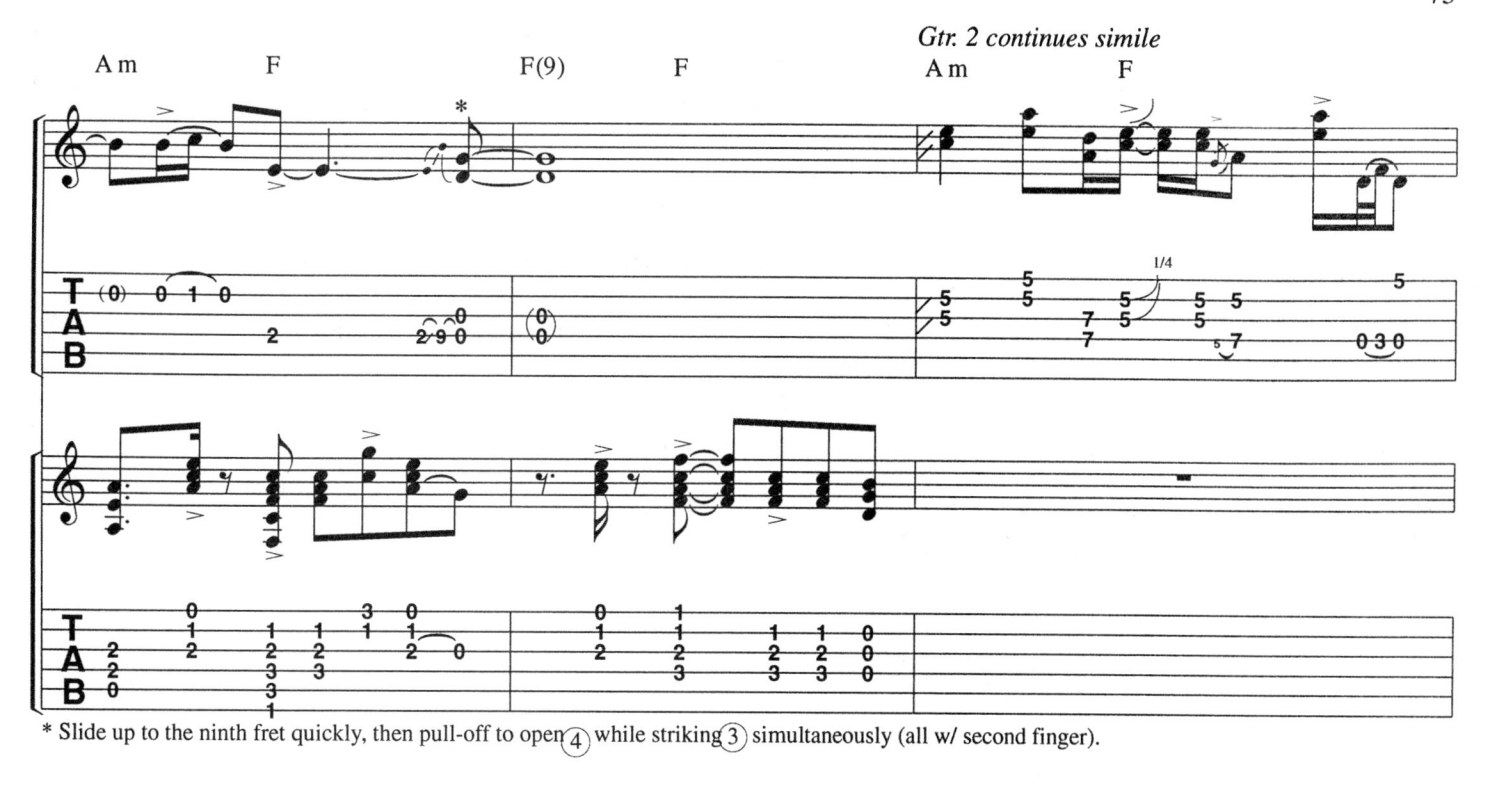

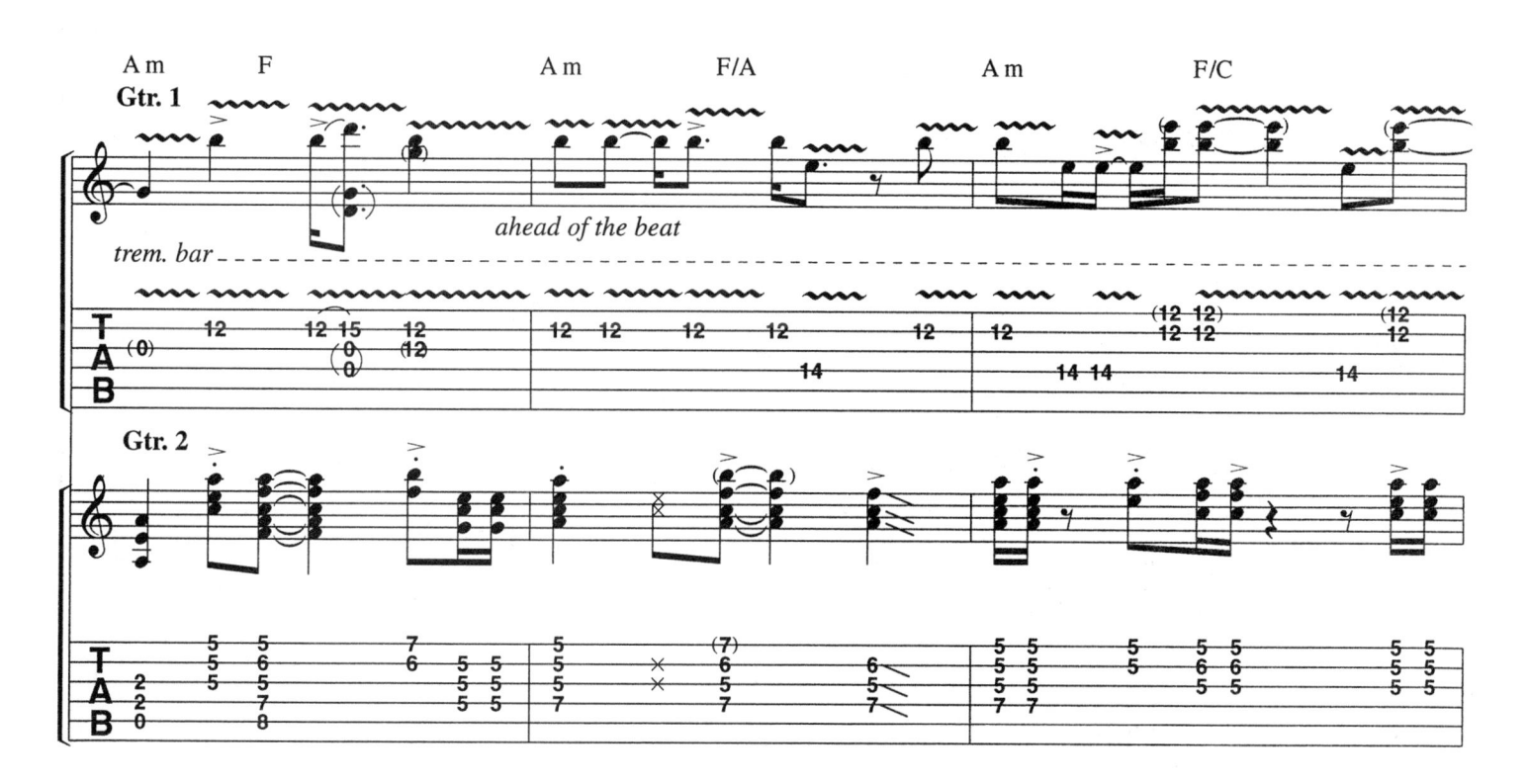

*Slide up to the ninth fret quickly, then pull-off to open ④ while striking ③ simultaneously (all w/ second finger).

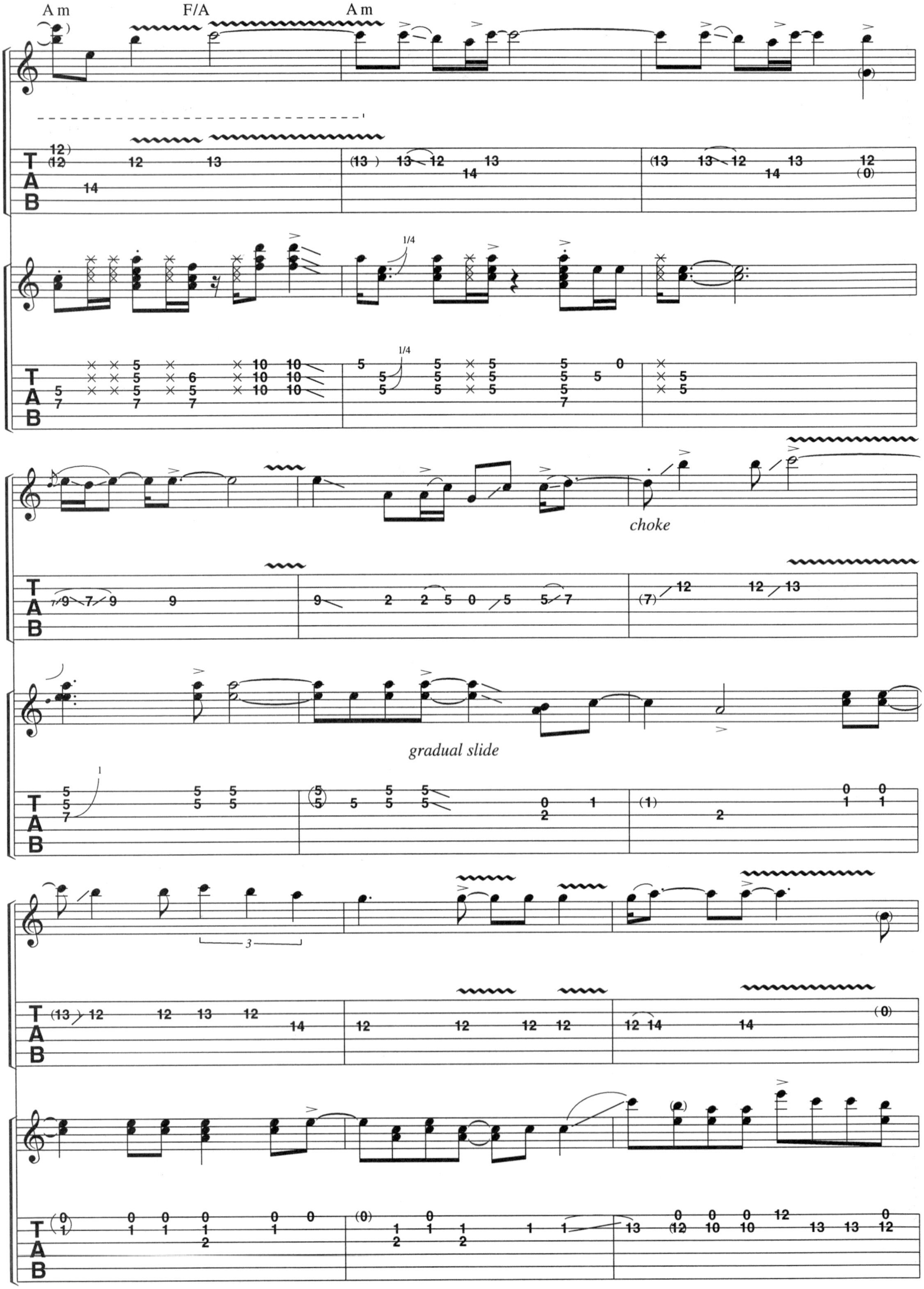
Am
F/A
Am
choke
gradual slide

77

*Distortion/tone sounds different here due to different amplifier.

Change Your Mind - 36 - 24
PG9502

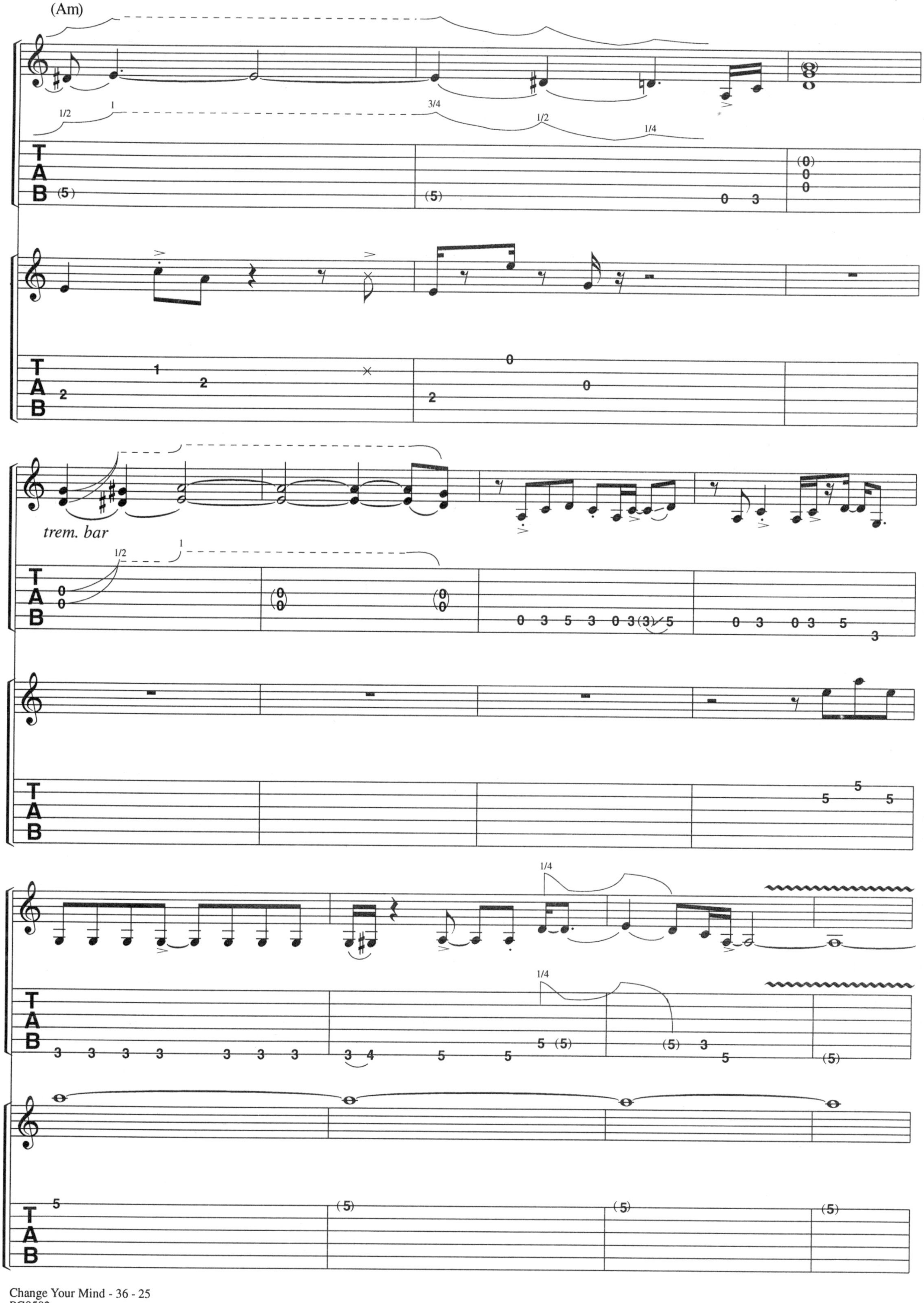
(Am)
trem. bar

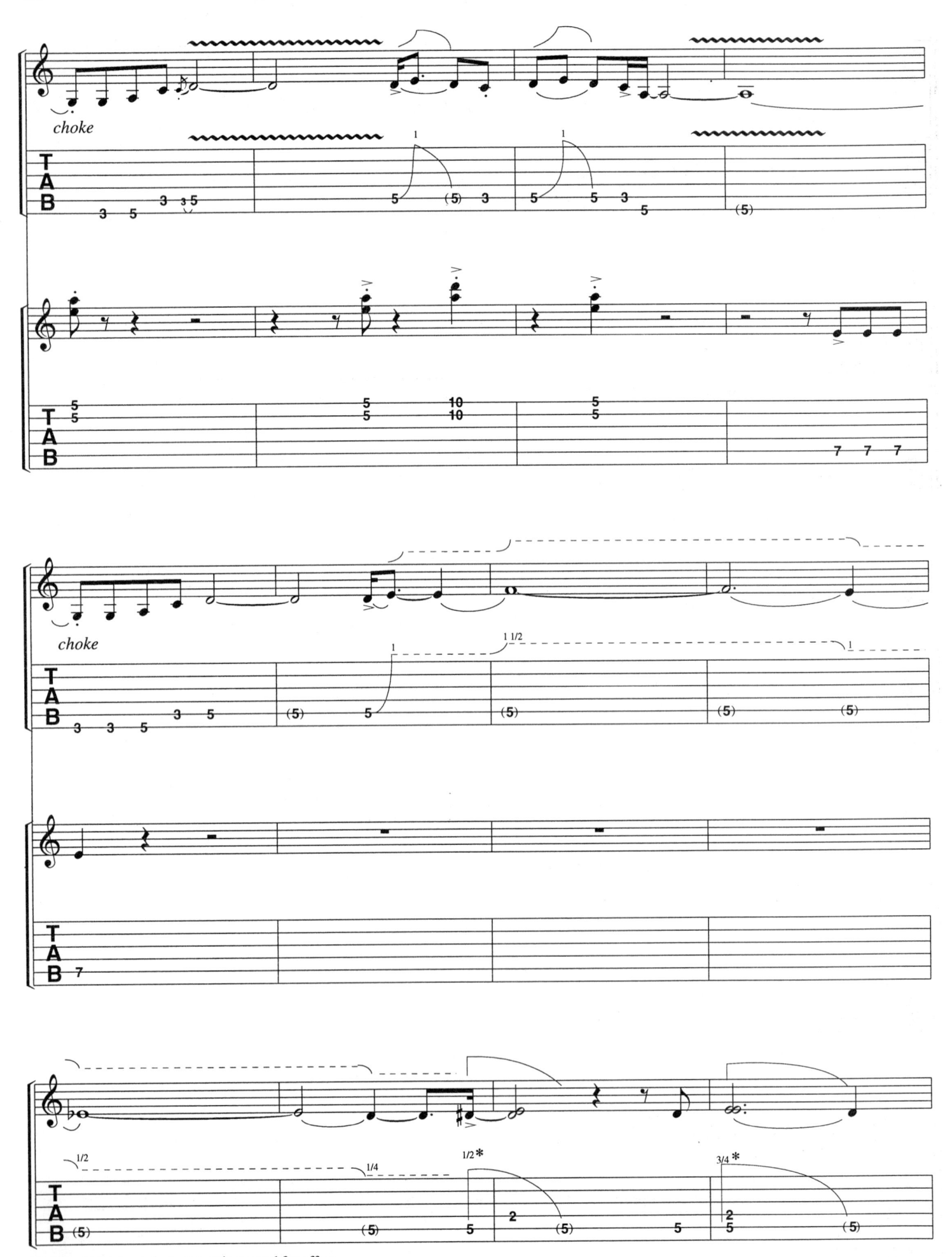

* Out of tune beats between strings used for effect.

*Out of tune beats between strings used for effect.

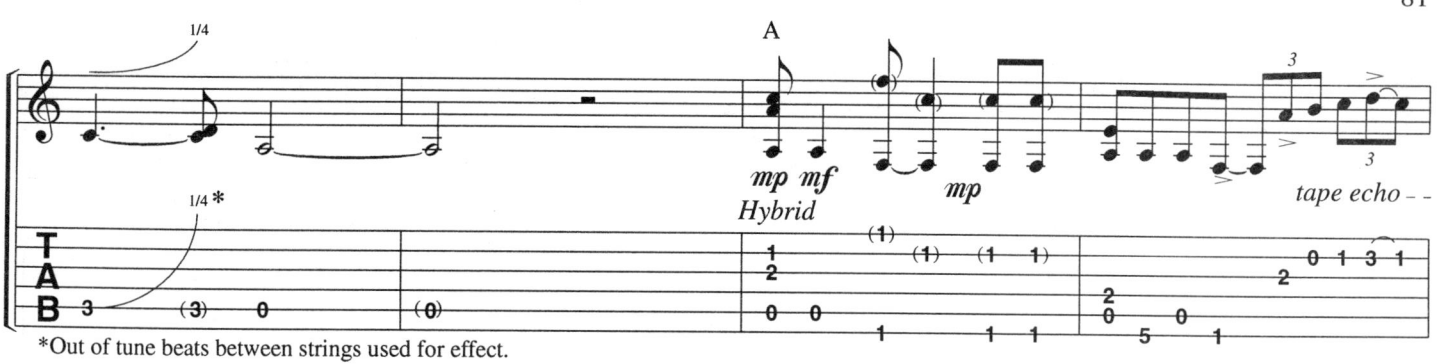

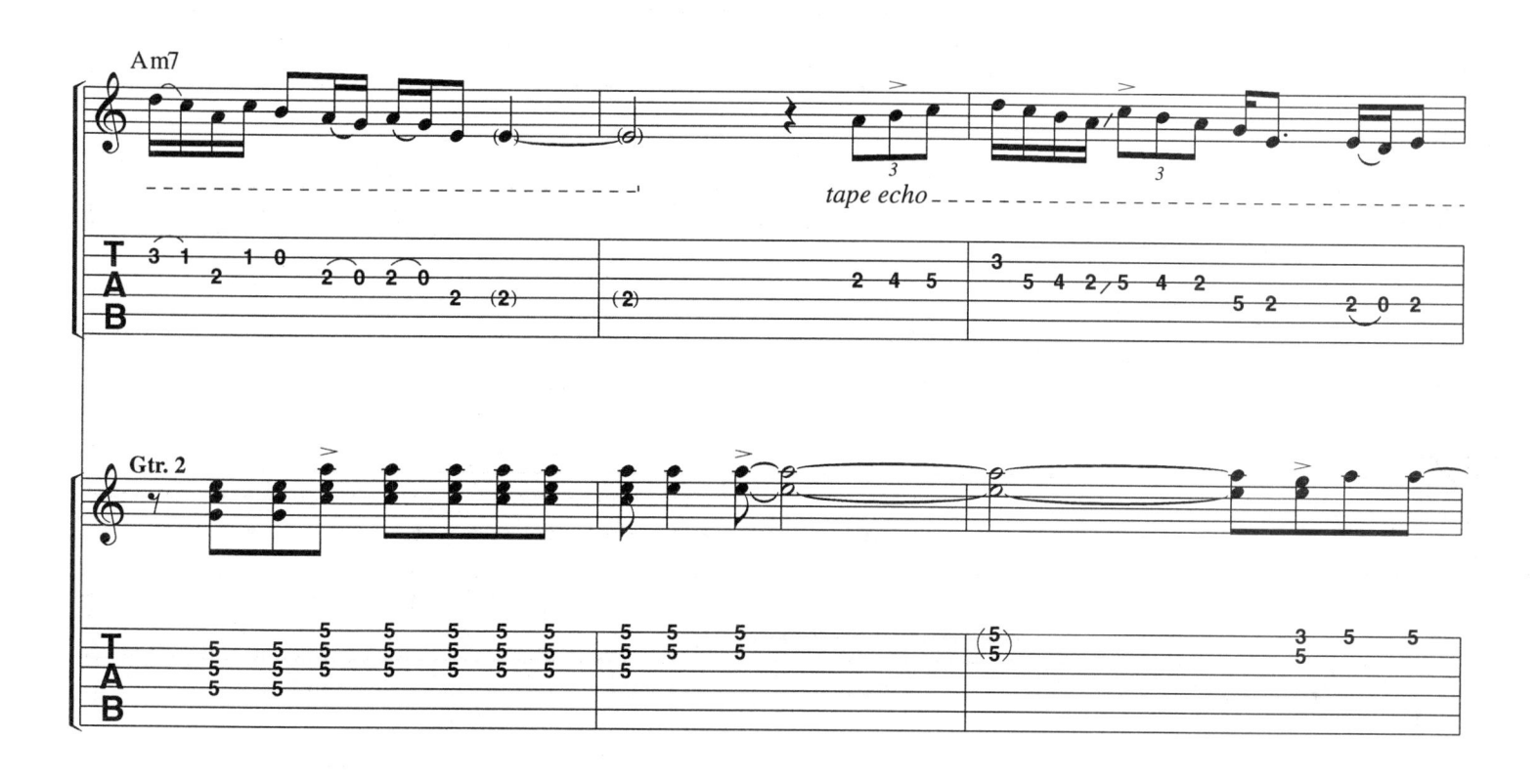

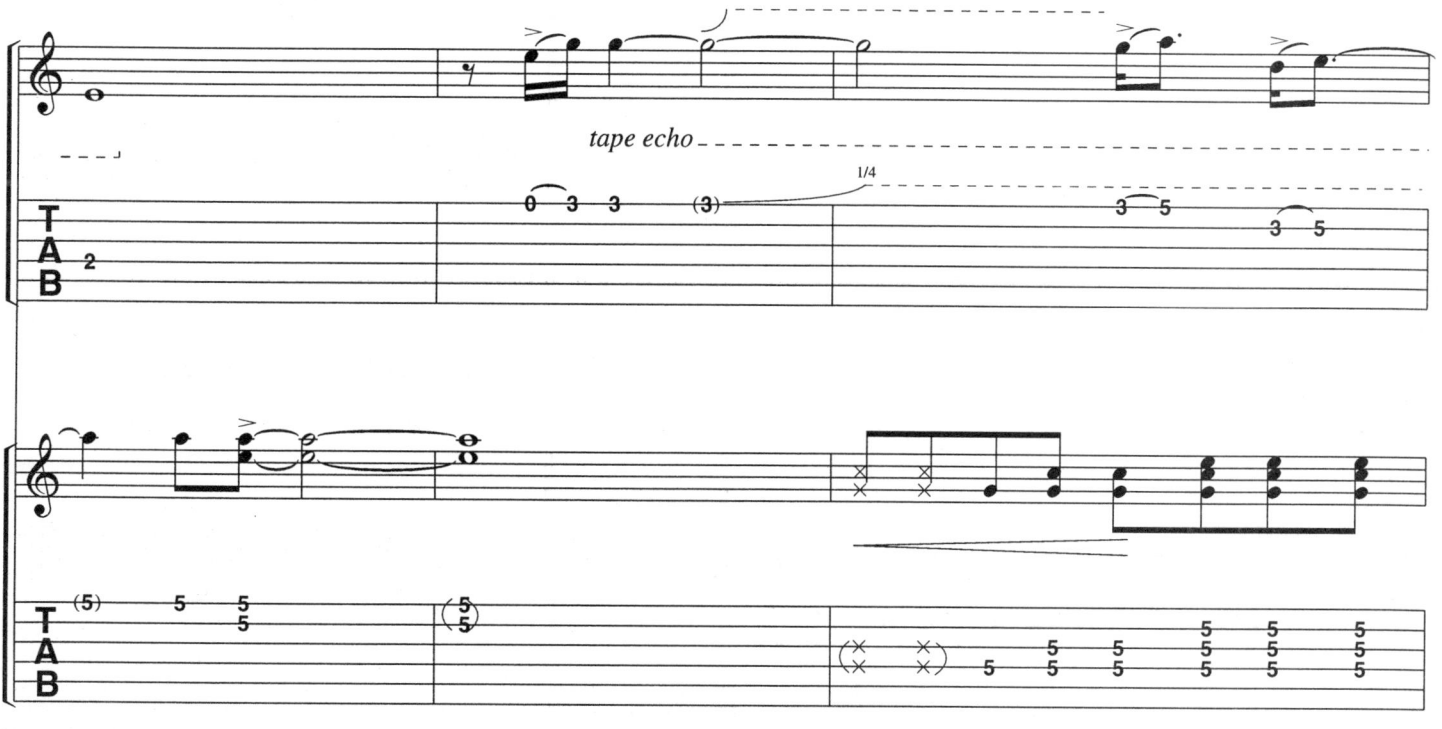

Change Your Mind - 36 - 27
PG9502

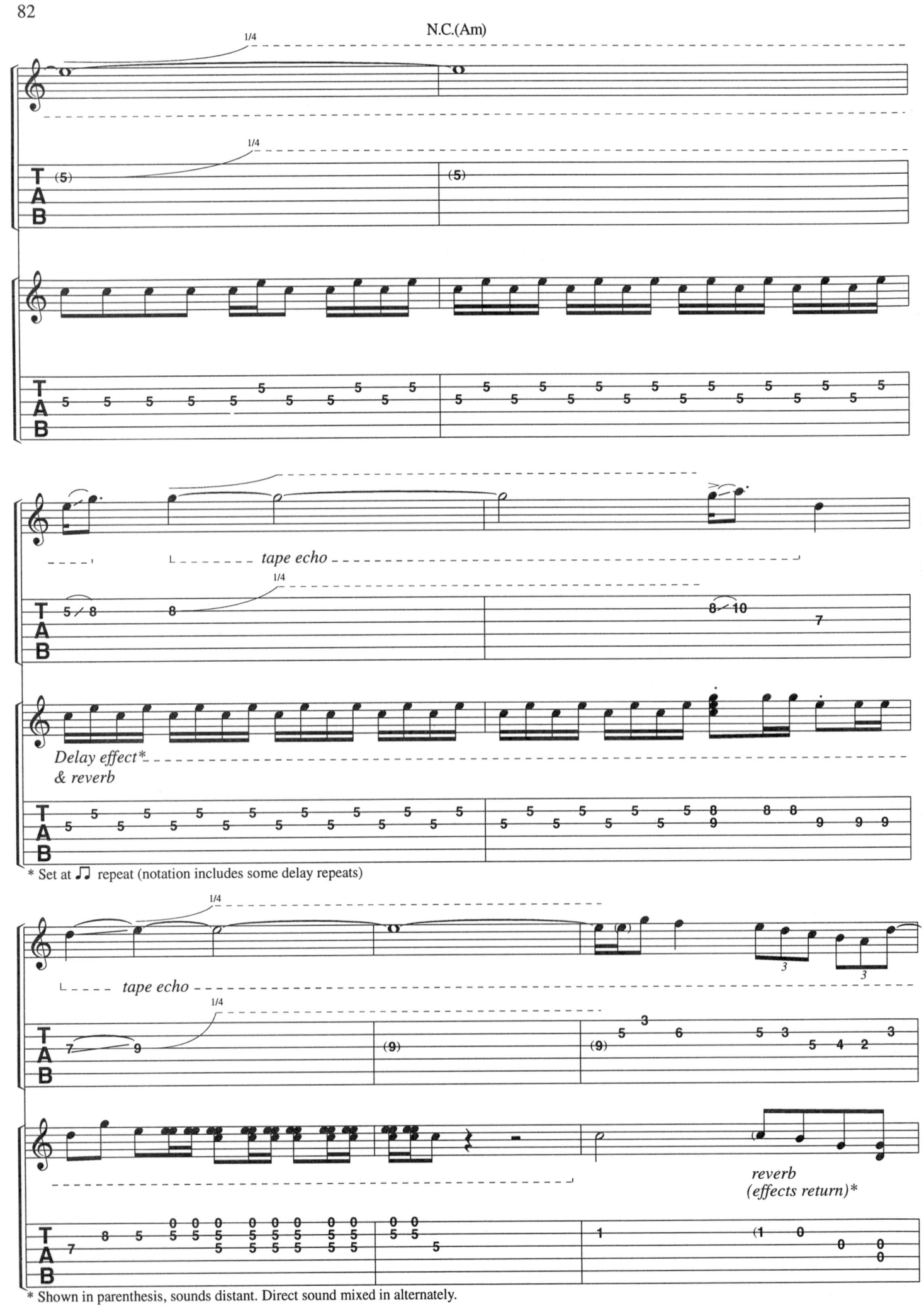

* Set at ♪ repeat (notation includes some delay repeats)

* Shown in parenthesis, sounds distant. Direct sound mixed in alternately.

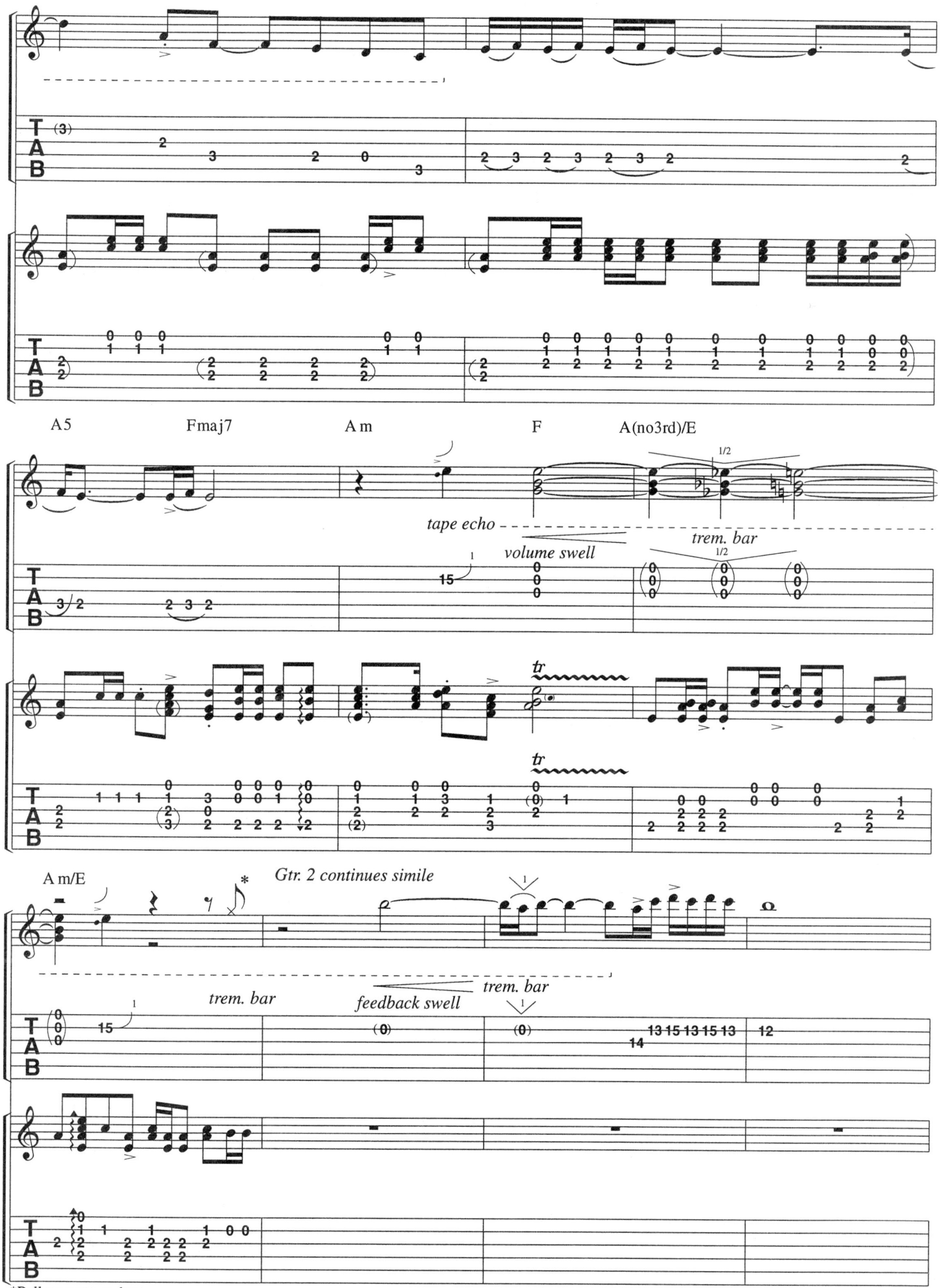

*Pull up on trem. bar.

tape echo
tape echo
1/4
1/2
harm.
Gtr. 1
A5
1
harm.
trem. bar
volume swell
tape echo
Gtr. 2
1/2
trem. bar *

* ♪ vibrato.

*Frethand slide on open strings.

** Open second string not palm muted.

Change Your Mind - 36 - 31
PG9502

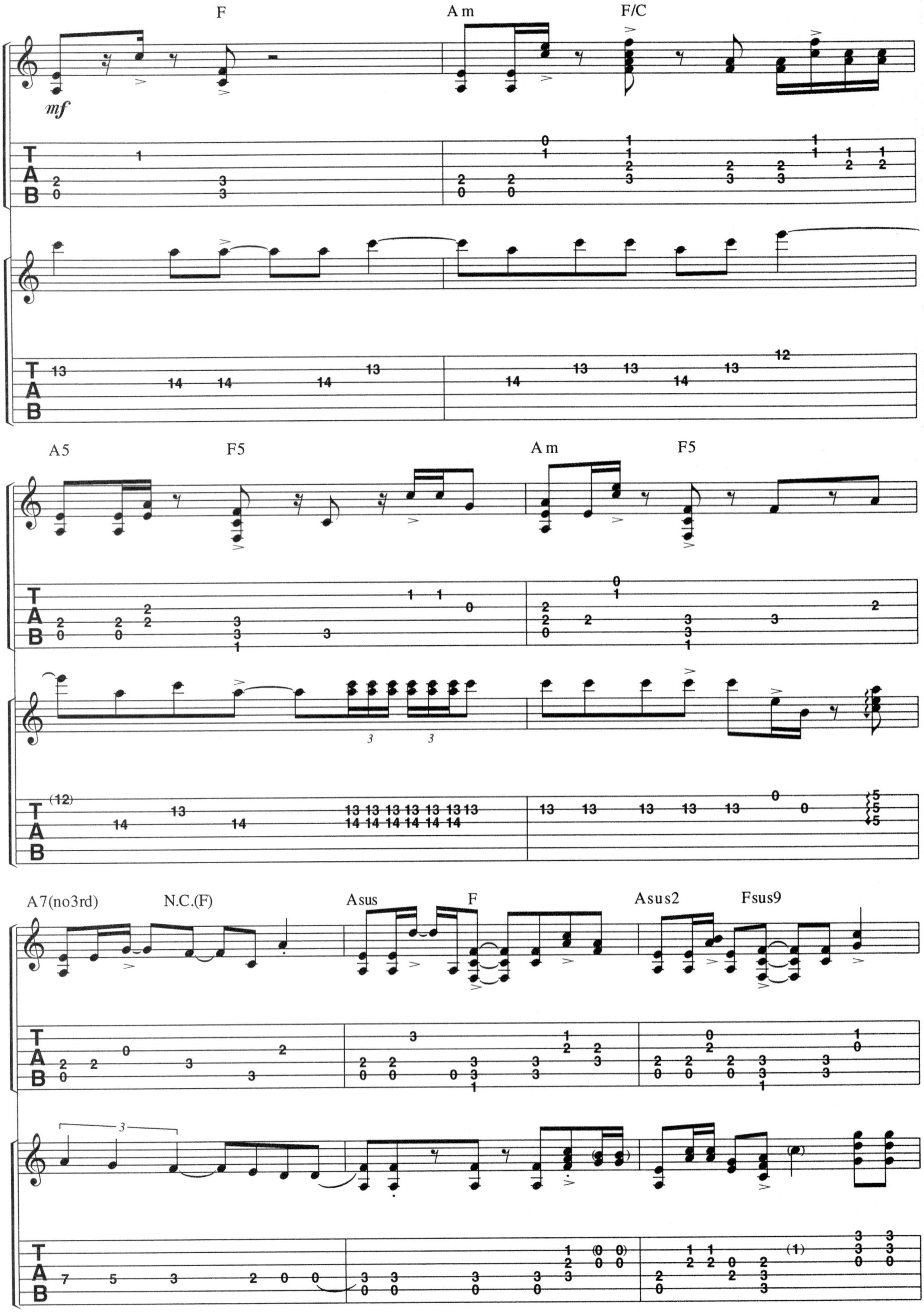
F
Am
F/C
mf
A5
F5
Am
F5
A7(no3rd)
N.C.(F)
Asus
F
Asus2
Fsus9
T
A
B

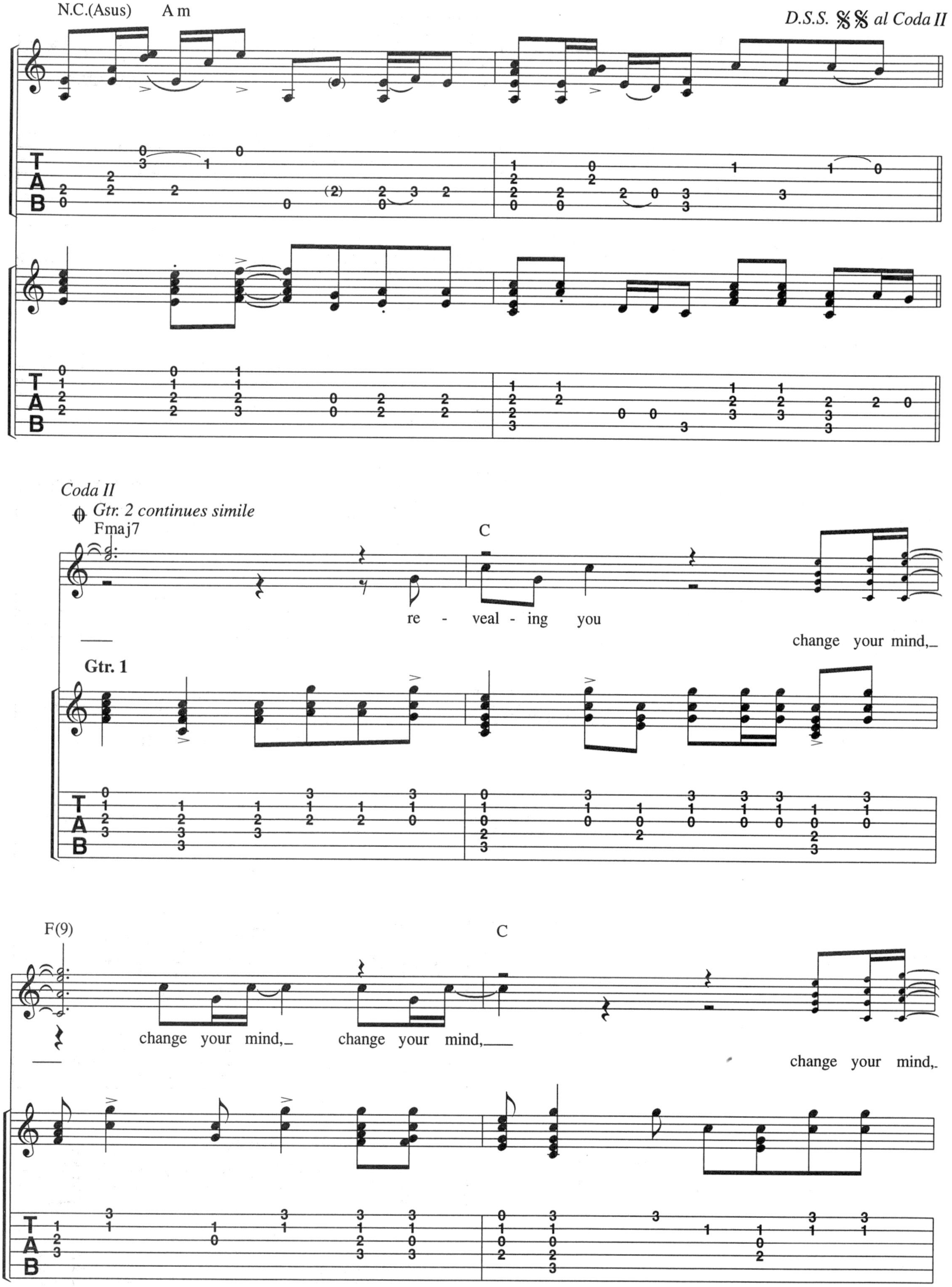
N.C.(Asus)
A m
D.S.S. 𝄋𝄋 al Coda II
Coda II
Gtr. 2 continues simile
Fmaj7
C
re - veal - ing you
change your mind,
Gtr. 1
F(9)
C
change your mind,
change your mind,
change your mind,

change your mind, change your mind, change your mind, change your mind, change your mind, change your mind, change your mind, change your mind, distant: change your mind,

Change Your Mind - 36 - 34
PG9502

F(9)
C
change your mind,
distant: change your
F
C
F(9)
change your mind,
change your mind,
mind,
change your mind,
change your mind,
C
F
change your mind,
change your mind,
change your mind,
Gtr. 1
mf
Gtr. 2
mf

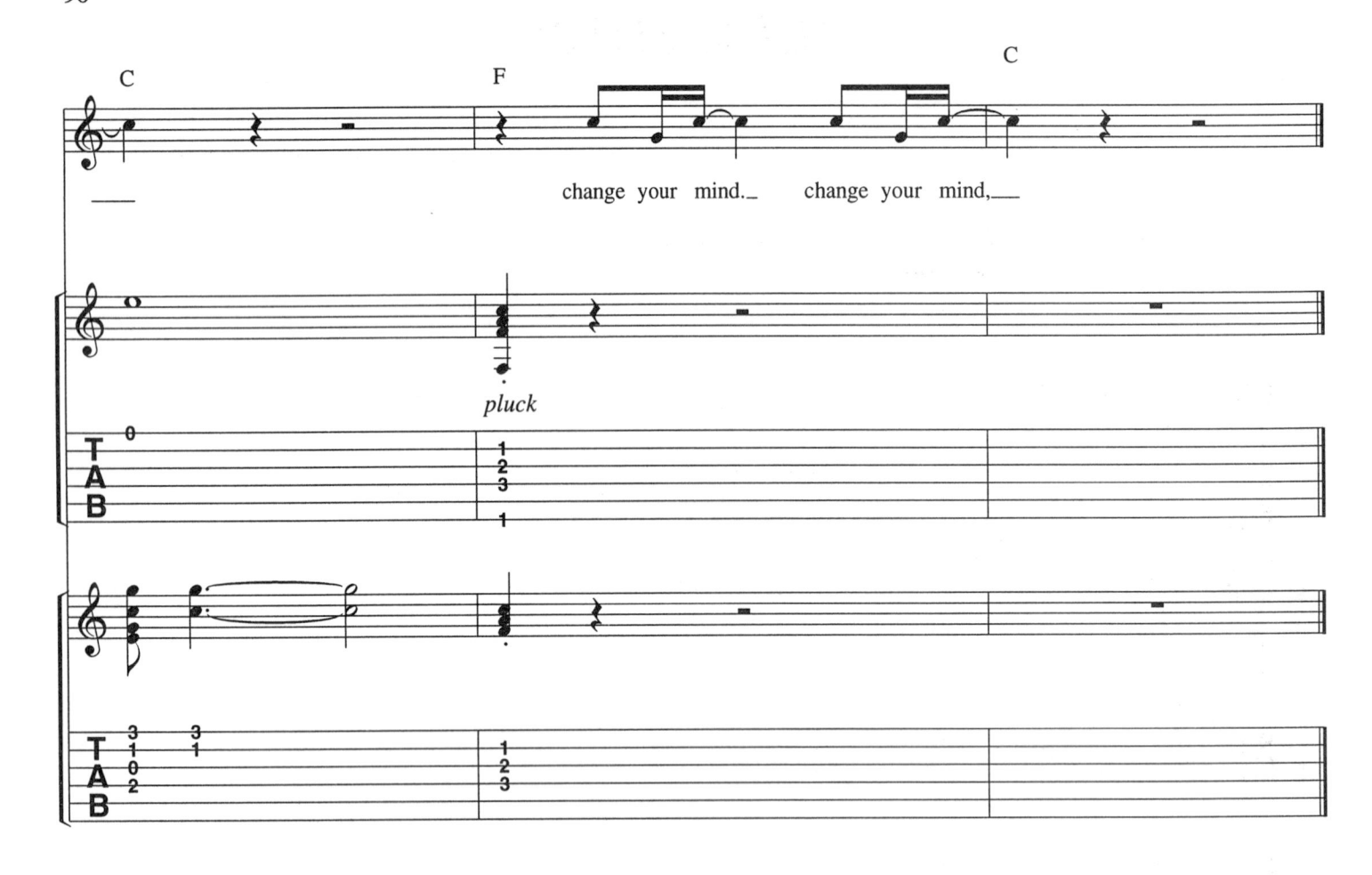

Verse 2:
When you're confused and the world has got you down.
When you feel used and you just can't play the clown.
Protecting you from this must be the one you love;
Must be the one whose magic touch can change your mind.
Don't let another day go by without the magic touch.
(To Chorus 2:)

Chorus 2:
Protecting you	(Change your mind)
Restoring you	(Change your mind)
Revealing you	(Change your mind)
Soothing you	(Change your mind)

Verse 4:
The morning comes, there's an odor in the room.
The scent of love, more than a million roses bloom.
Embracing you with this, must be the one you love;
Must be the one whose magic touch can change your mind.
(To Chorus 4:)

Chorus 4:
Embracing you	(Change your mind)
Concealing you	(Change your mind)
Protecting you	(Change your mind)
Revealing you	(Change your mind)

BLUE EDEN

**Words and Music by
NEIL YOUNG, FRANK "PONCHO" SAMPEDRO
BILLY TALBOT and RALPH MOLINA**

*Electric guitars: Gtr. 1 (right channel) Gtr. 1 with tape echo (setting: ♪♪♪). Gtr. 2 (left channel).

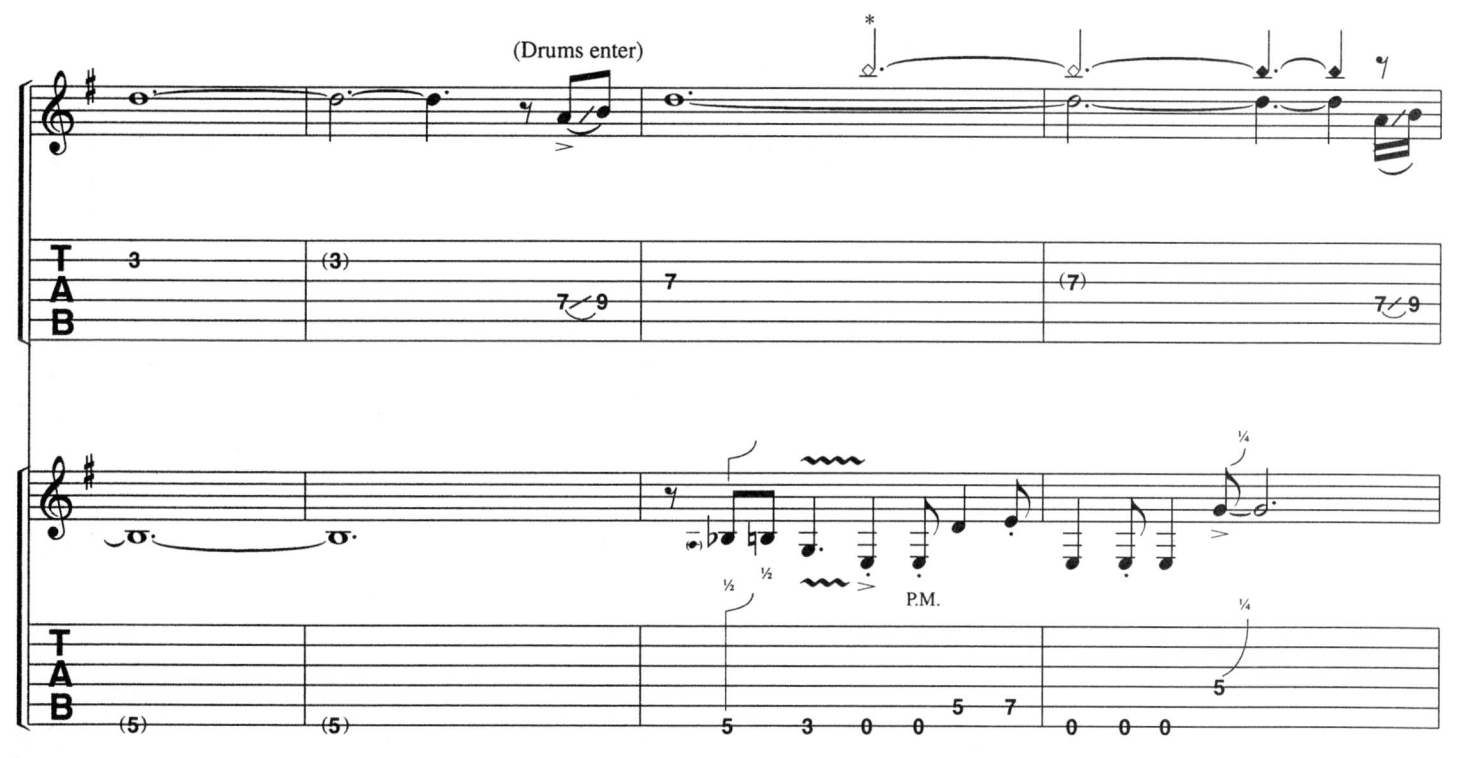

*Amplifier feedback/overtone (sounds one octave higher).

Blue Eden - 15 - 1
PG9502

© 1994 BROKEN FIDDLE MUSIC (BMI), SILVER FIDDLE MUSIC (ASCAP) and FALMOUTH MUSIC (BMI)
All rights on behalf of FALMOUTH MUSIC administered by BROKEN FIDDLE MUSIC (BMI)
All Rights Reserved

*Flip 3-way switch back and forth between "rhythm" and middle positions.

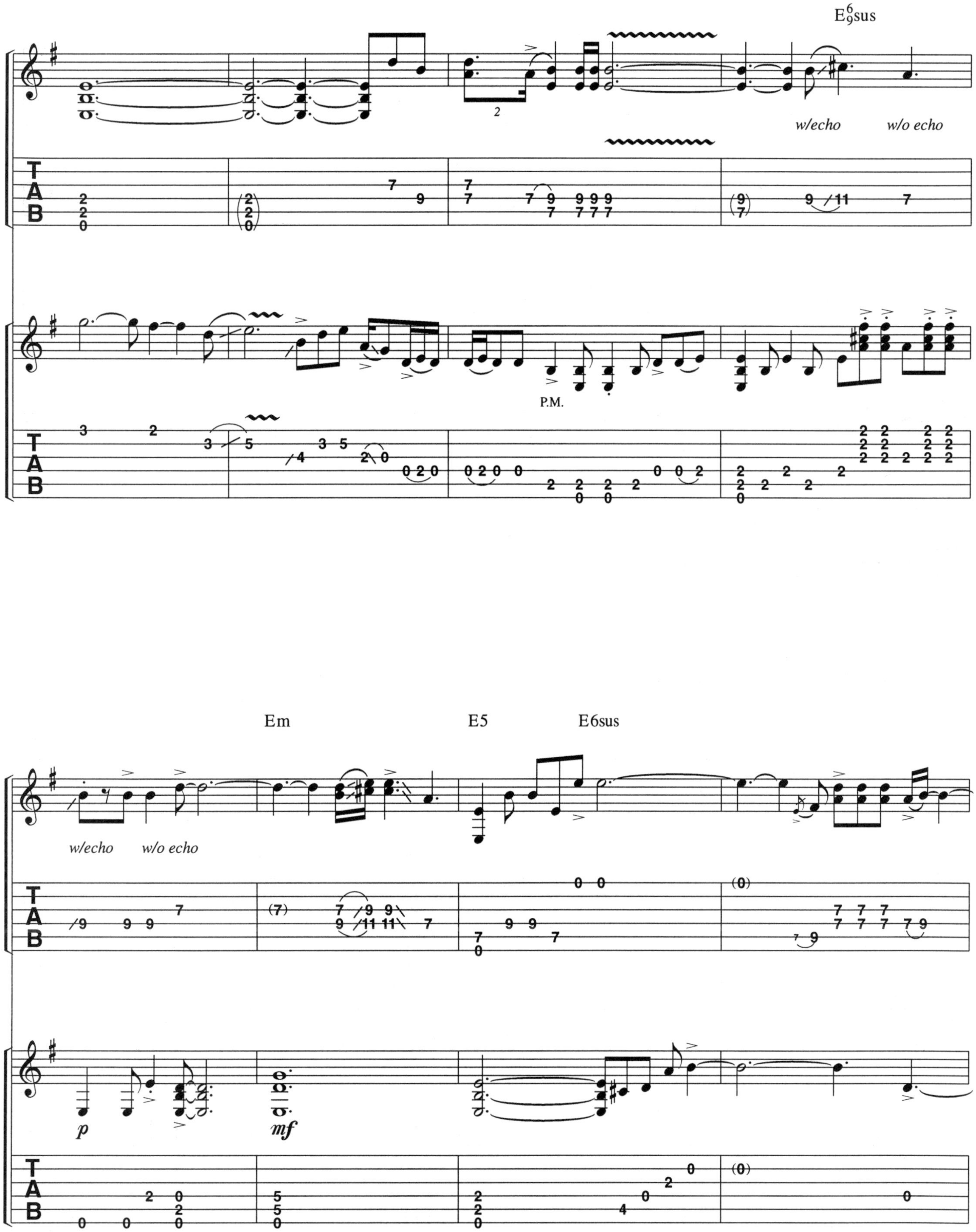
E6/9sus
w/echo
w/o echo
P.M.
Em
E5
E6sus
w/echo
w/o echo
p
mf

Verse:

(Em) - brac - ing (you), dis-

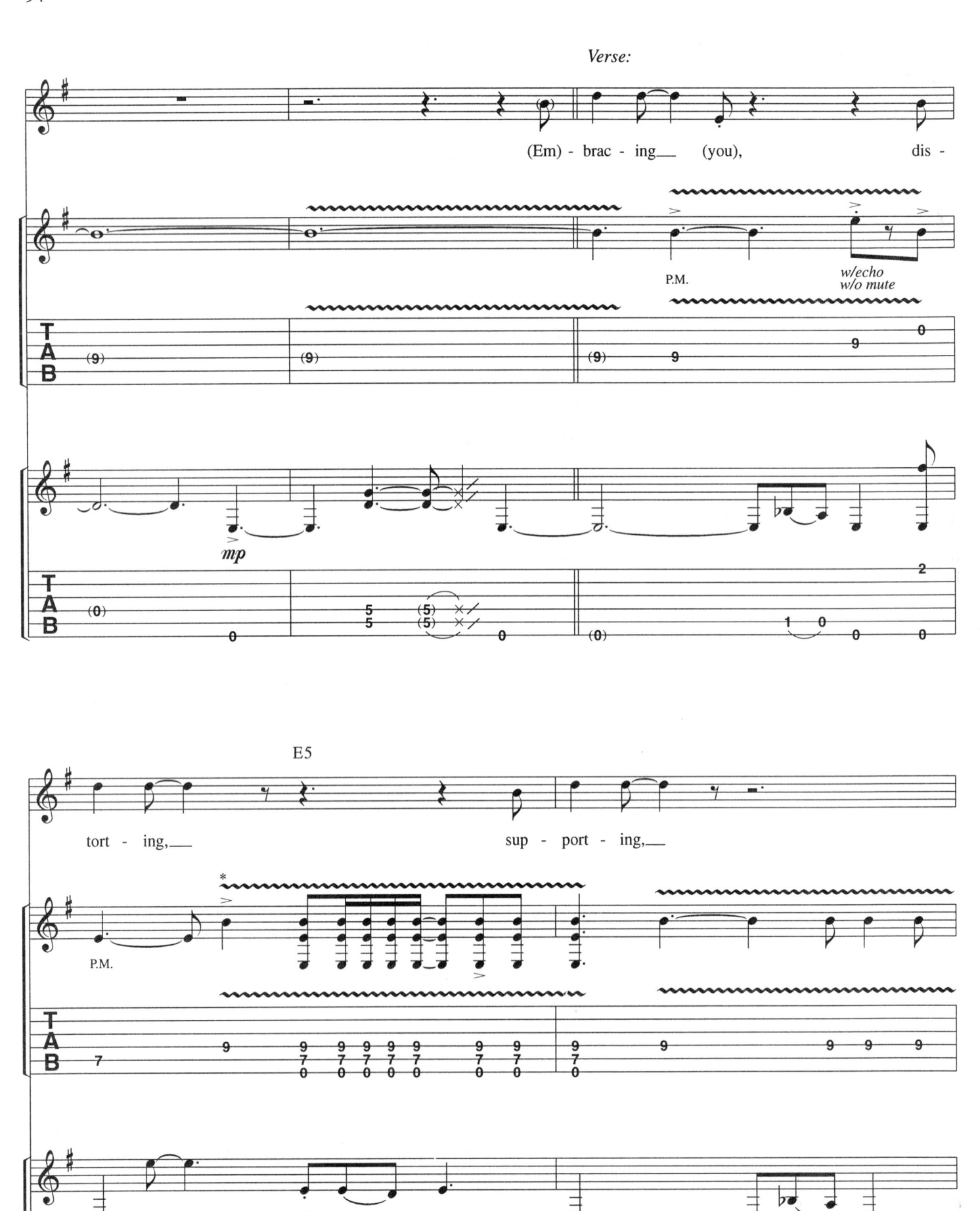

tort - ing, sup - port - ing,

*Vibrato is continuous throughout this section on ④ and ⑤.

com - fort - ing,   con - vinc - ing   you,   con -

sol - ing   you,   con - trol - ling   you,   de -

stroy - ing___ you,   all o - ver___ you.___

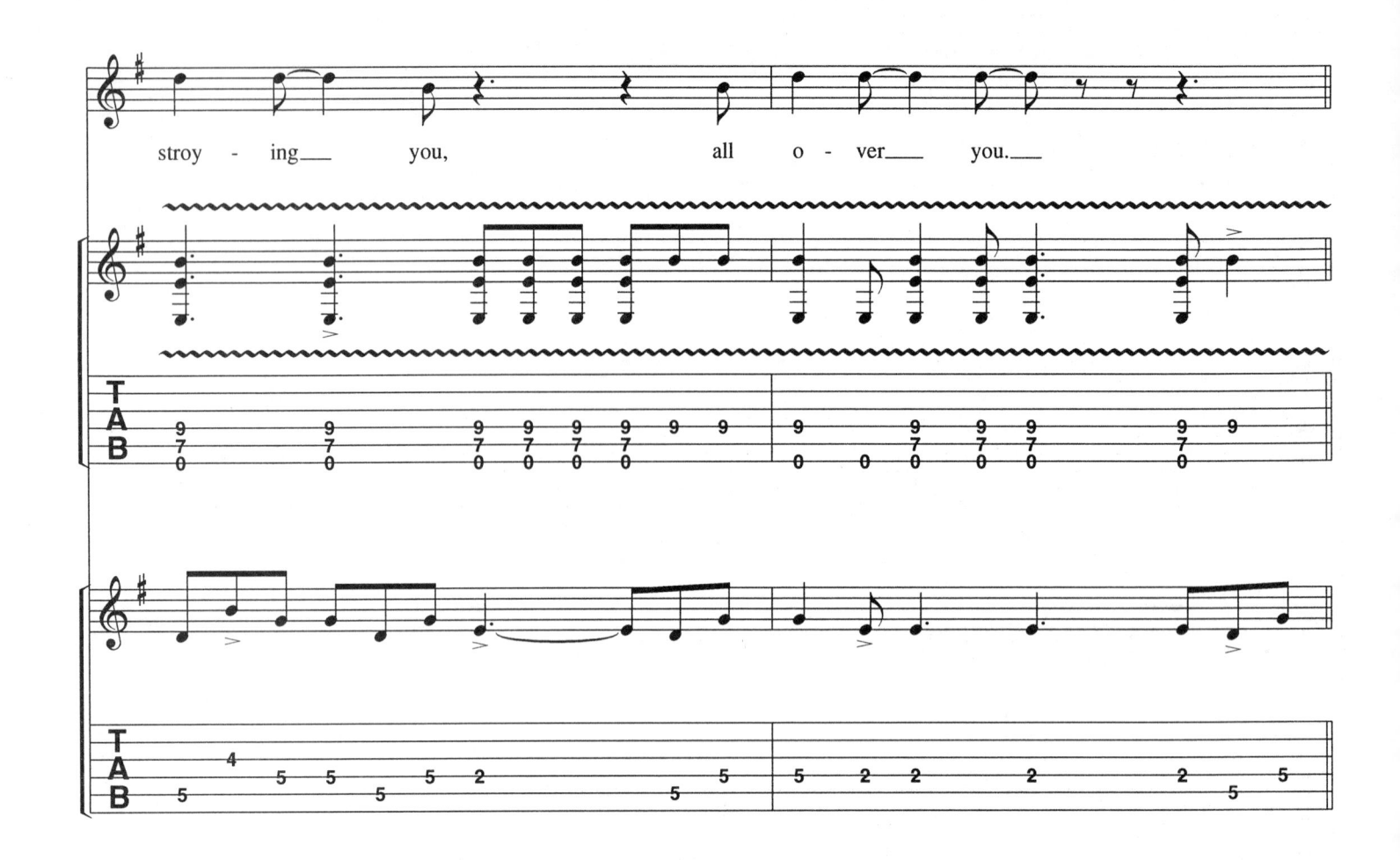

Interlude:
N.C.(Em7)

f
w/echo

mf   *mp*   *mf*

Blue Eden - 15 - 6

E7(no3rd)

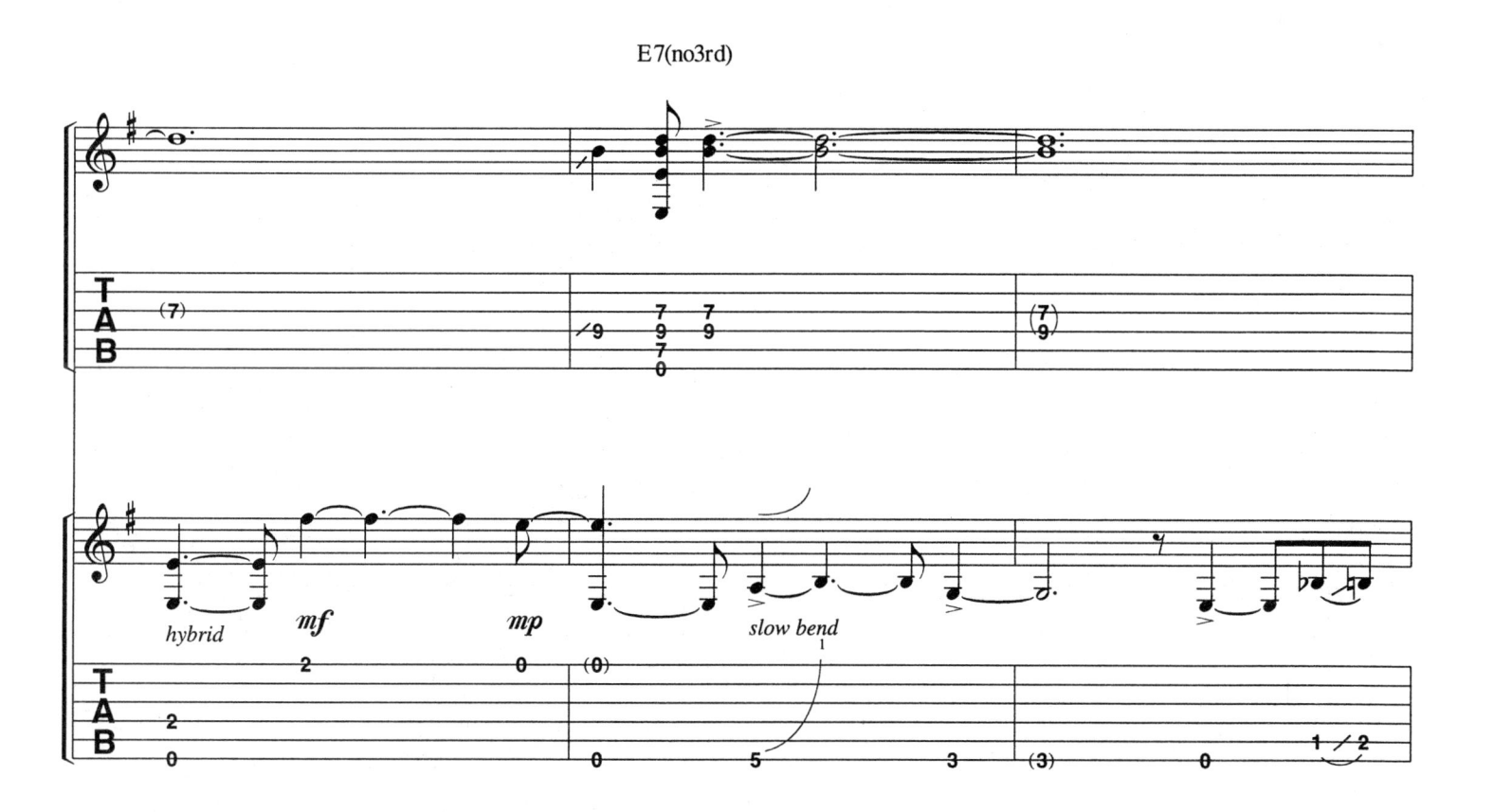

hybrid *mf* *mp* *slow bend*

Blue Eden - 15 - 7
PG9502

*w/ increased distortion due to volume.

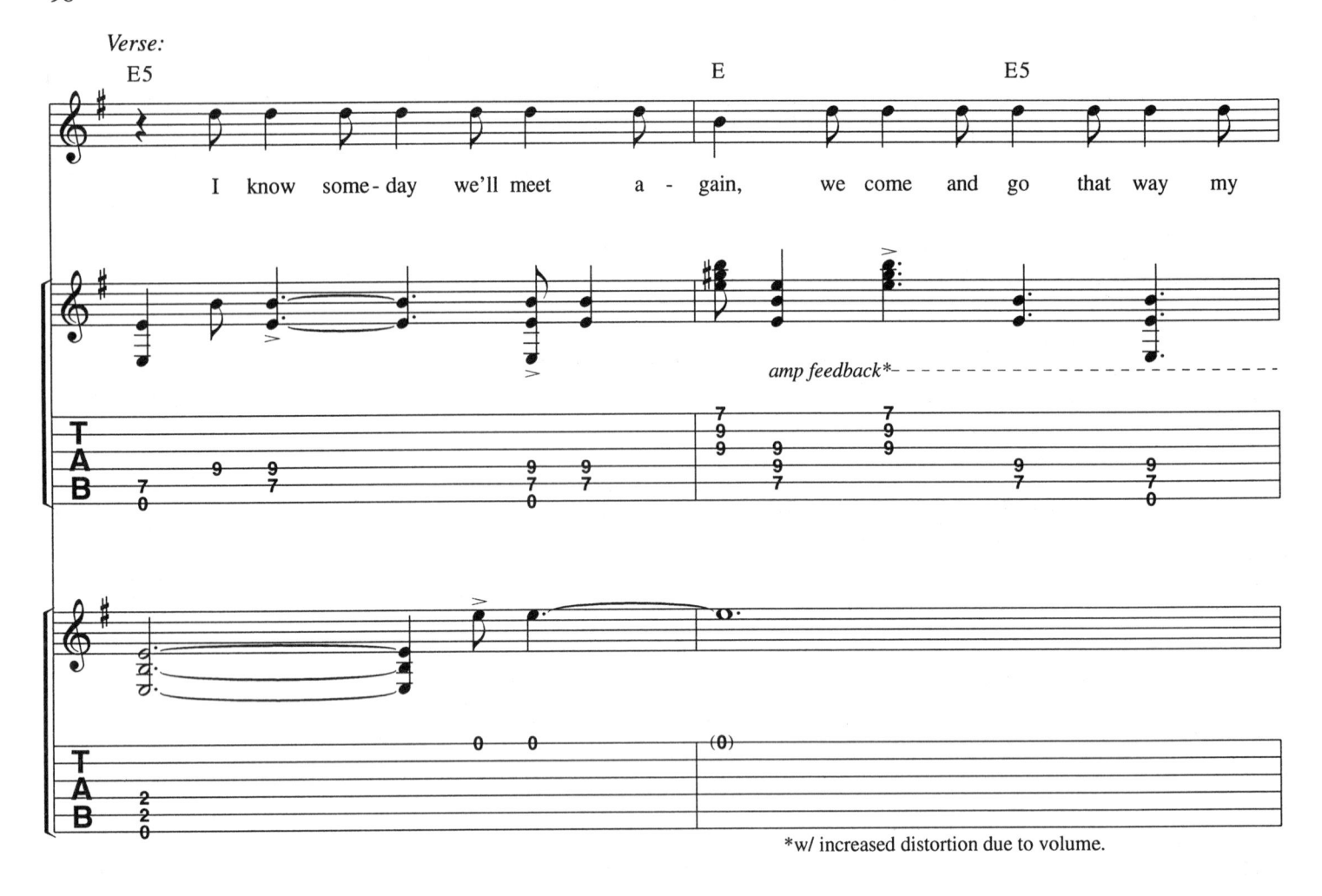

99

Guitar Solo:
N.C.(Em7)

w/trem. bar*

feedback: 8va

*Hold while picking from here on.

(tape echoes)

Blue Eden - 15 - 9
PG9502

*Amp. feedback/overtone.

(You)

Verse:

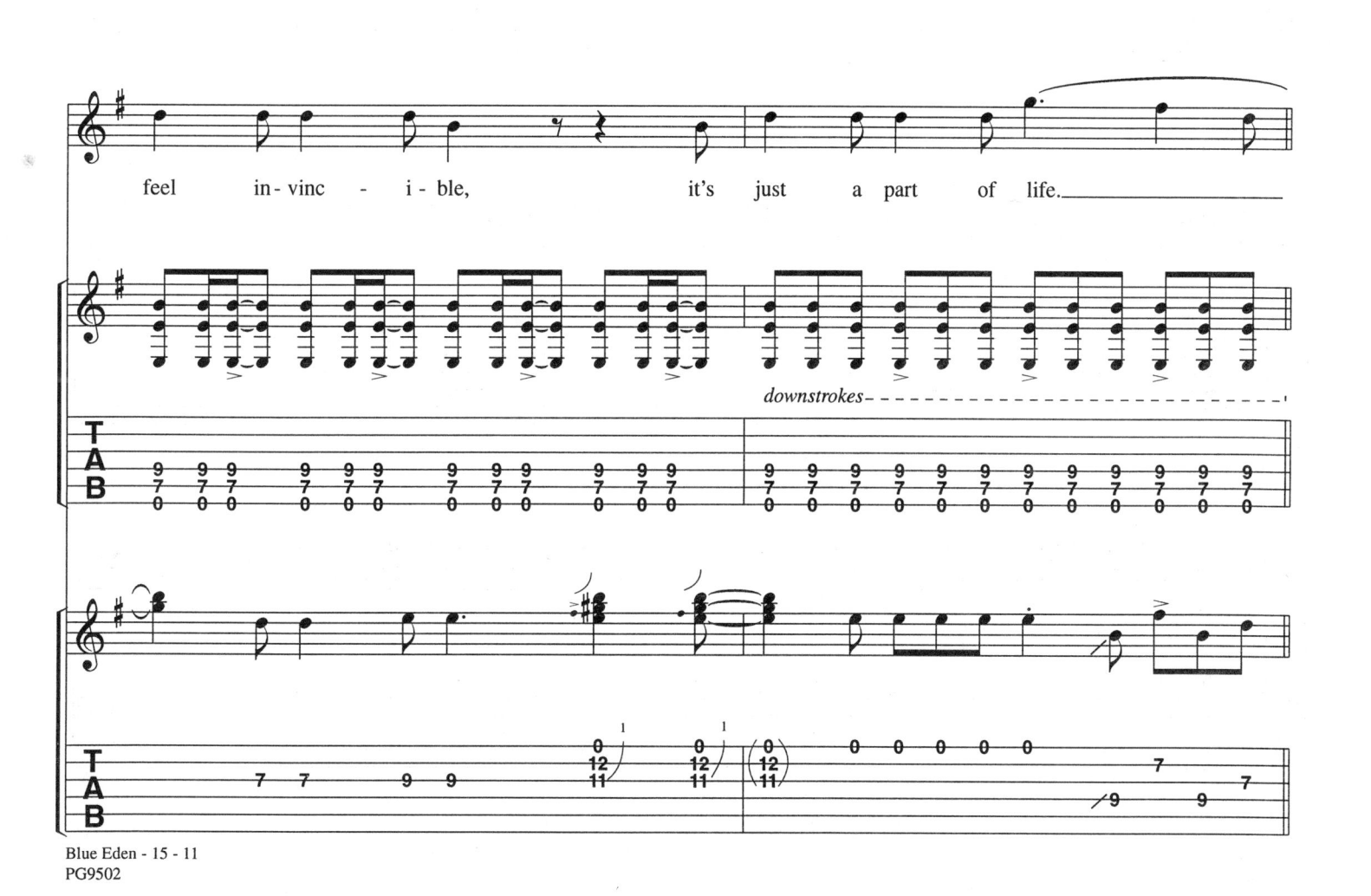

feel in - vinc - i - ble, it's just a part of life, (you)

feel in - vinc - i - ble, it's just a part of life.

downstrokes

Outro:

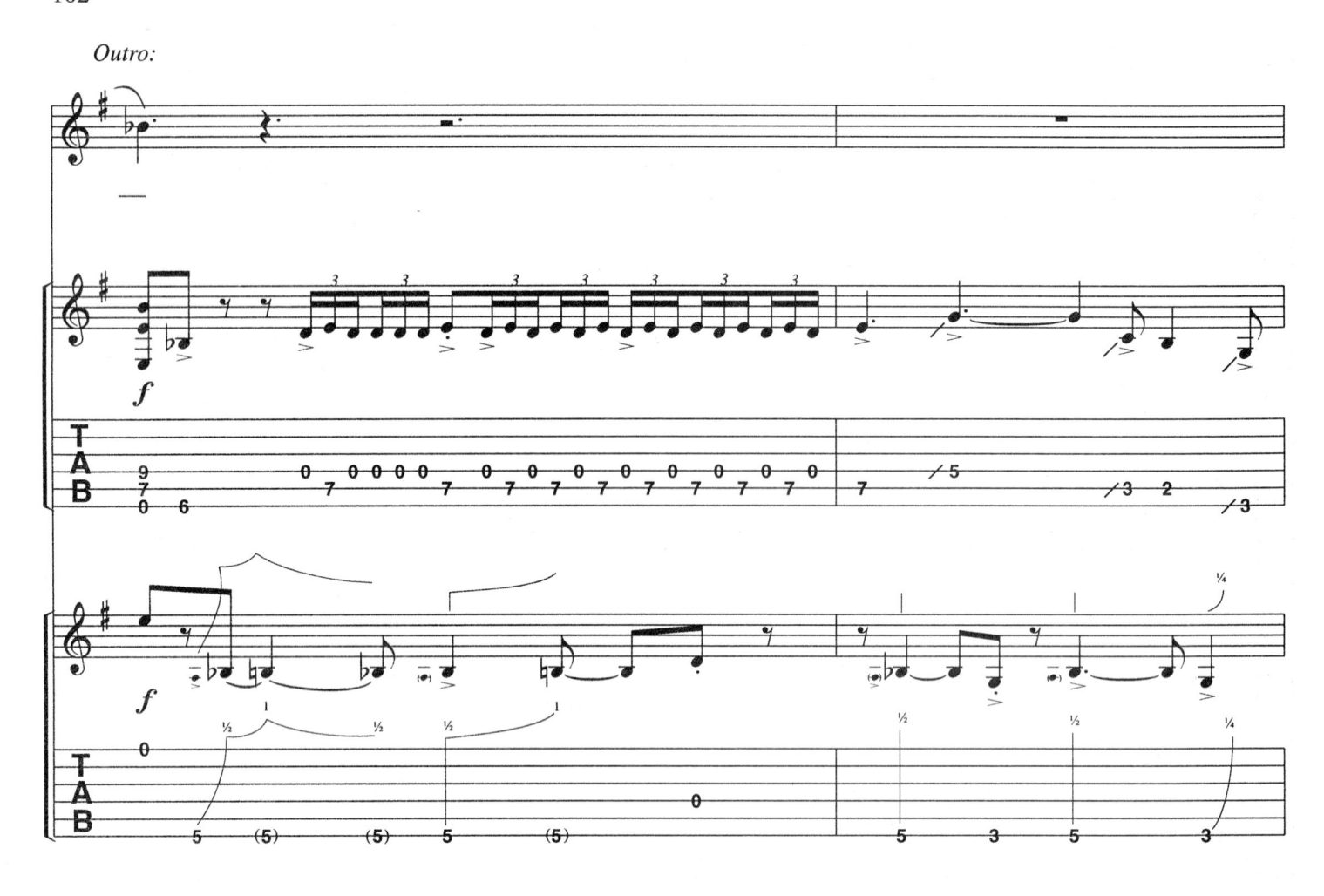

Blue Eden - 15 - 13
PG9502

*Pick approx. 3/4" behind rhythm pickup.

(Esus9)

Triplet rhythm.   *"Pound" bar w/palm.

Blue Eden - 15 - 14
PG9502

Blue Eden - 15 - 15

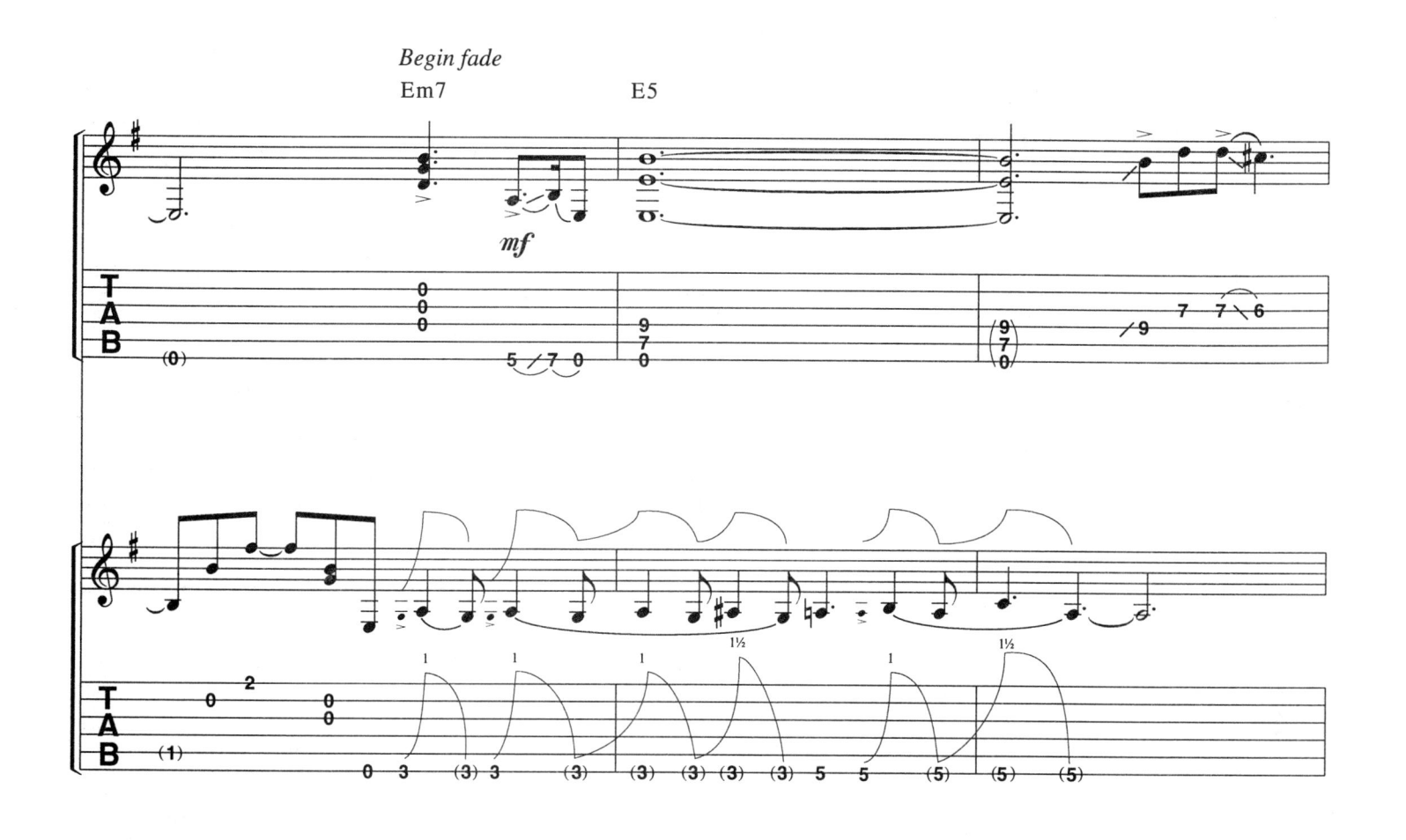

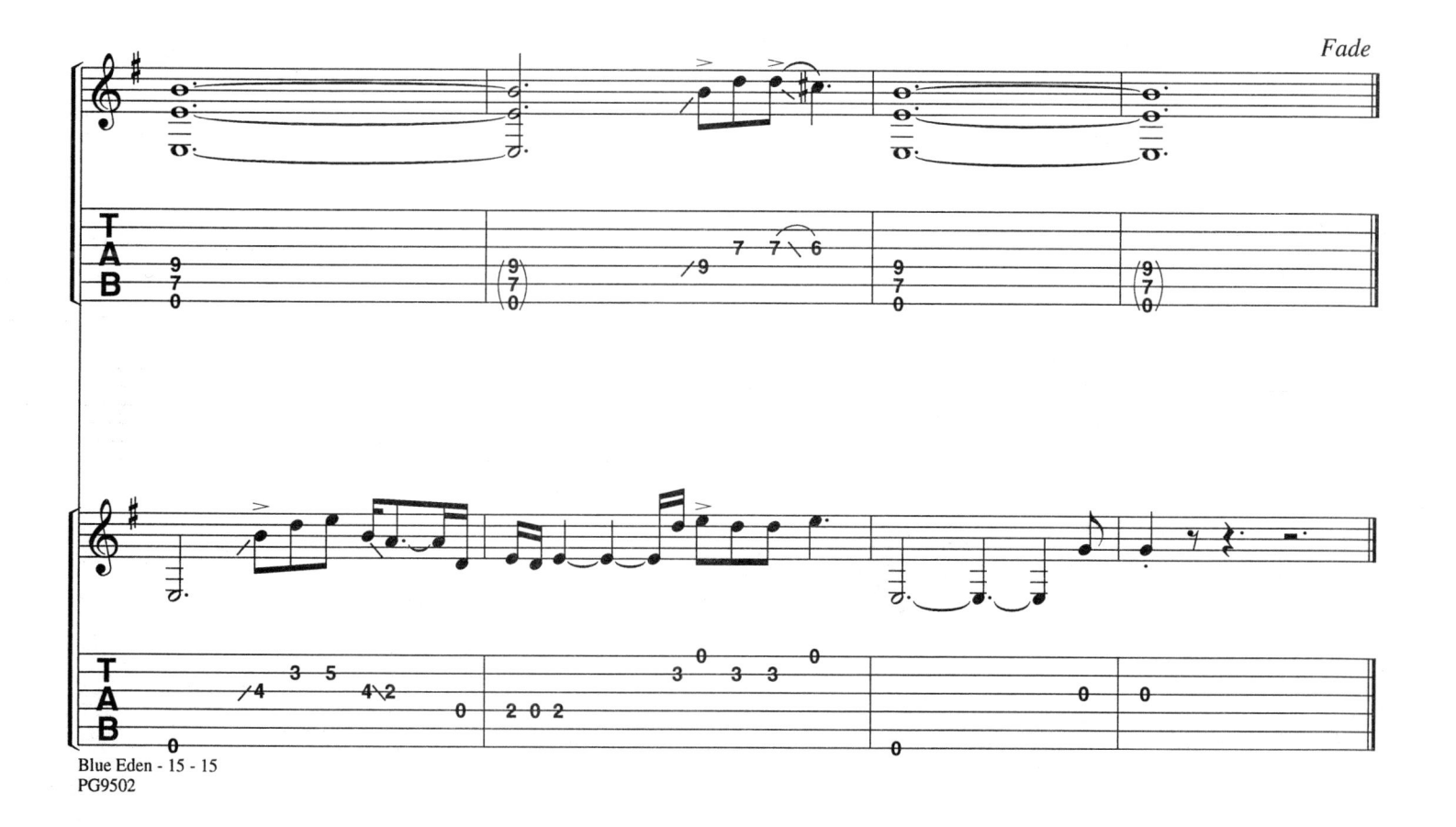

SAFEWAY CART

Words and Music by
NEIL YOUNG

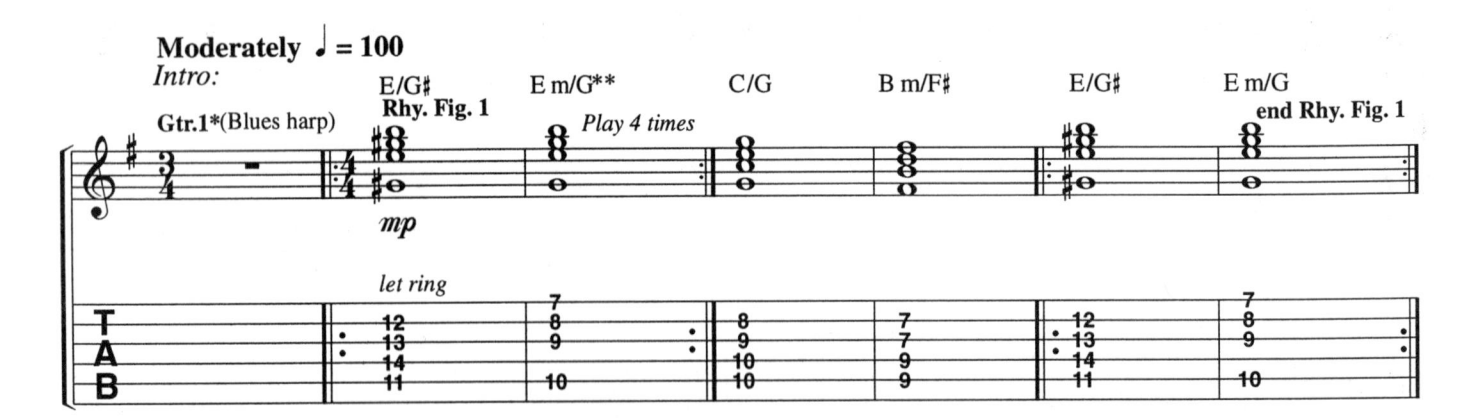

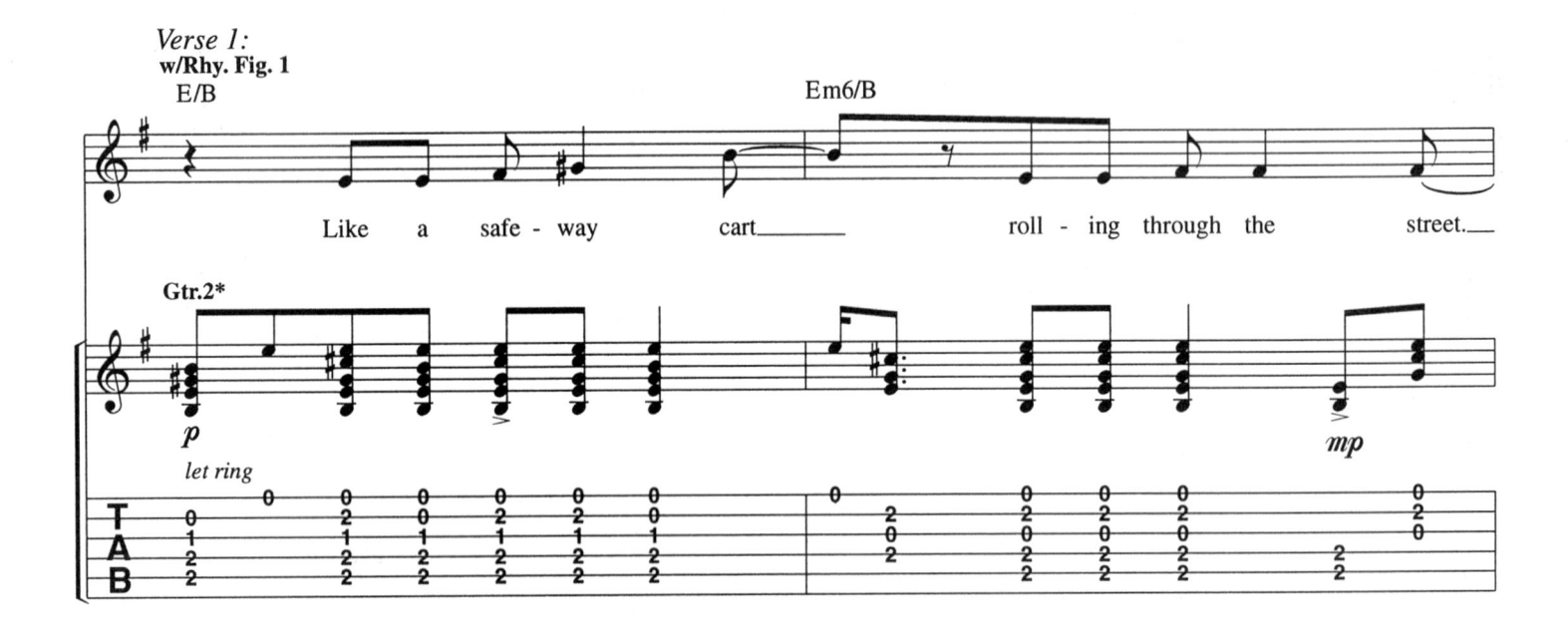

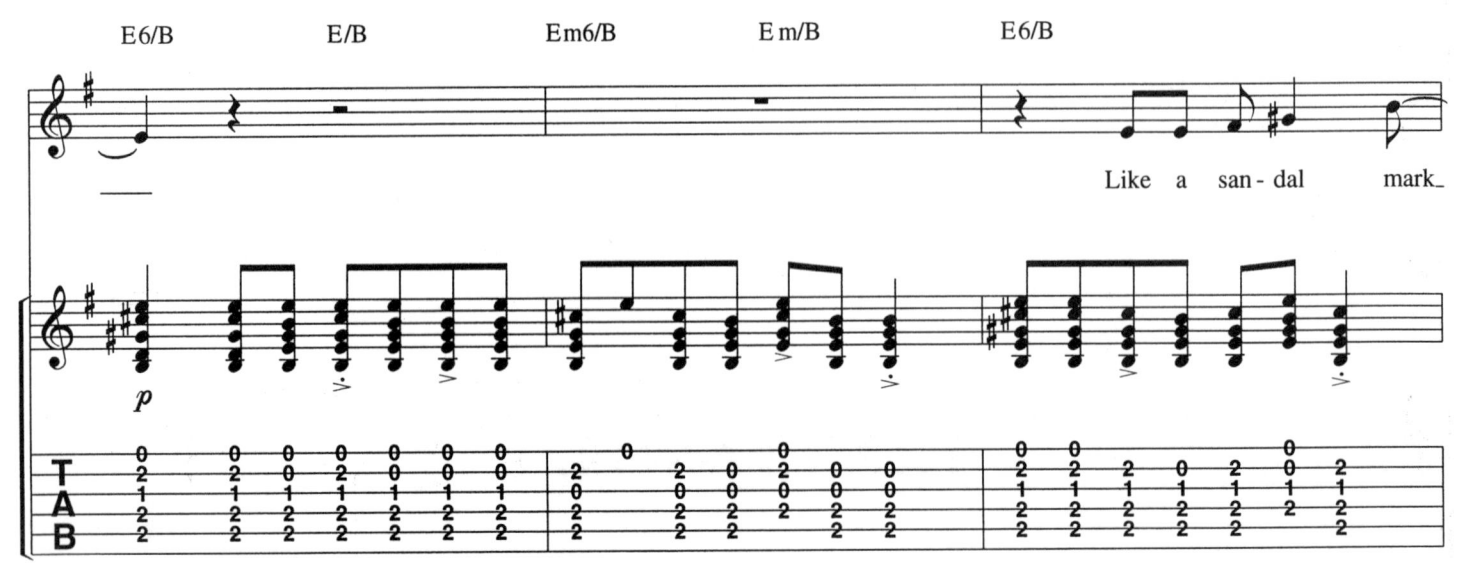

*Gtr.1=synth. arranged for guitar, Gtr.2=Electric guitar.
**G is played beneath this chord by the bass guitar throughout the song.

© 1994 SILVER FIDDLE MUSIC (ASCAP)
All Rights Reserved

107

on the savior's feet.

just keep rolling on, it's a ghetto dawn.

Verse 2:
w/Rhy. Fig. 1

Baby looks so bad with her TV eyes,

Safeway Cart - 6 - 2
PG9502

E6/B
Em6
E6
go - ing, go - ing, gone_
Em6
E6/B
Em6
and the pic - ture cries.
C/G
C
Bm/F♯
E
It's a ghet - to dawn.
Em
E/B
E7
E/B
Em7/B
harm.
TAB

*Bass drones E throughout.

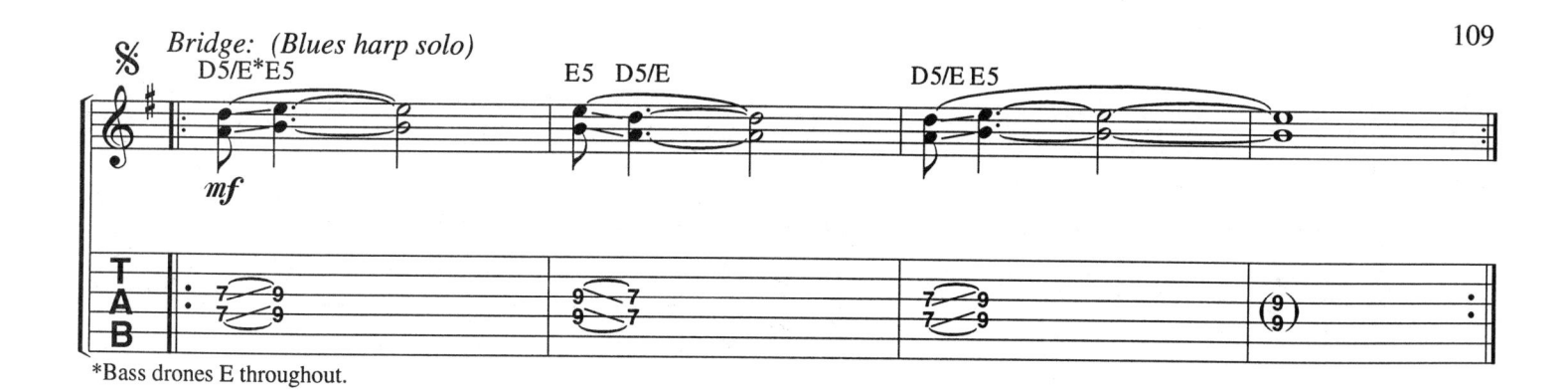

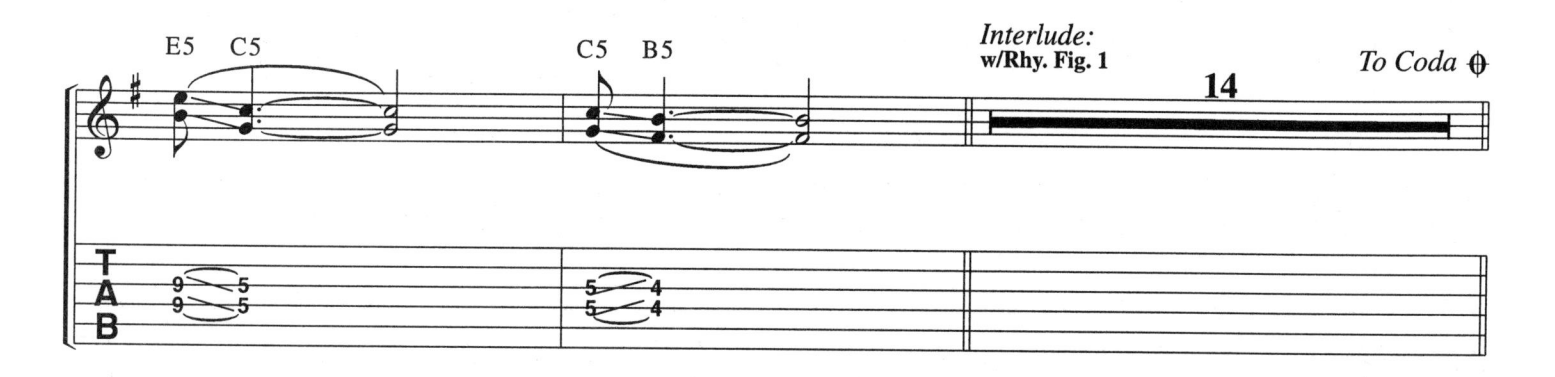

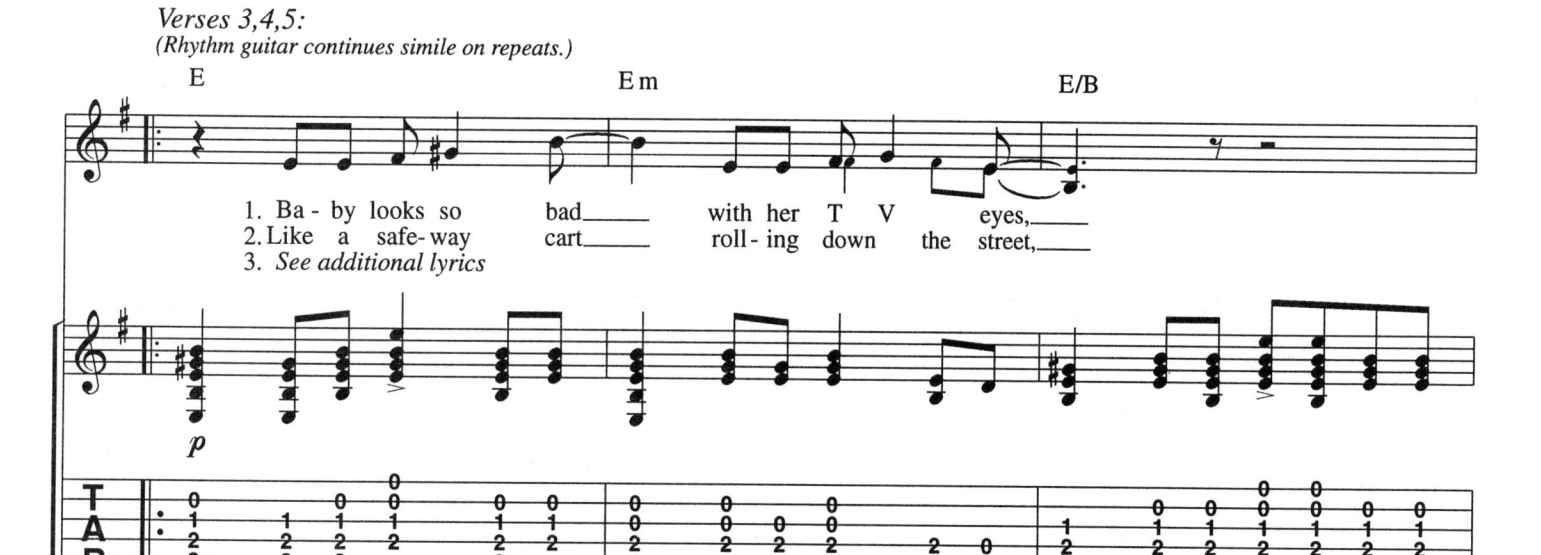

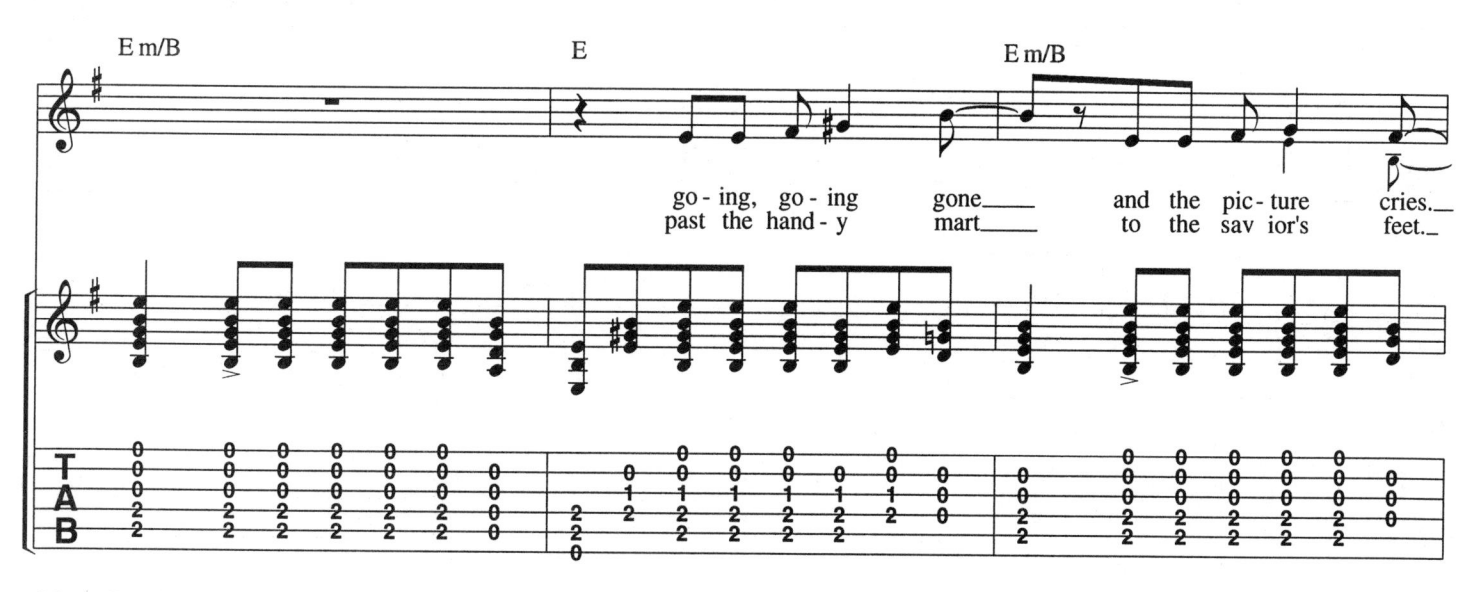

Verses 3,4,5:
(Rhythm guitar continues simile on repeats.)

1. Ba-by looks so bad___ with her T V eyes,___
2. Like a safe-way cart___ roll-ing down the street,___
3. *See additional lyrics*

go-ing, go-ing gone___ and the pic-ture cries.___
past the hand-y mart___ to the sav-ior's feet.___

Safeway Cart - 6 - 4
PG9502

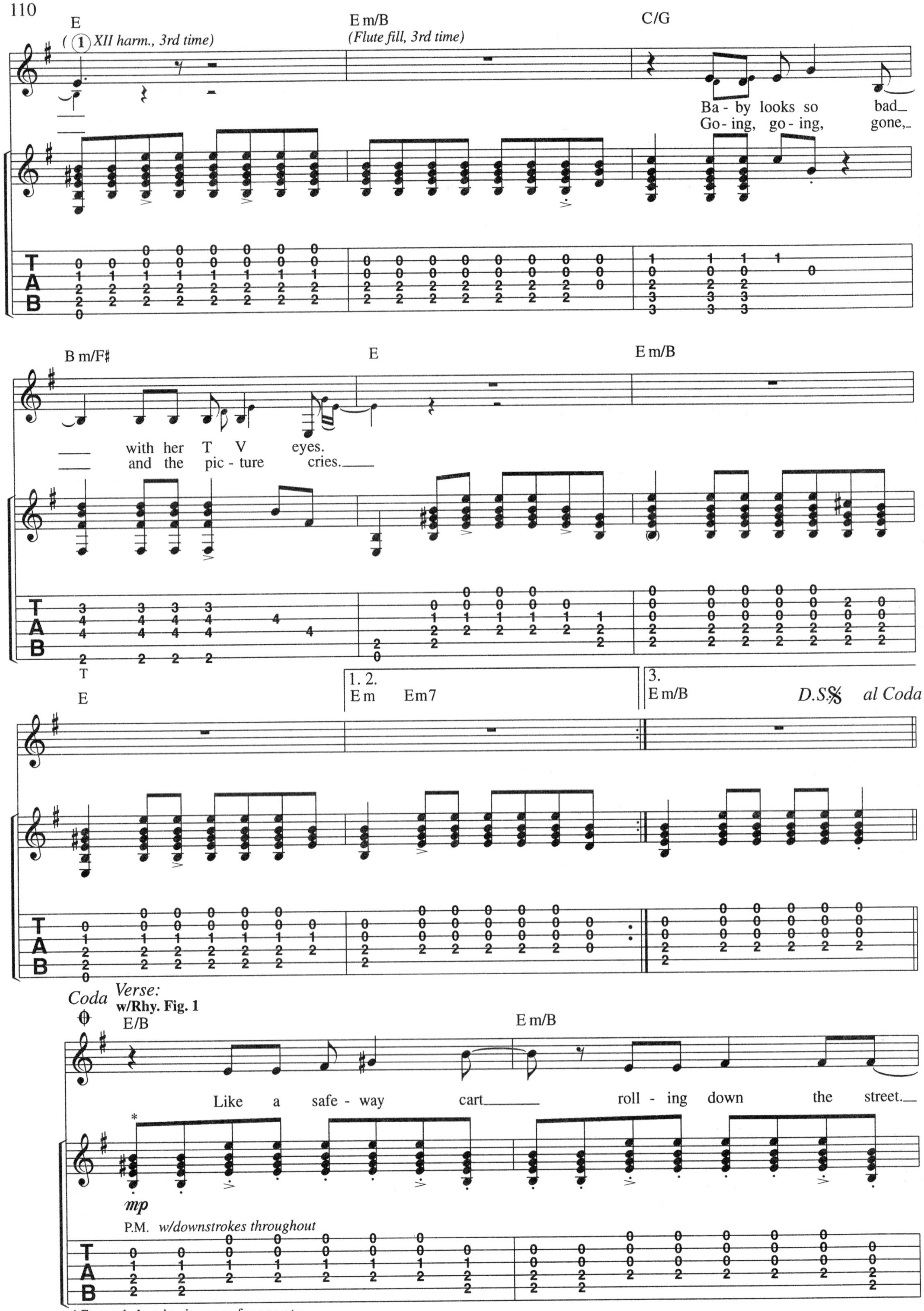

*Gtr. and electric piano arr. for one gtr.

Verse 5:
Baby looks so sad (Baby looks)
Baby look so bad (Baby looks)
It's a ghetto dawn

TRAIN OF LOVE

Words and Music by
NEIL YOUNG

Train of love, racing from heart to heart.

© 1993 SILVER FIDDLE MUSIC (ASCAP)
All Rights Reserved

113

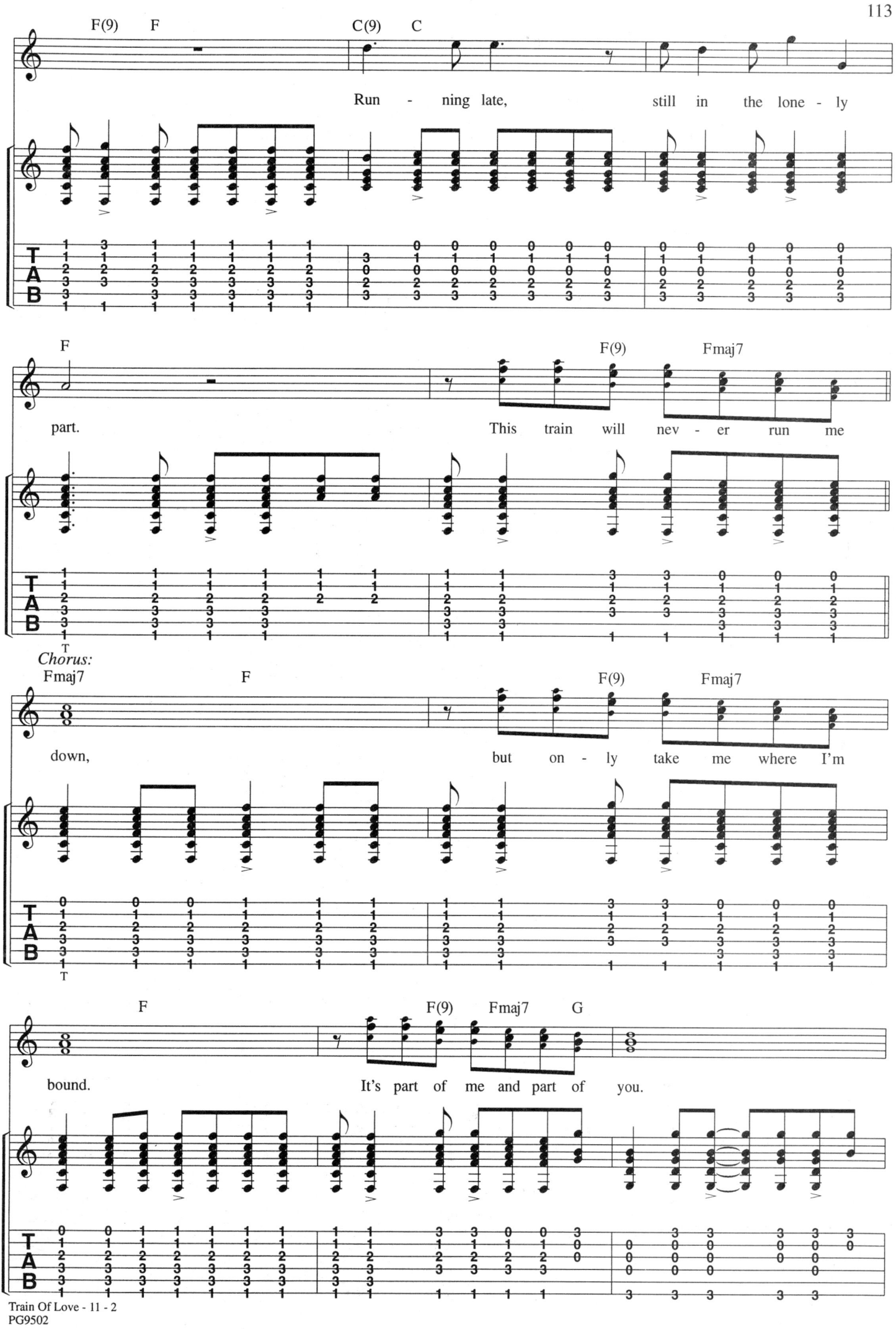

Running late, still in the lonely part.

This train will never run me

Chorus:
down, but only take me where I'm

bound. It's part of me and part of you.

Train Of Love - 11 - 2
PG9502

I'll al - ways be a part of you.

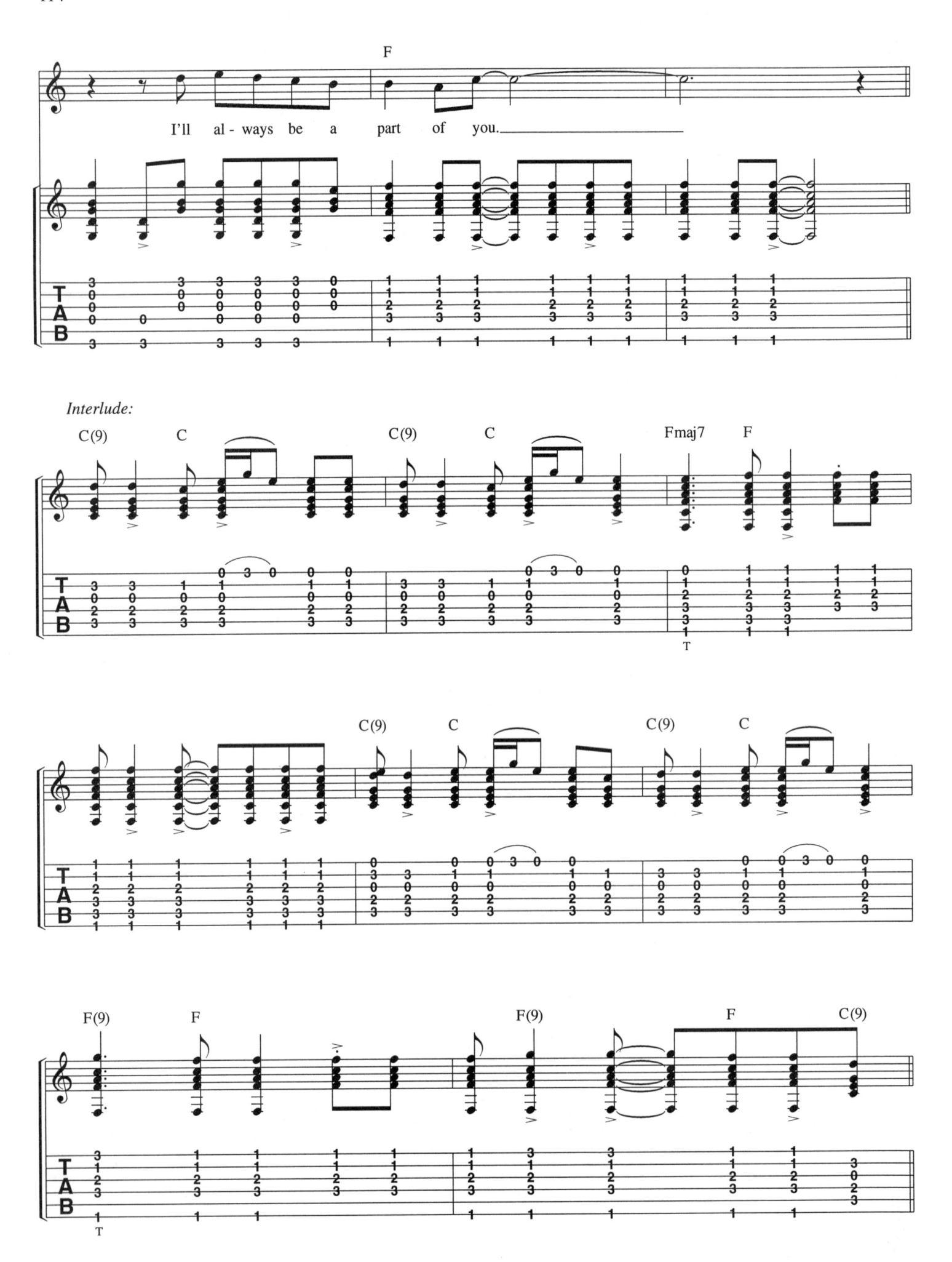

Interlude:

115

Verse:

Sail a-long, sail a-long, sil-ver moon. Don't be blue. Throw shad-ows in my room. I know in time we'll meet a-gain.

Chorus:

We come and go that way, my friend.

Train Of Love - 11 - 4
PG9502

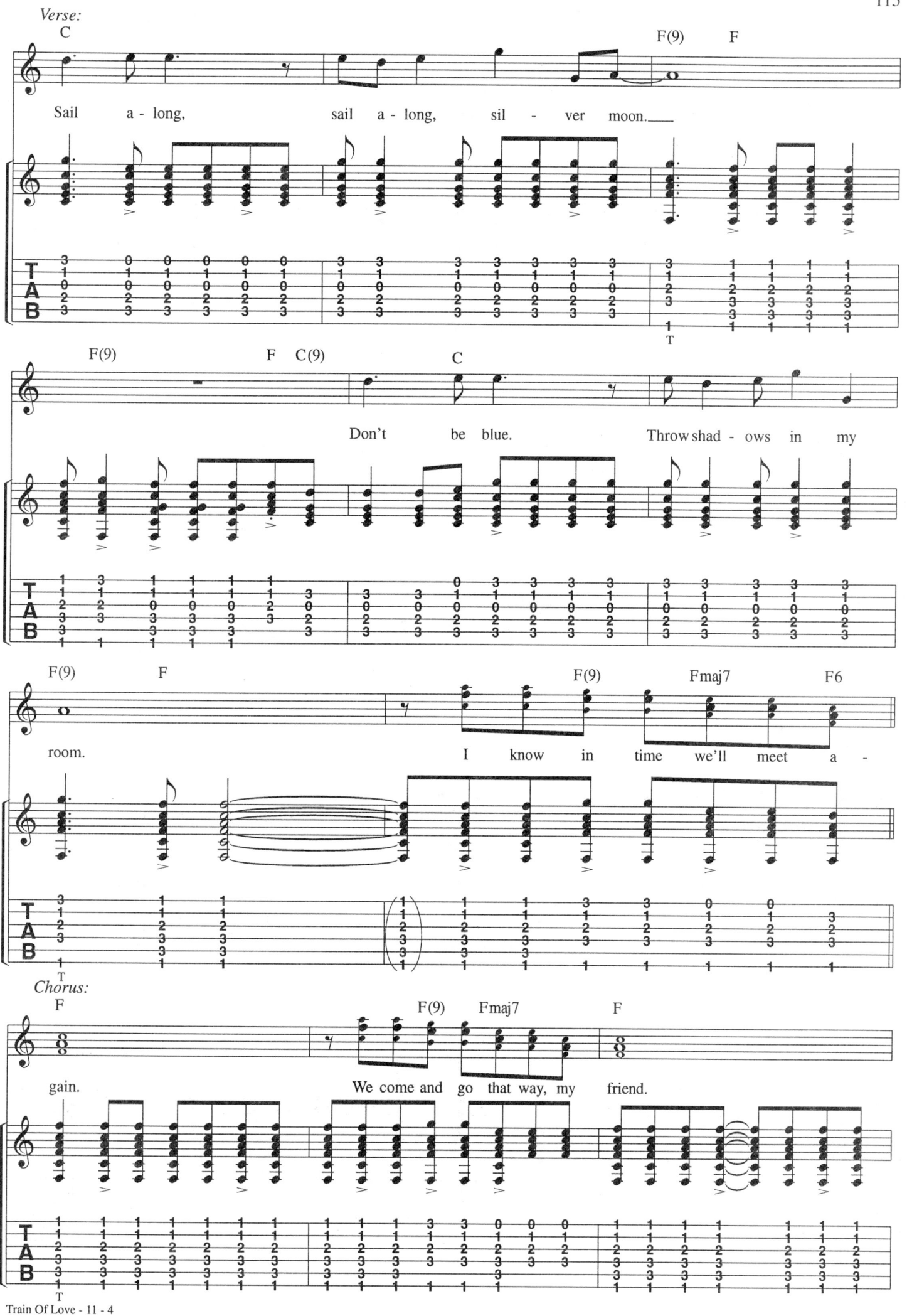

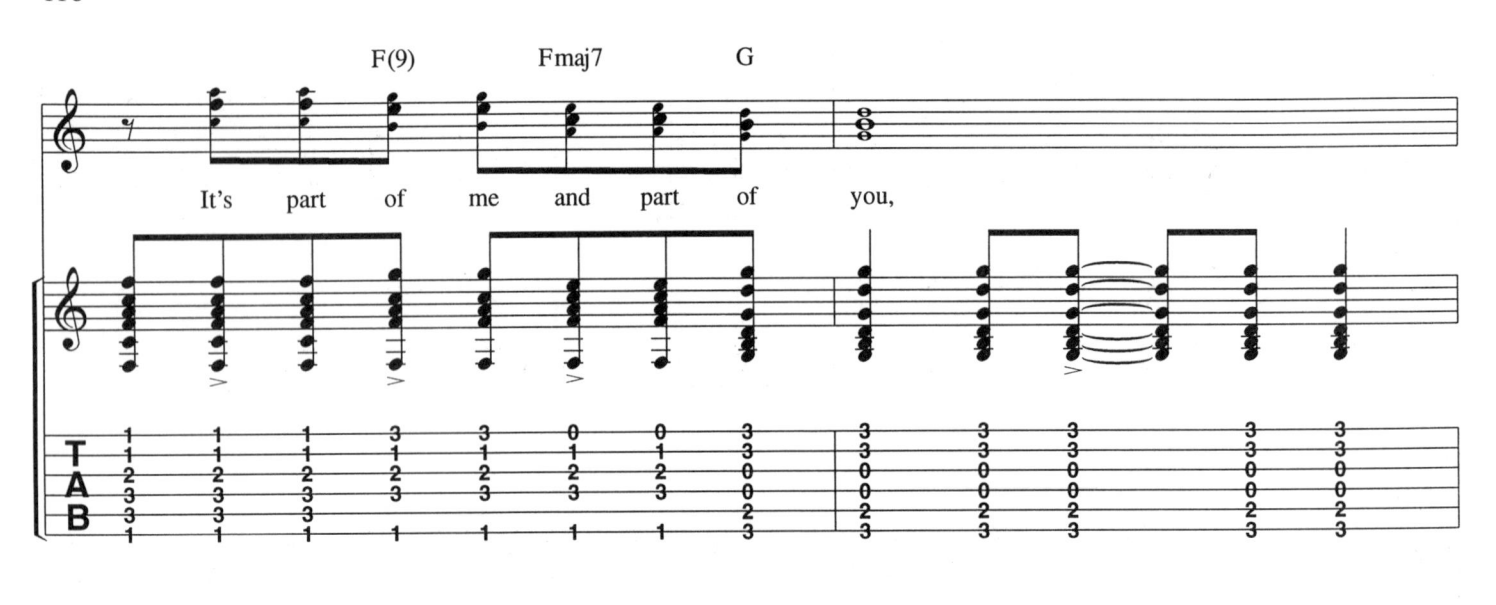

Train Of Love - 11 - 5

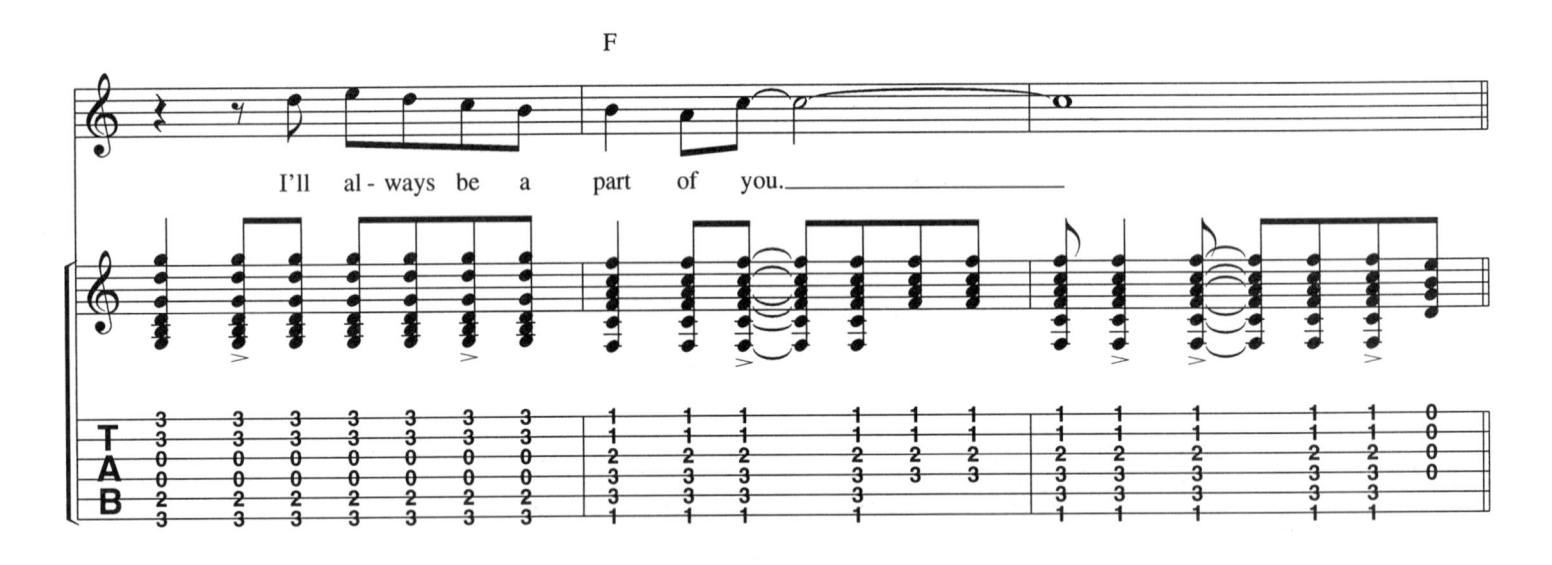

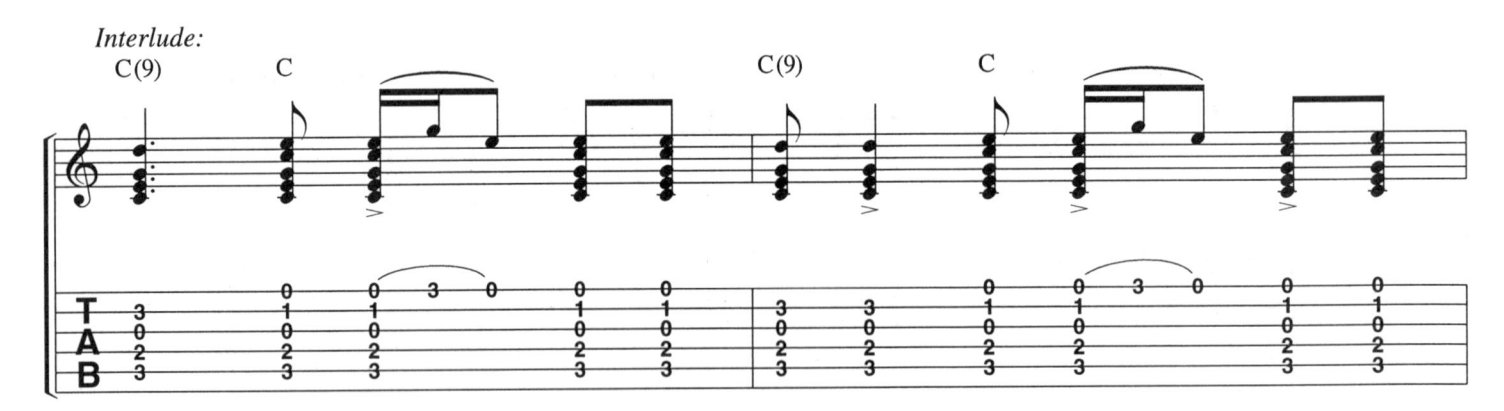

Bridge:

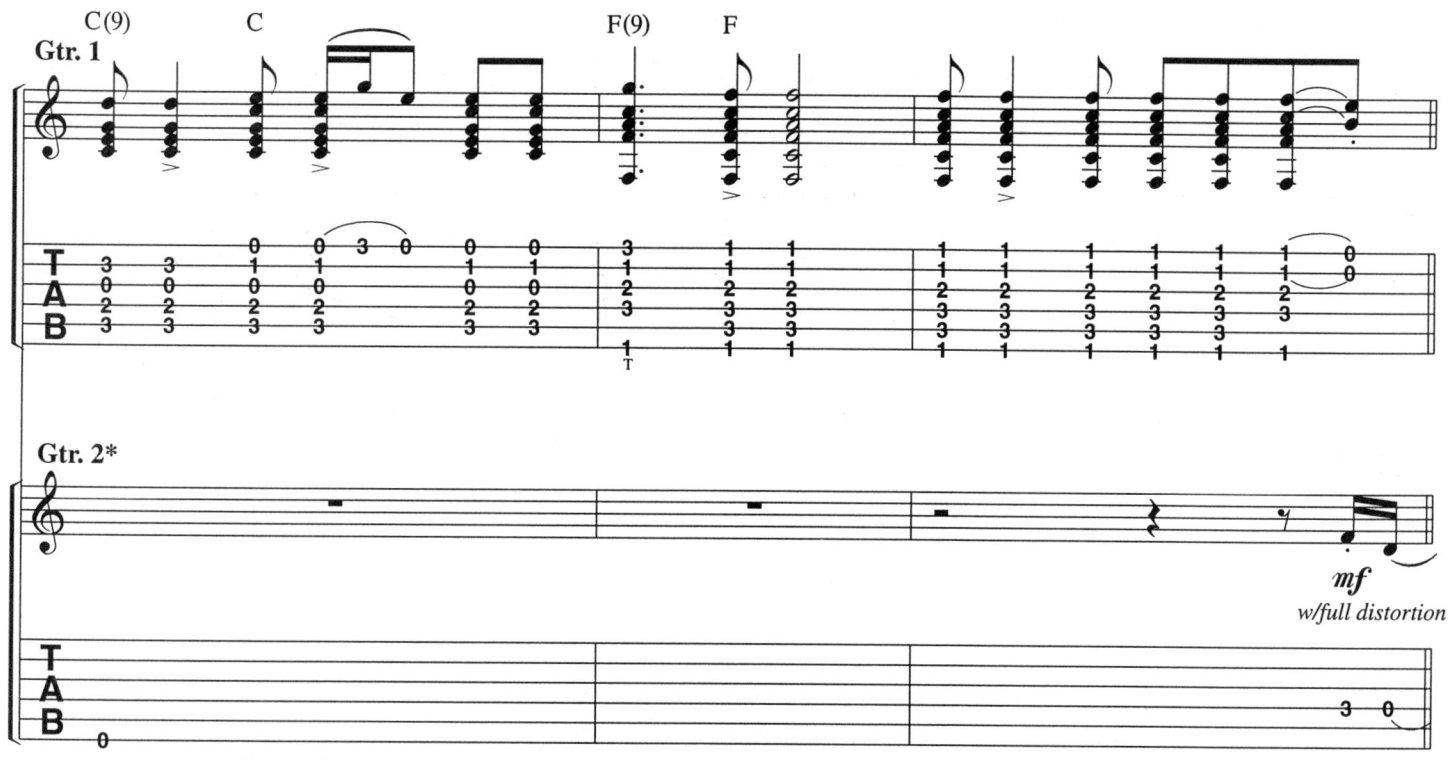

"To love and hon-or 'til death do us part."

Electric gtr. tuning: ⑥ = D ⑤ = G ④ = C ③ = F ② = A ① = D.

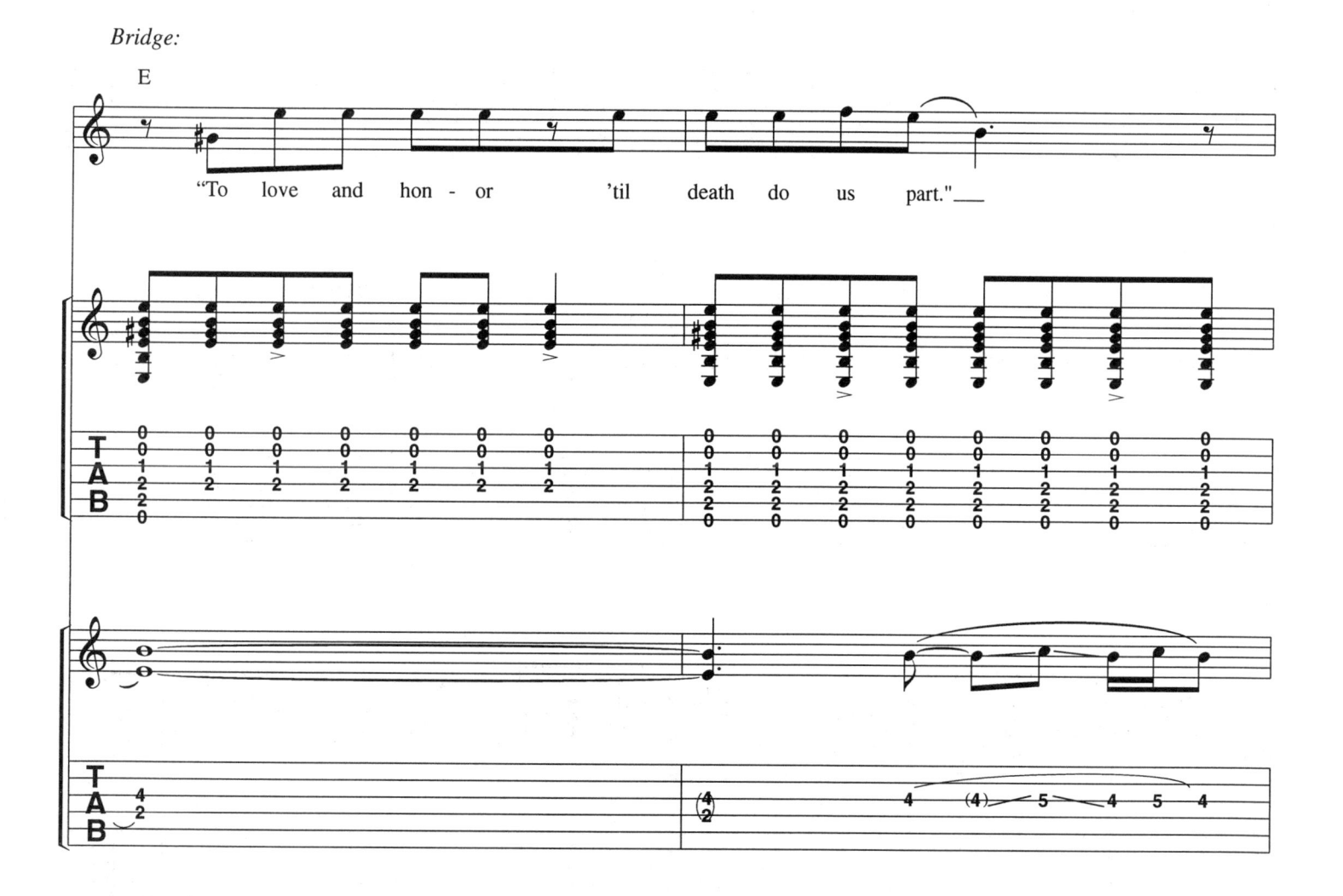

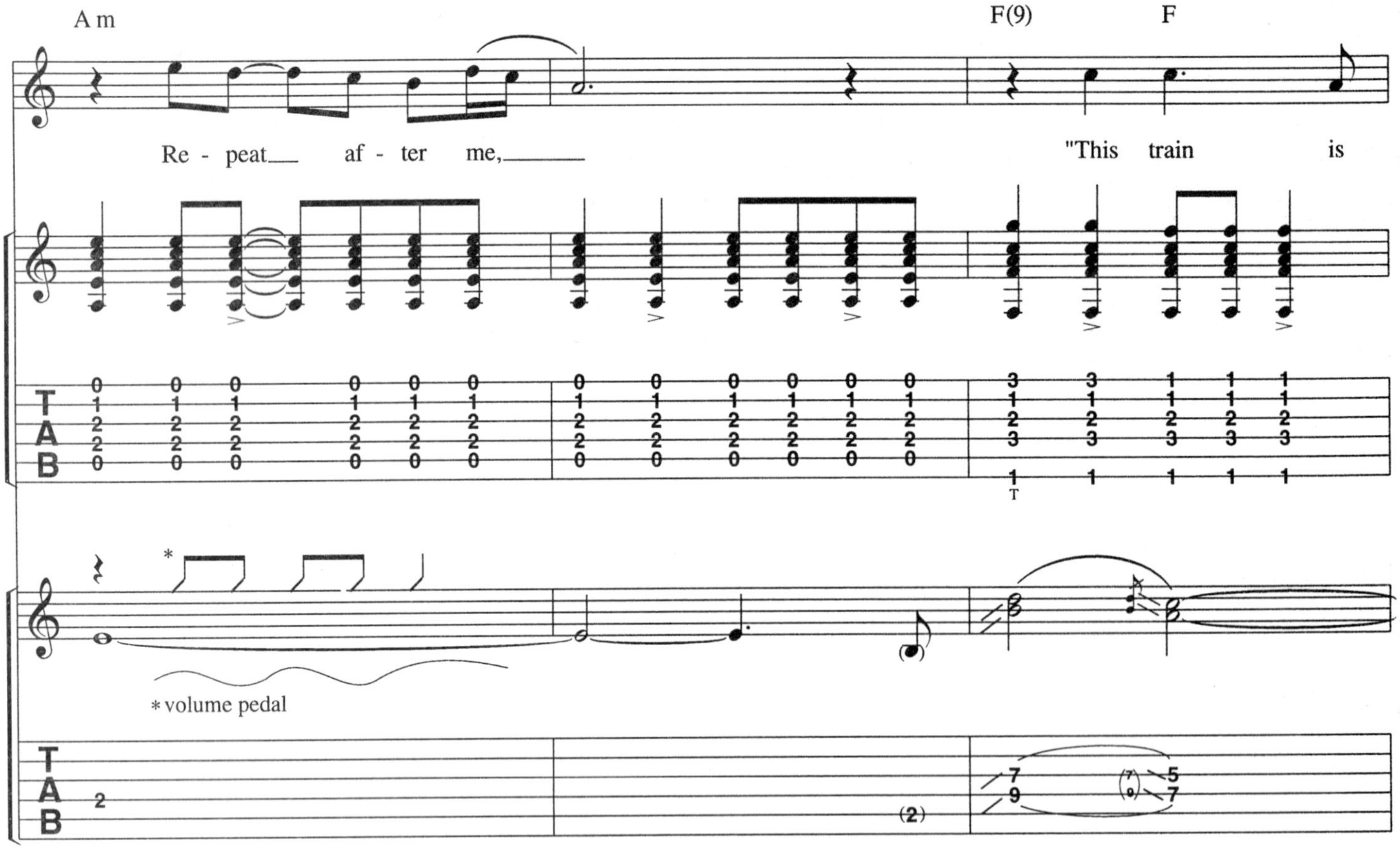
Am
F(9)
F
Re - peat af - ter me,
"This train is
*volume pedal

G
nev - er go - ing back."
harm.
harm.

Background Vocals:
E
Am
Where the lone - some whis - tle blows,
Where the lone - some whis - tle blows,
Gtr. 1
F
G
no one knows,
no one knows.
no one knows,
no one know.

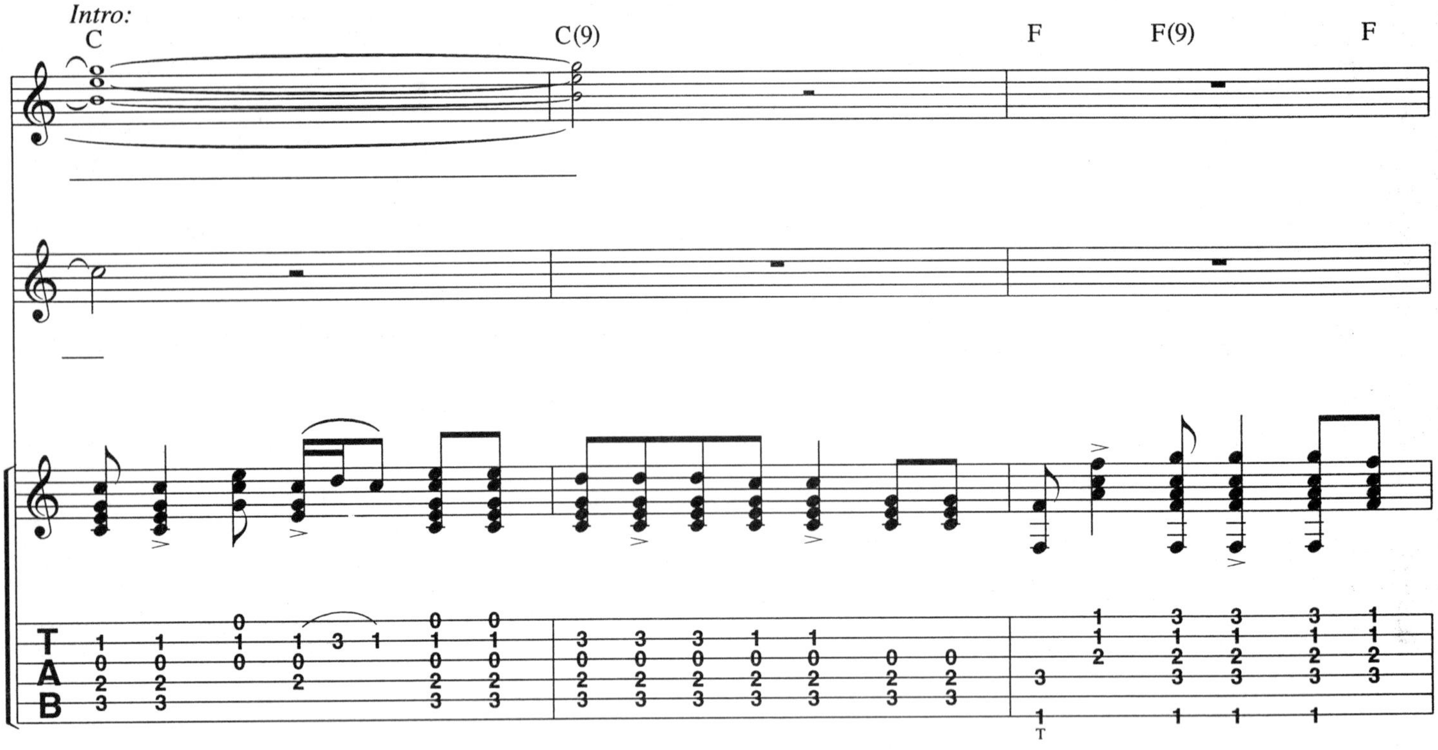
Intro:
C
C(9)
F
F(9)
F
TAB

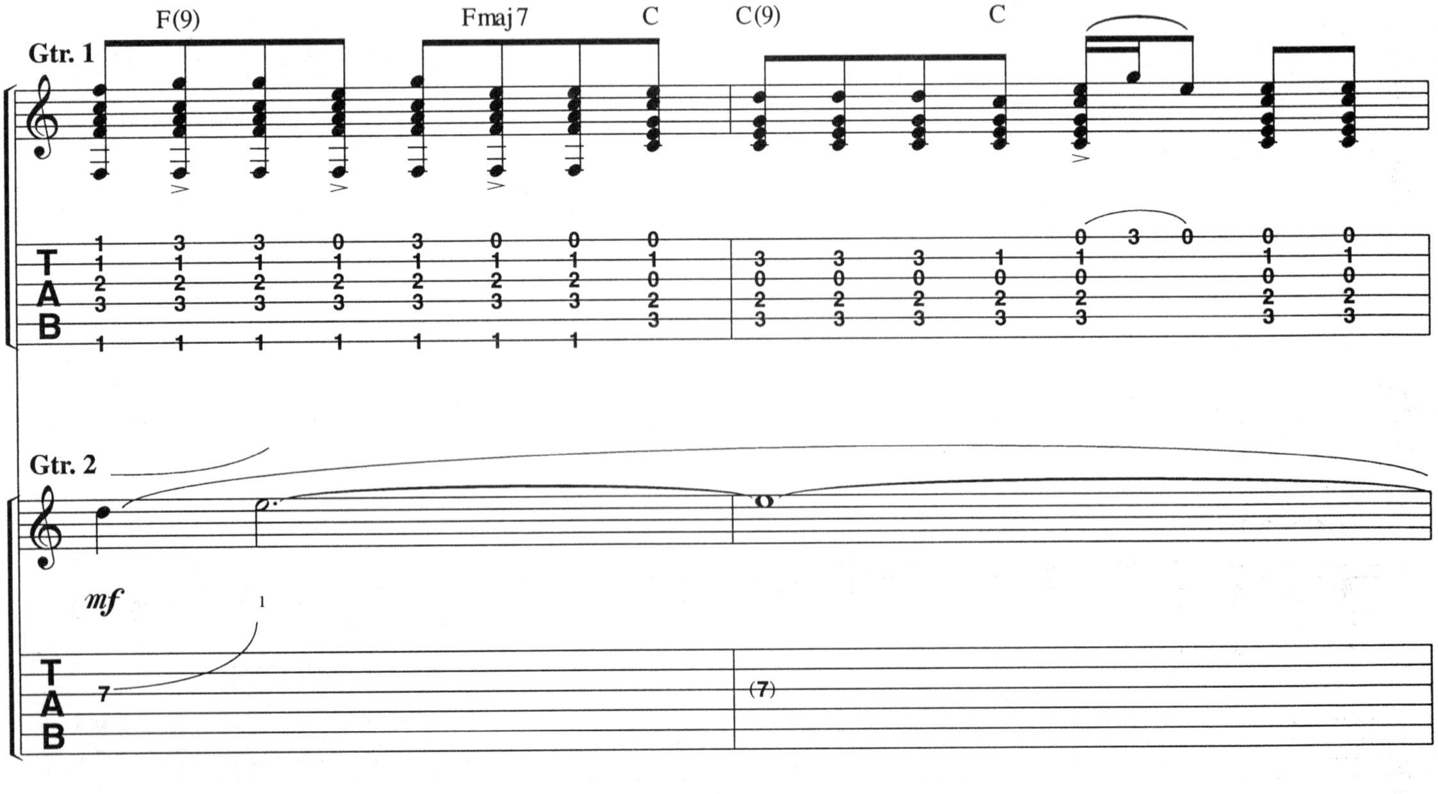
Gtr. 1
F(9)
Fmaj7
C
C(9)
C
TAB
Gtr. 2
mf
TAB

121

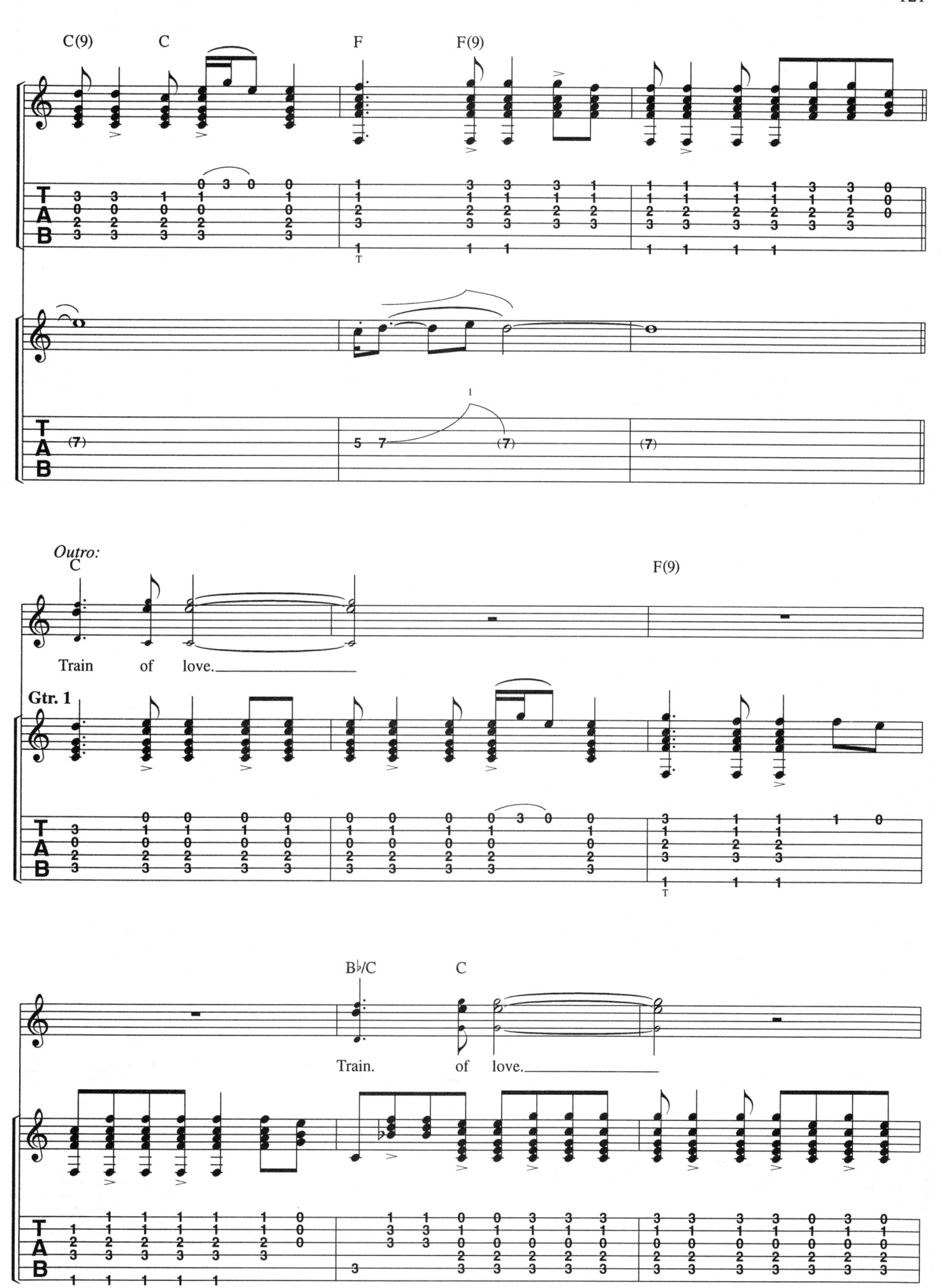

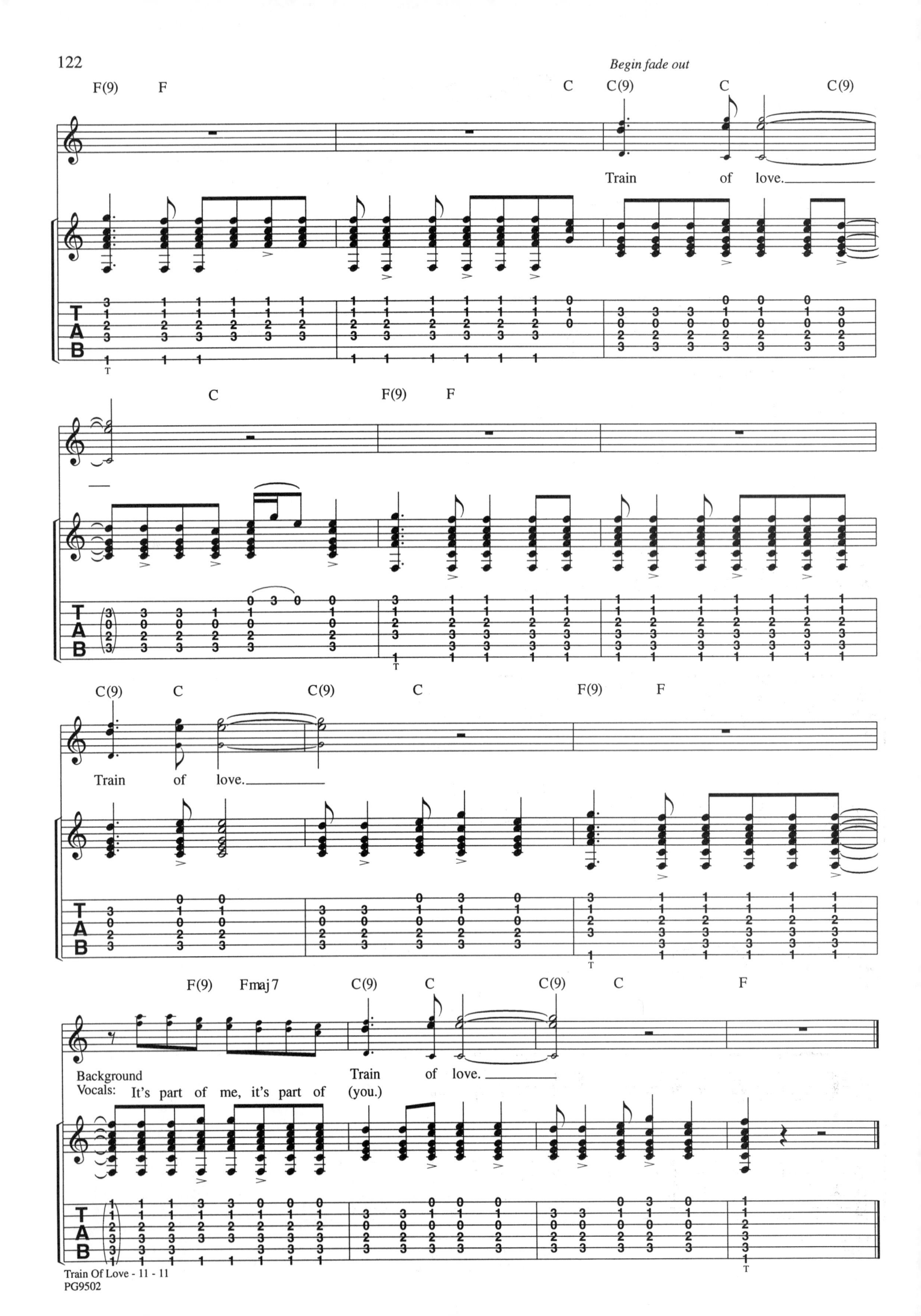

Train of love.

Train of love.

Background Vocals: It's part of me, it's part of (you.) *Train of love.*

TRANS AM

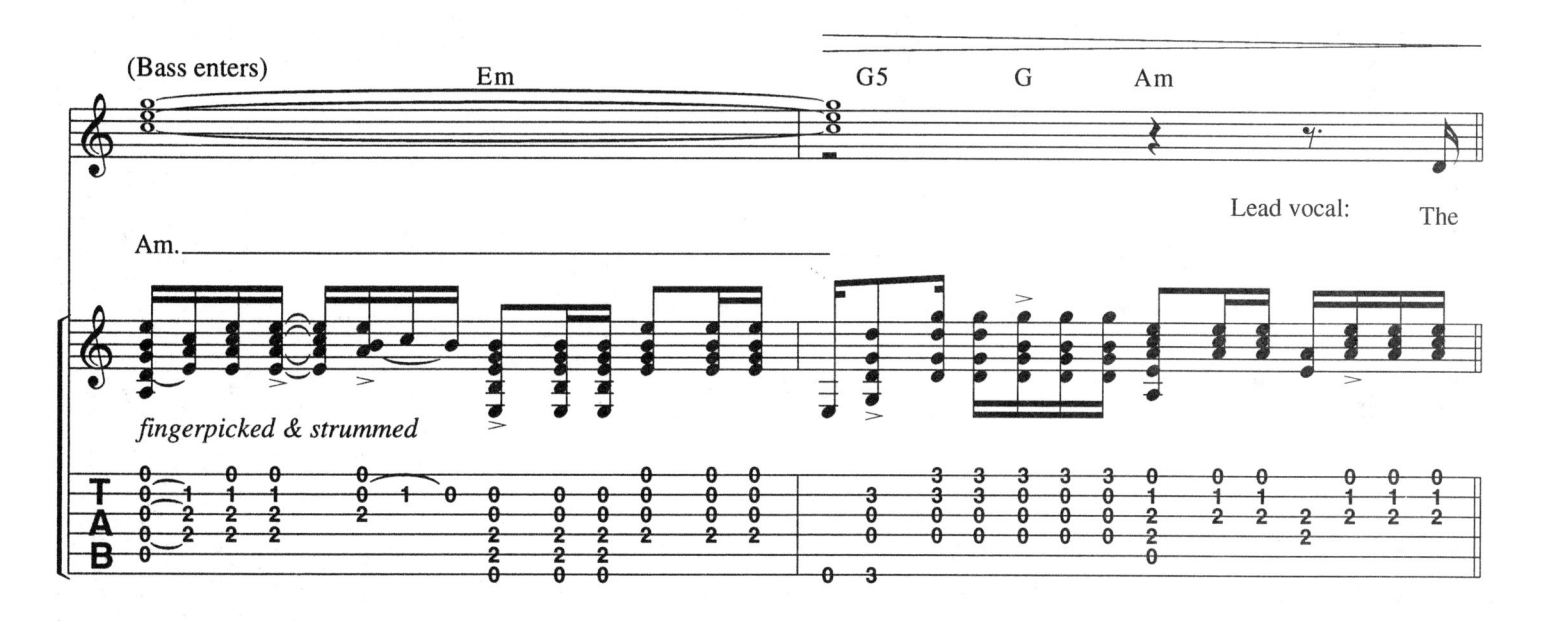

Words and Music by
NEIL YOUNG

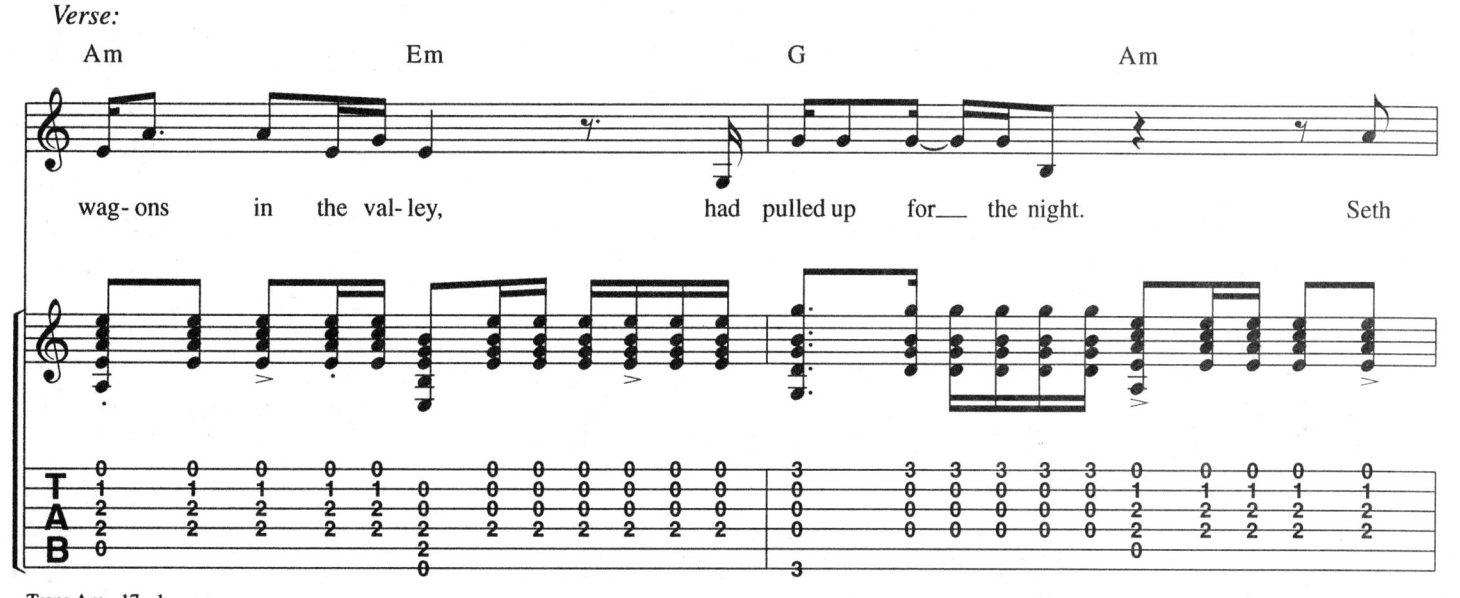

Slowly ♩ = 69

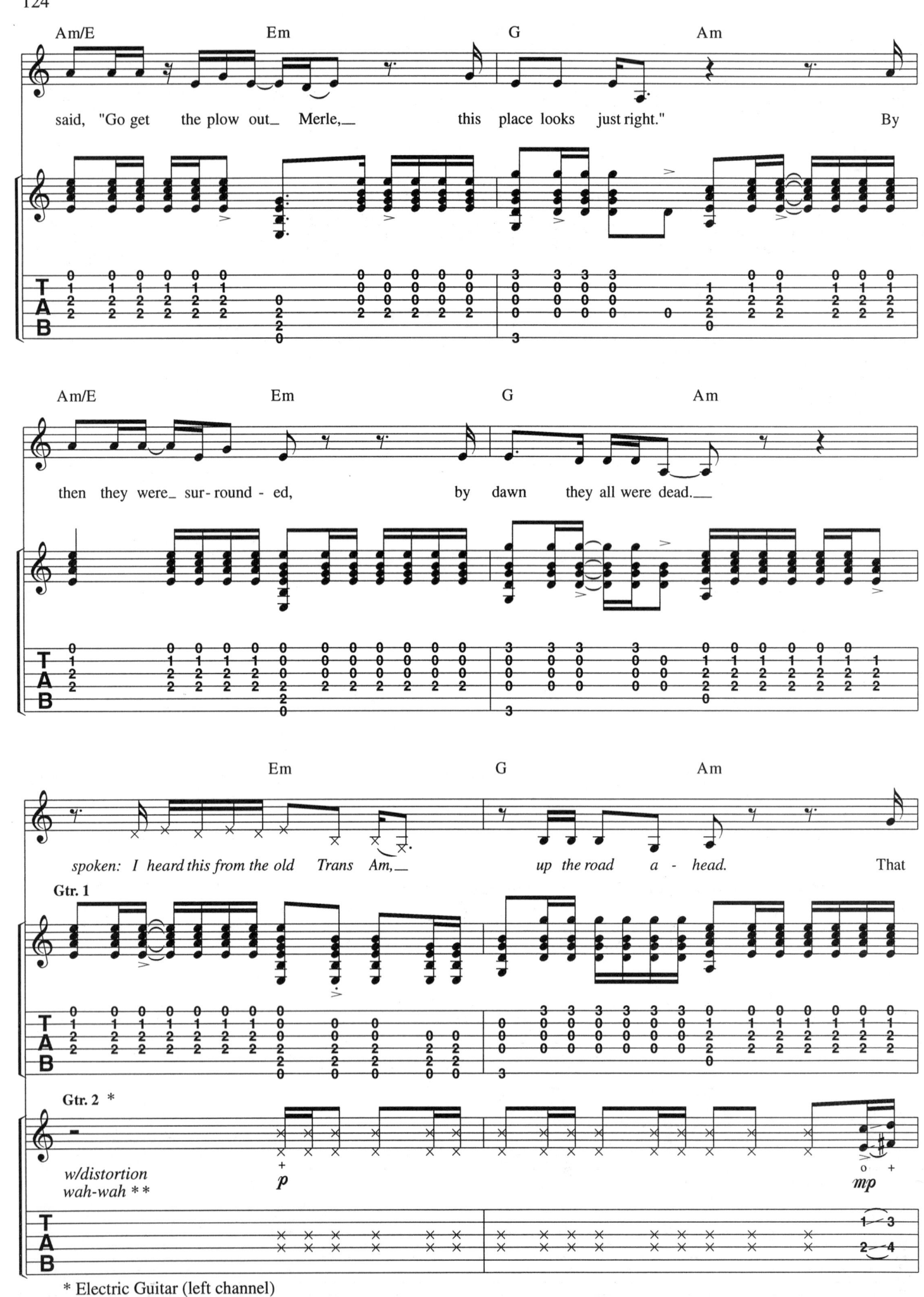

Lyrics:
said, "Go get the plow out Merle, this place looks just right." By then they were surrounded, by dawn they all were dead.

spoken: I heard this from the old Trans Am, up the road ahead. That

Gtr. 1

Gtr. 2 *

w/distortion
wah-wah **

* Electric Guitar (left channel)
**Wah-wah pedal: o = down, + = up.

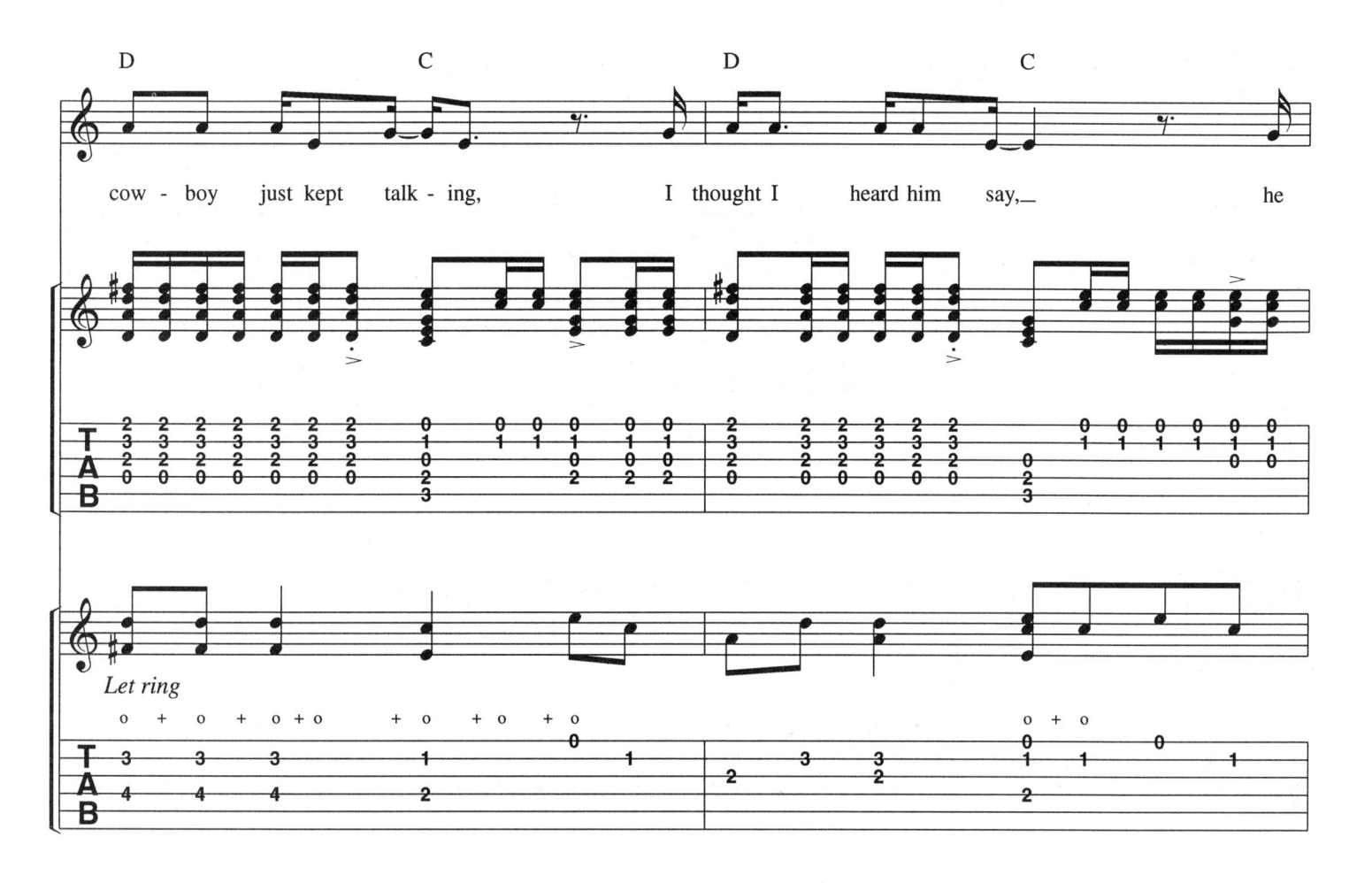

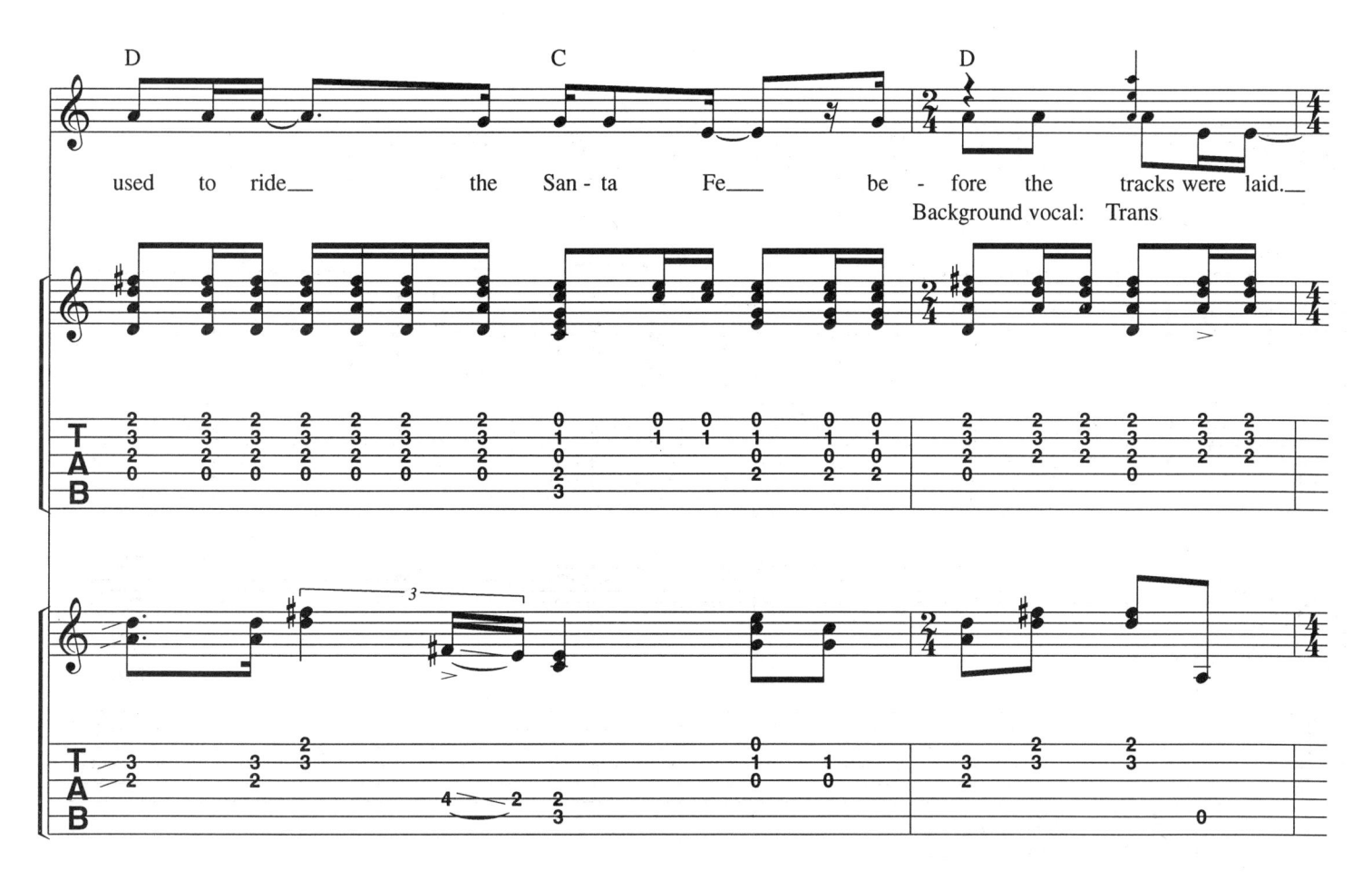

cow - boy just kept talk - ing, I thought I heard him say,— he

used to ride— the Santa Fe— be - fore the tracks were laid.—
Background vocal: Trans

Verse:

nas-ty wind was blow-ing through the gates of Ed-en Park.

palm mute throughout*

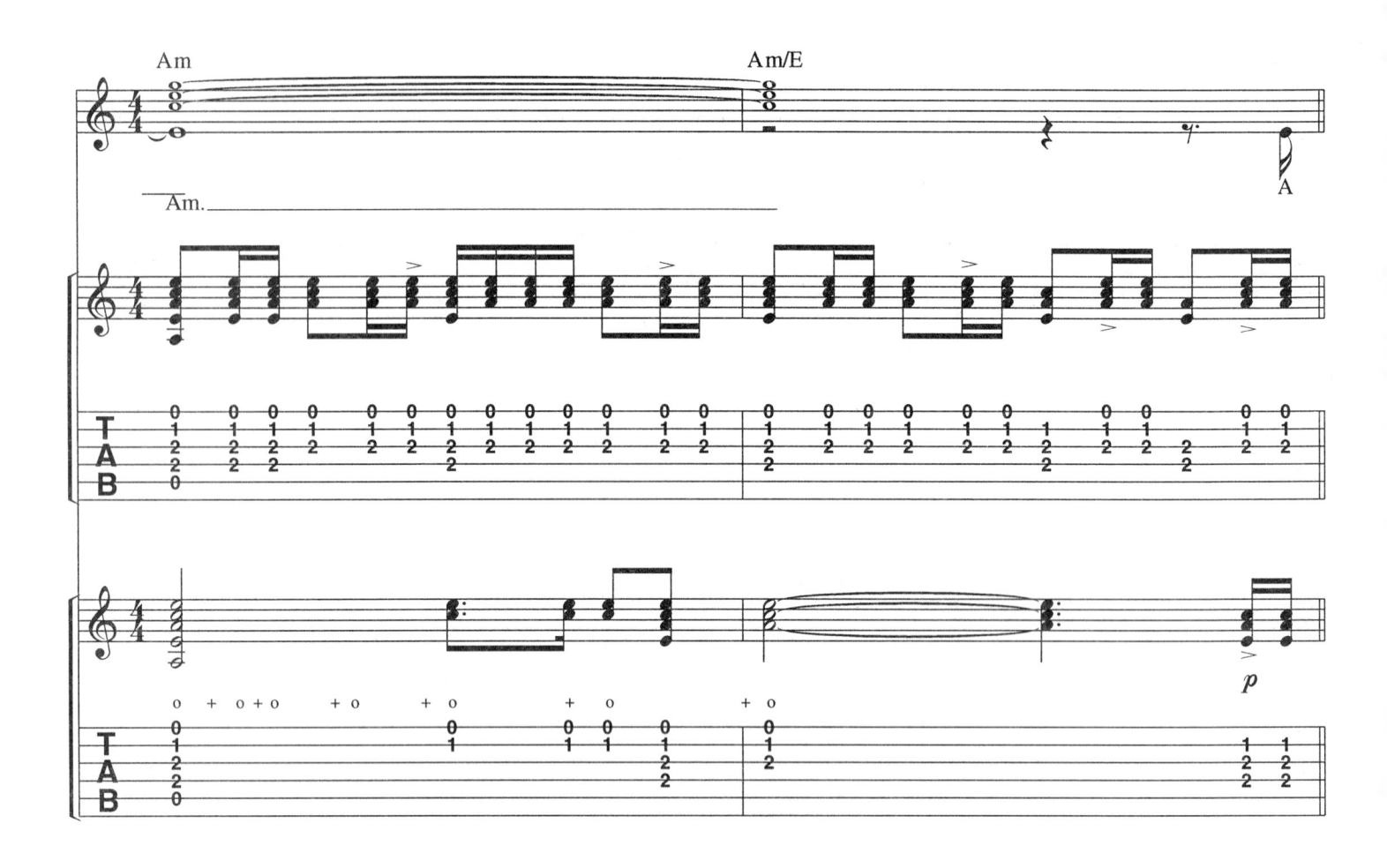

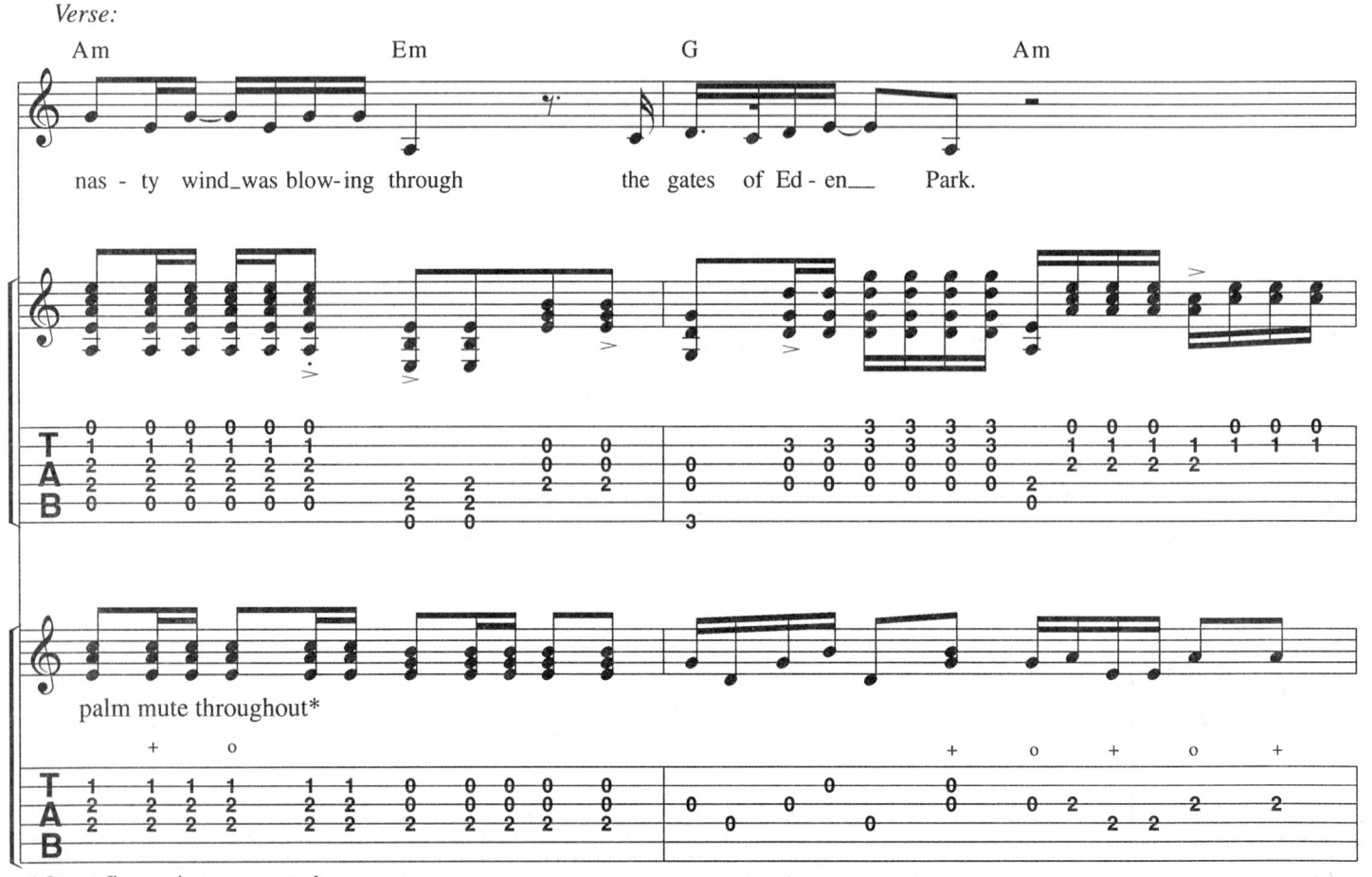

*Open first string not muted.

Trans Am - 17 - 4

127

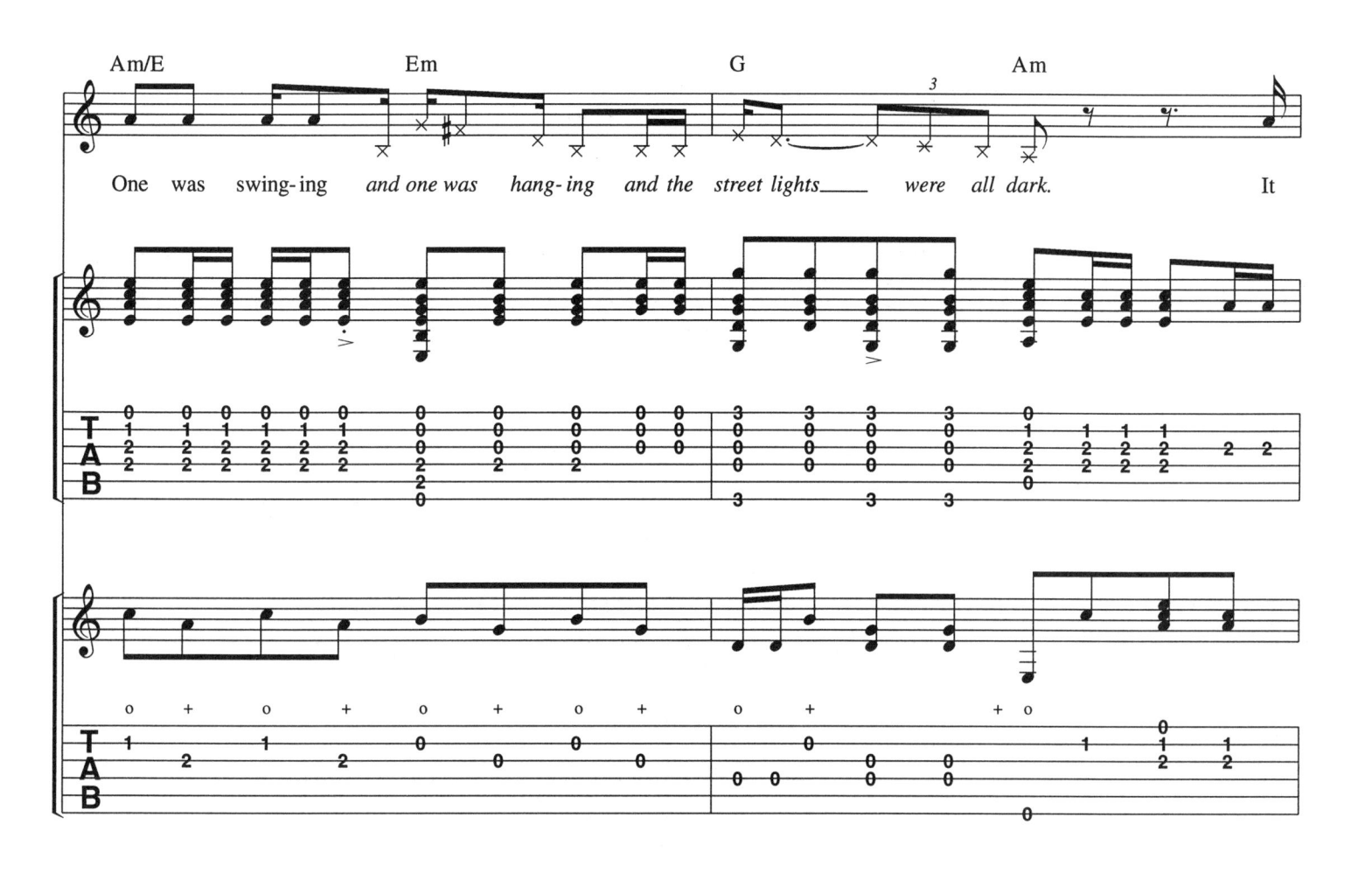

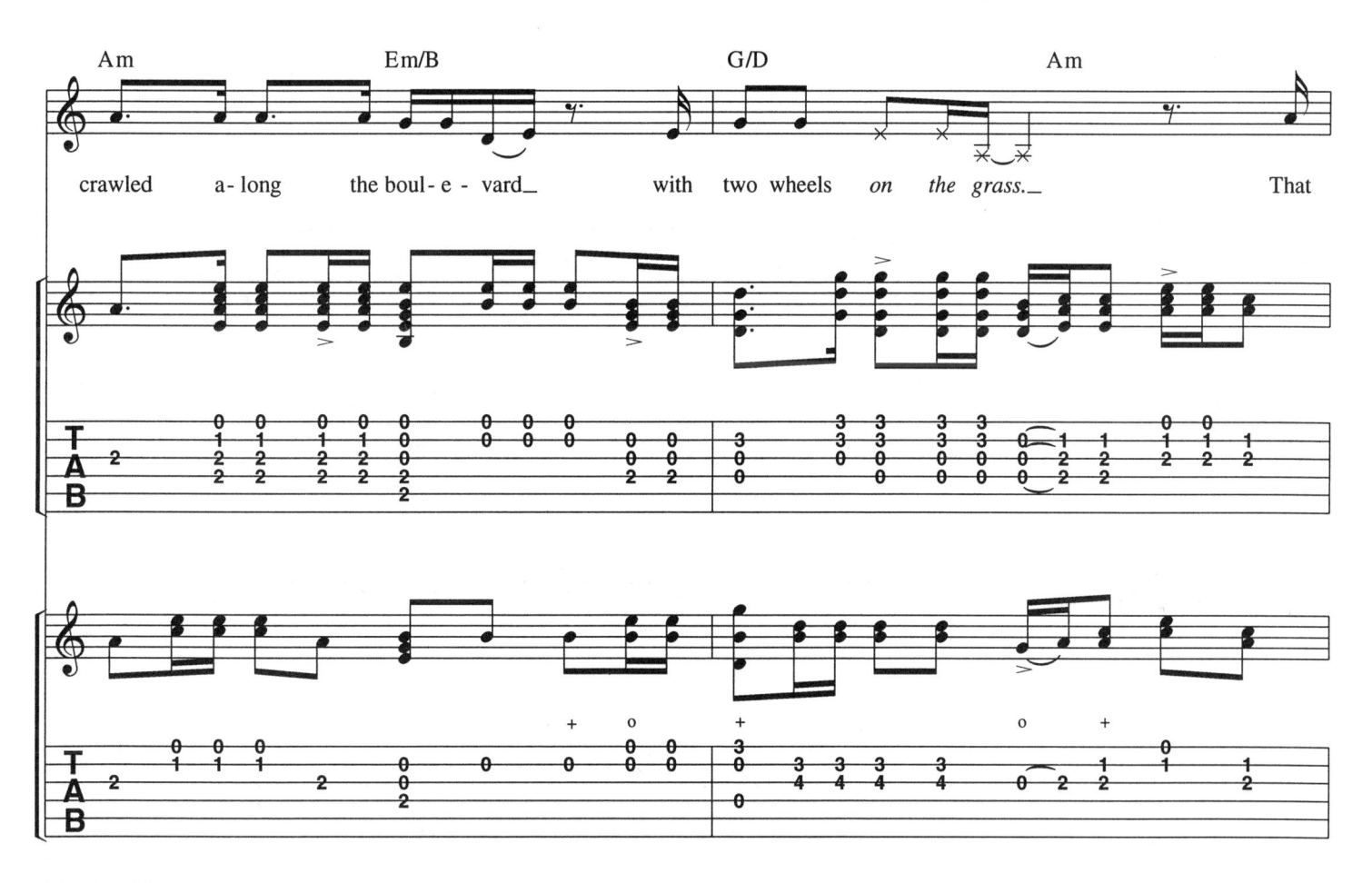

One was swing-ing *and one was hang-ing* and the street lights_____ were all dark. It crawled a-long the boul-e-vard___ with two wheels *on the grass.___* That

Trans Am - 17 - 5
PG9502

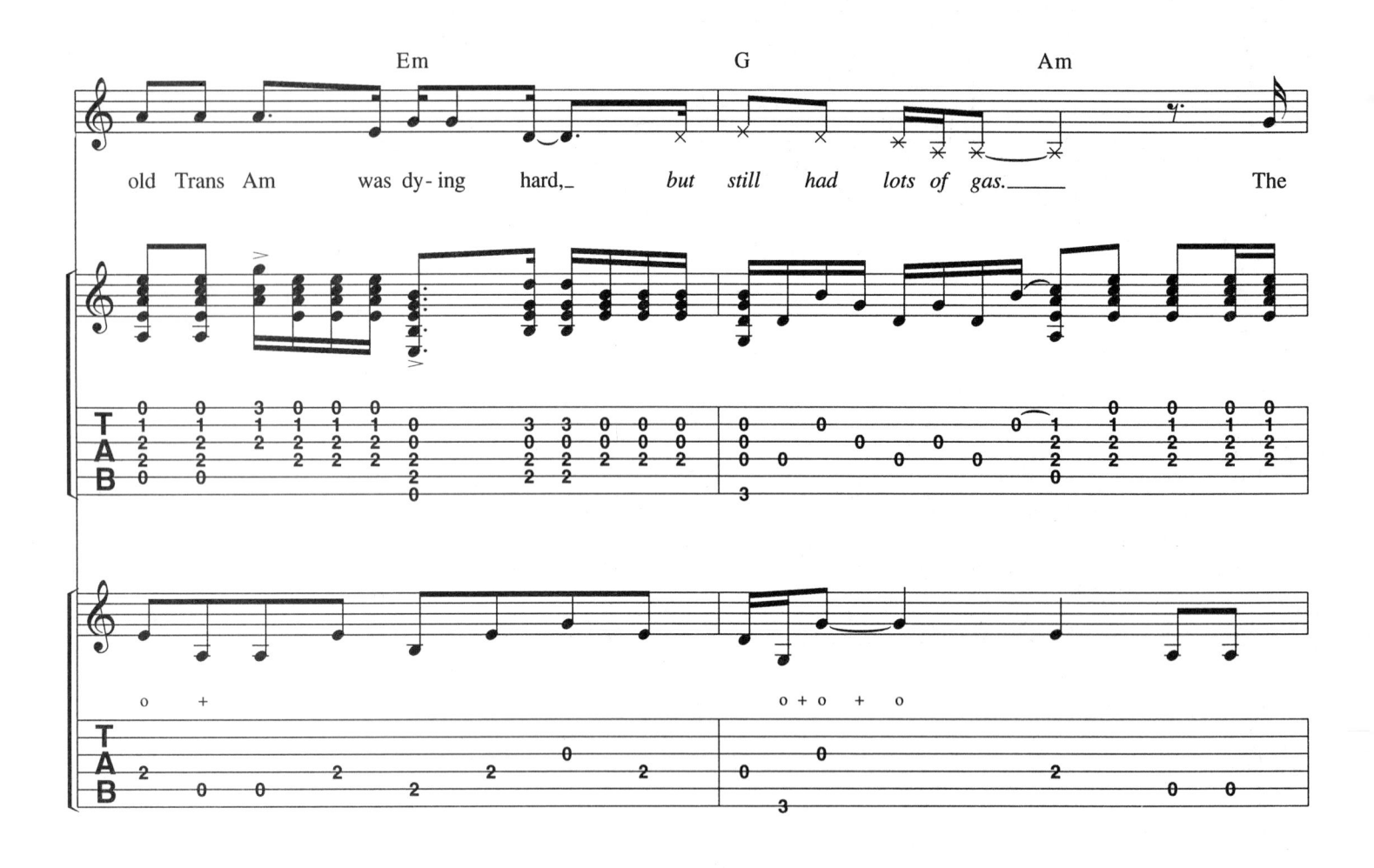

old Trans Am was dying hard, but still had lots of gas. The golden gate was open wide, the sun came shining through. Where

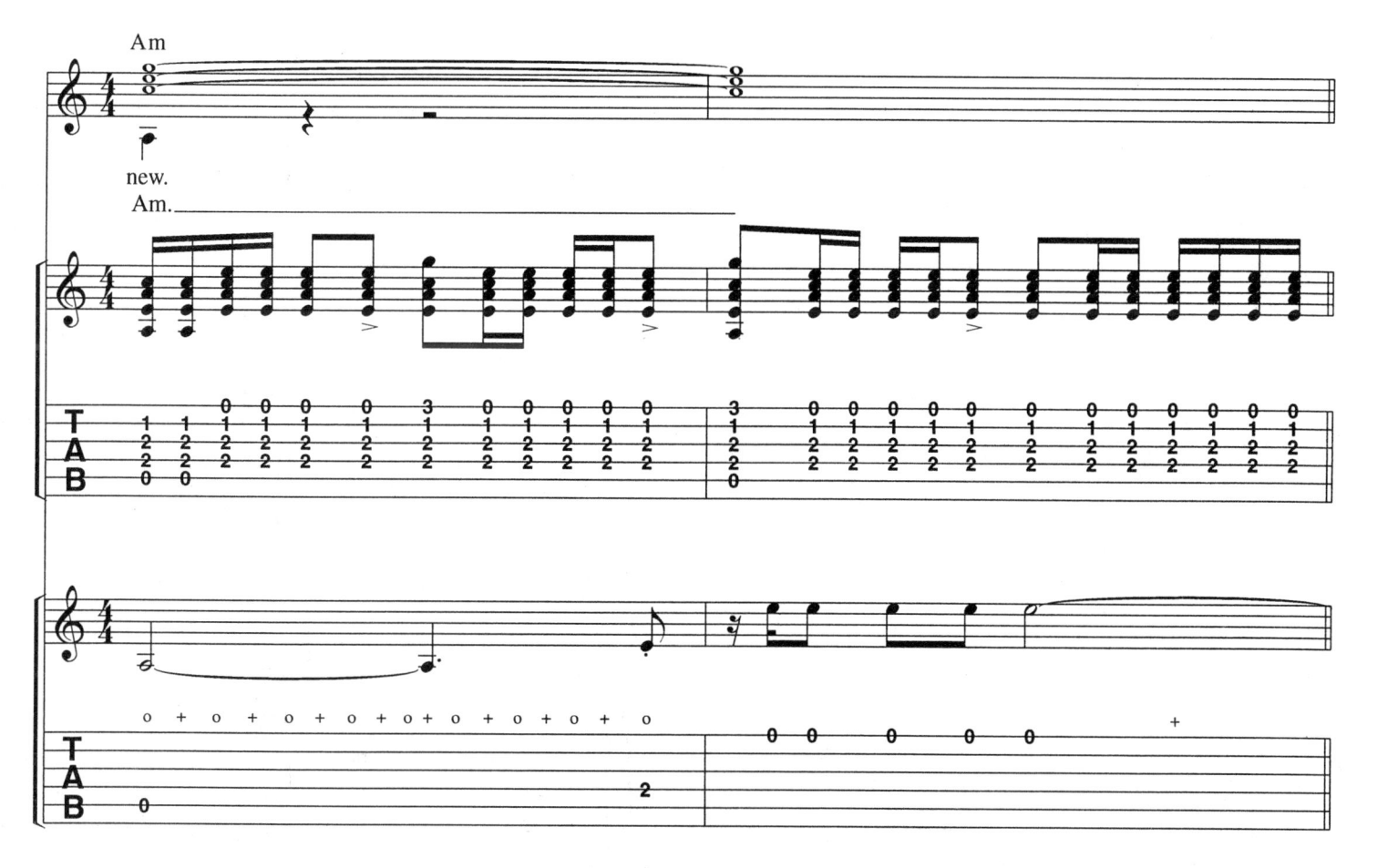

once the an - gels *stood and cried* eve'ry-thing___ was
Background vocal: Trans

new.
Am.___

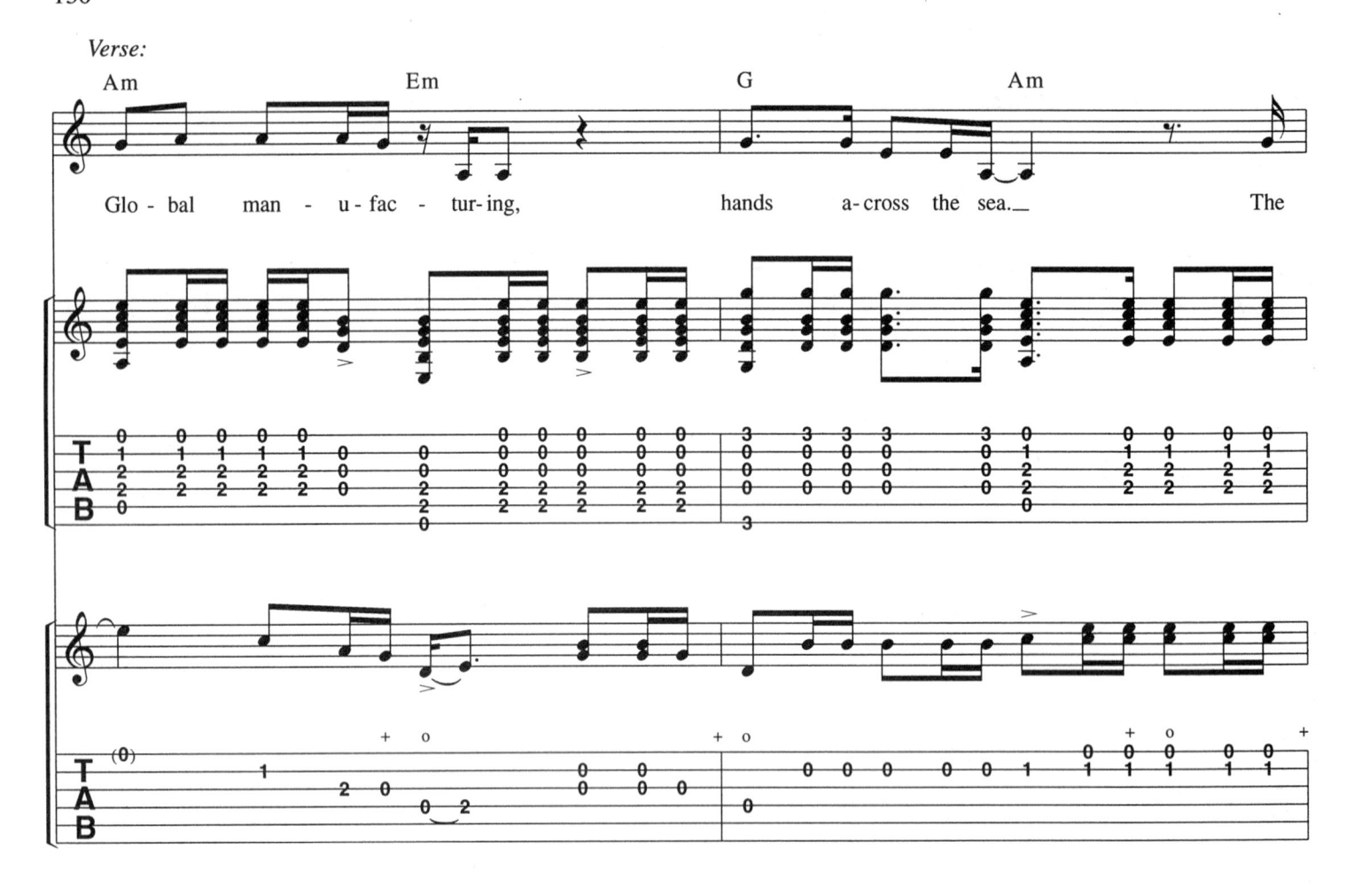

130

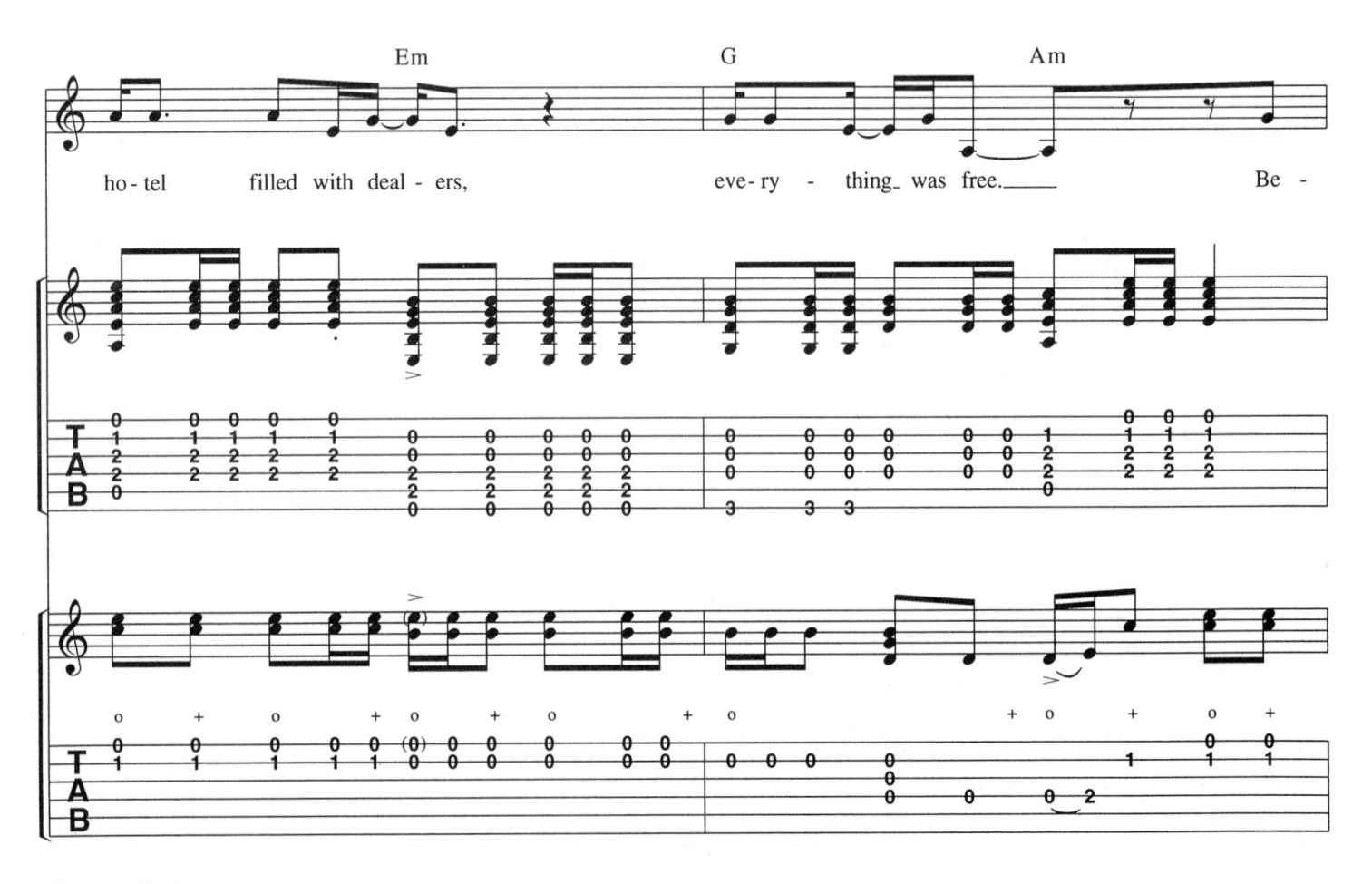

Verse:

Glo-bal man-u-fac-tur-ing, hands a-cross the sea.___ The ho-tel filled with deal-ers, eve-ry-thing_ was free.___ Be-

Trans Am - 17 - 8
PG9502

fore the comp-e-ti-tion, a-head of all the rest, the

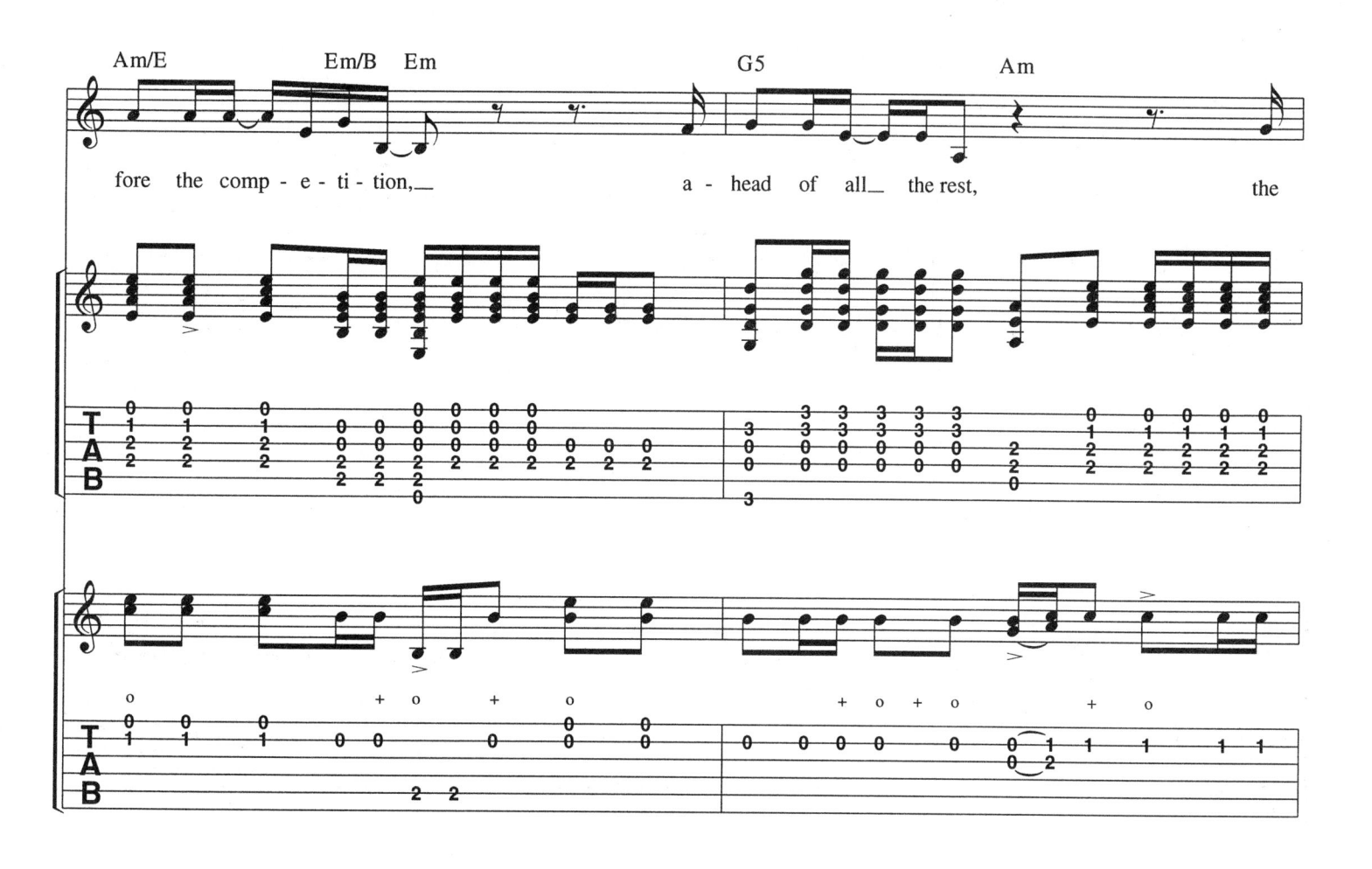

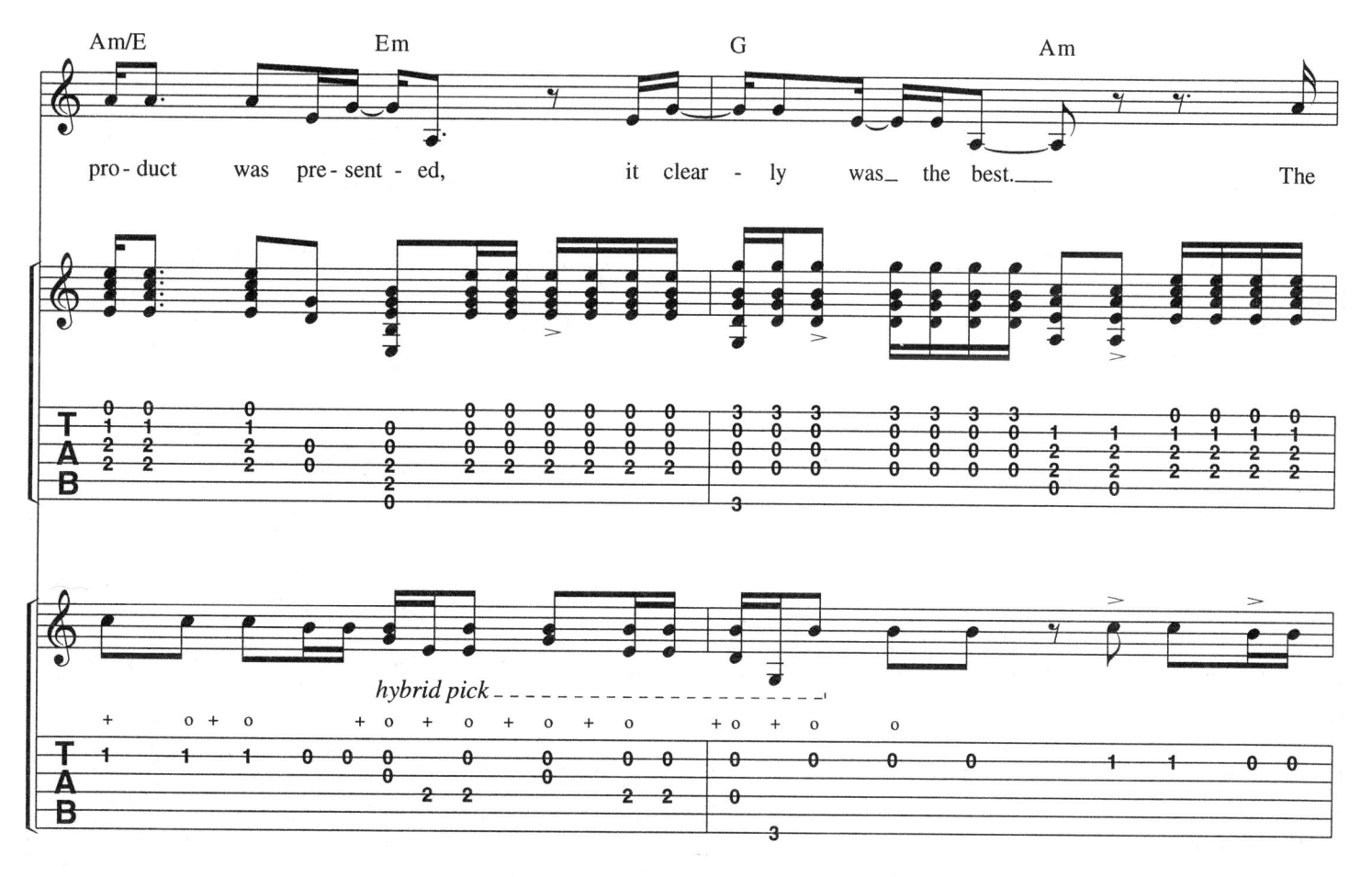

pro-duct was pre-sent-ed, it clear-ly was the best. The

hybrid pick

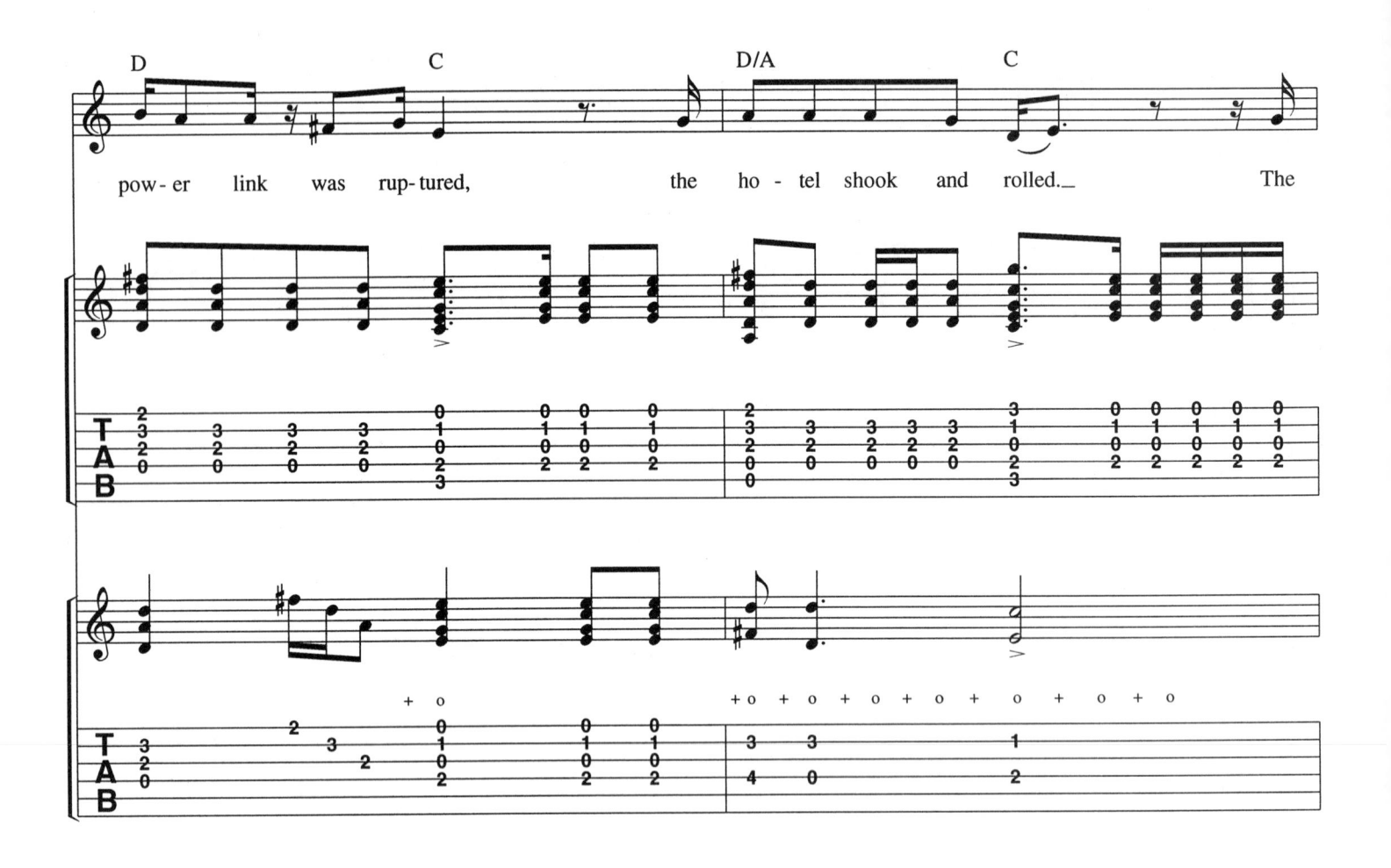

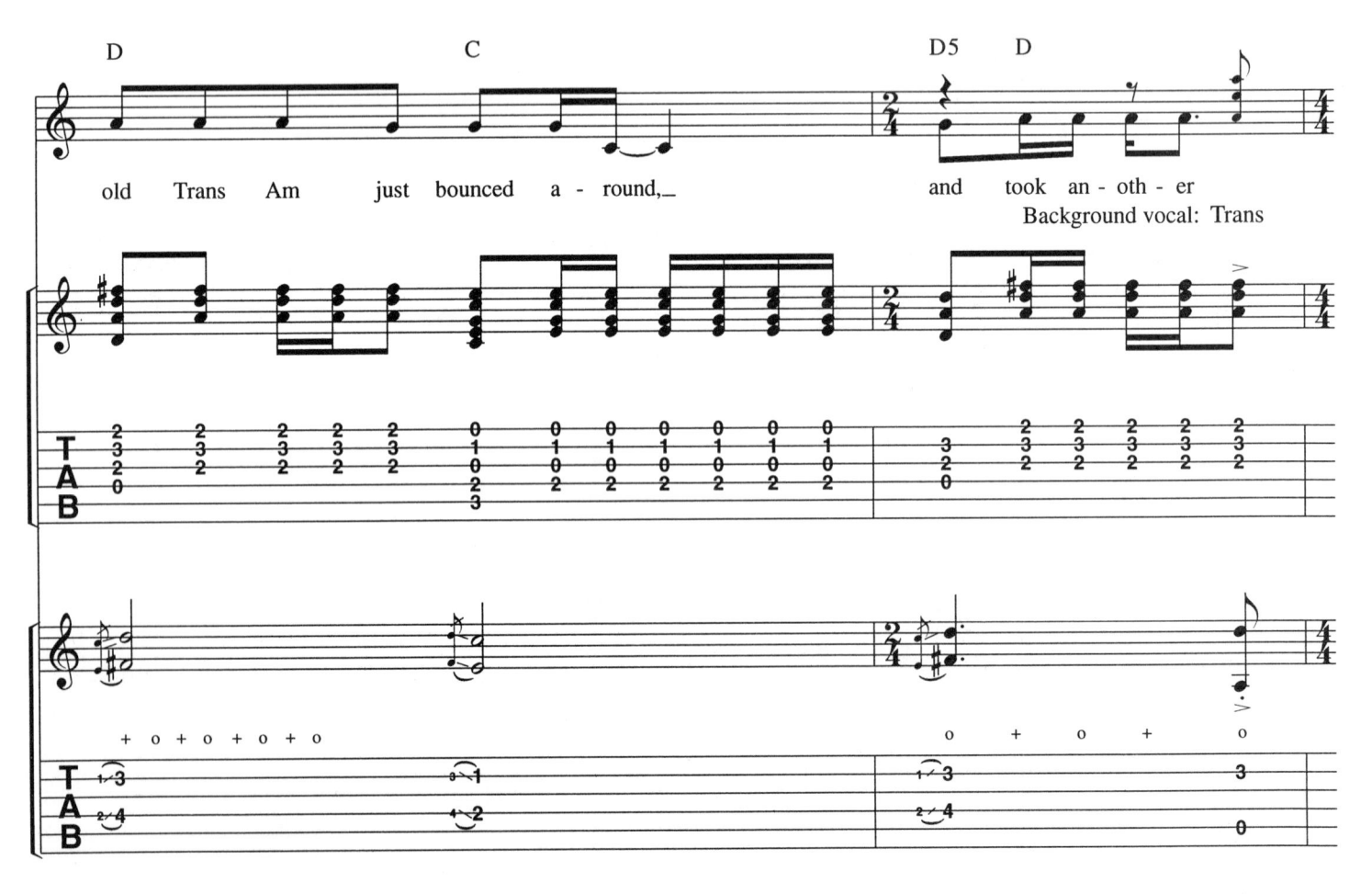

132

pow- er link was rup- tured, the ho- tel shook and rolled.___ The old Trans Am just bounced a- round,___ and took an- oth- er

Background vocal: Trans

Trans Am - 17 - 10
PG9502

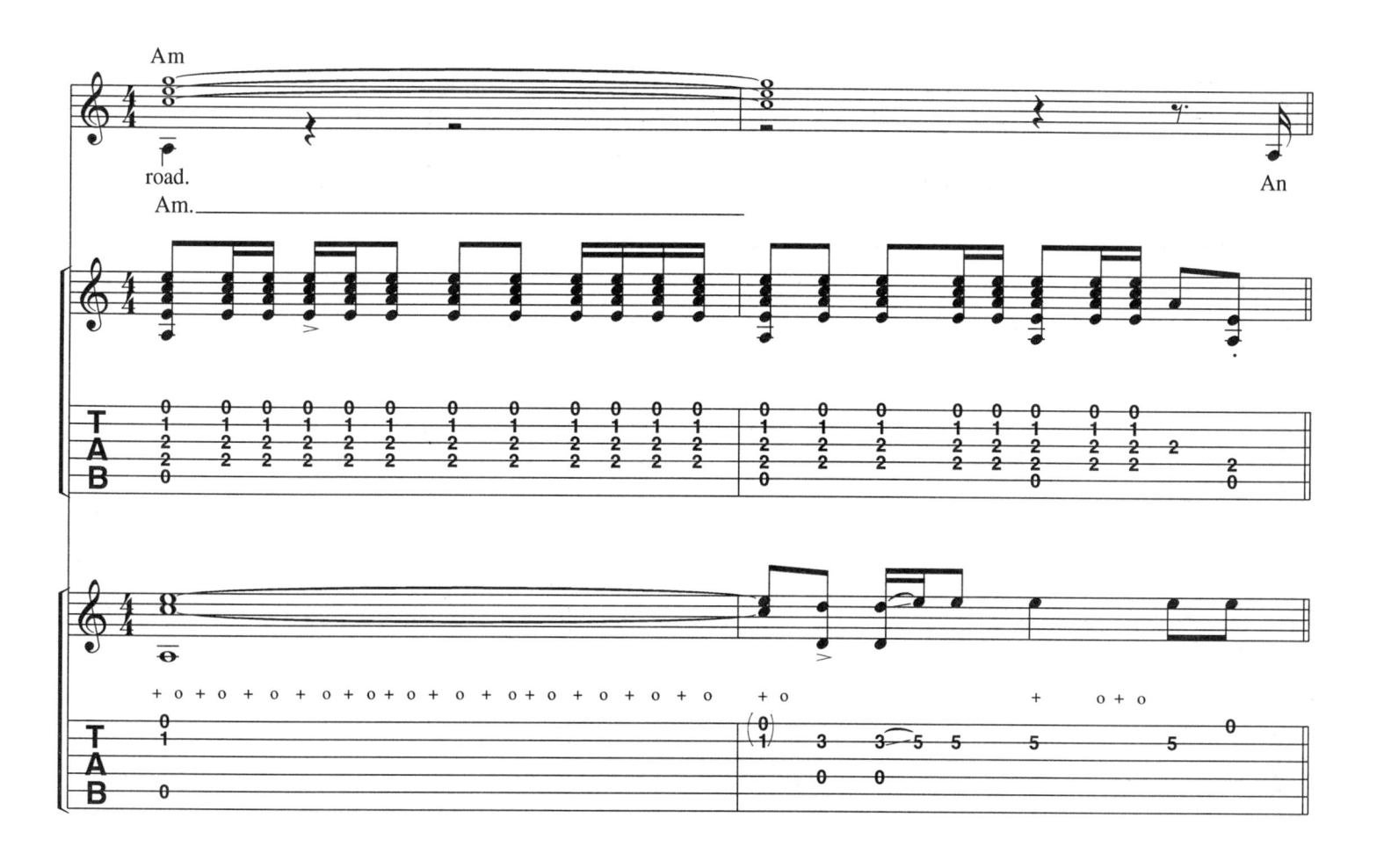

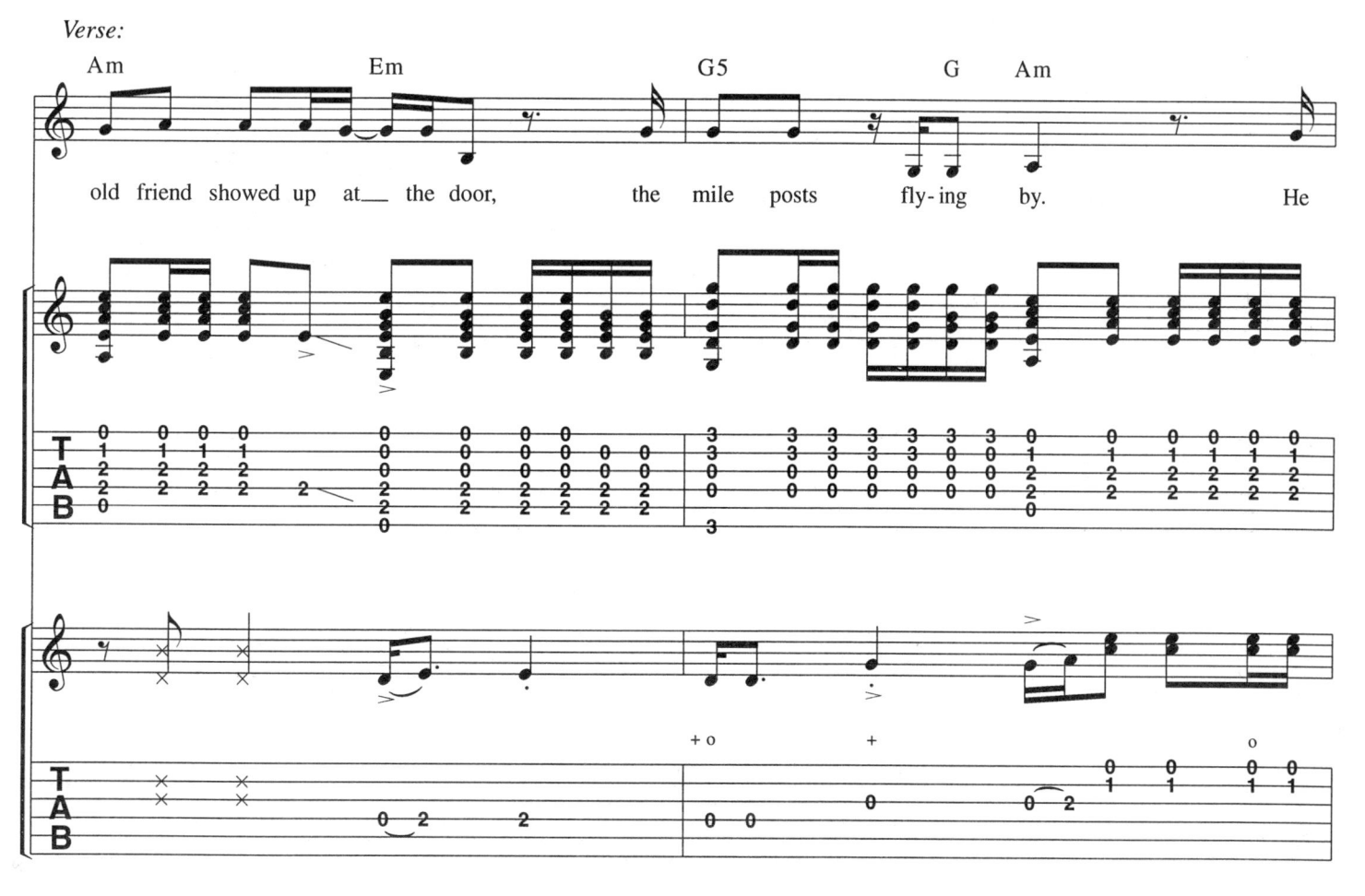

Verse:

road. An old friend showed up at the door, the mile posts flying by. He

Trans Am - 17 - 11
PG9502

Em G5 Am
said, "Come on." I said "What for?" He said, "I'll show you why." I
Am Em7 Em G/D Am
got a call from north of here they said some girl's broke down. There's

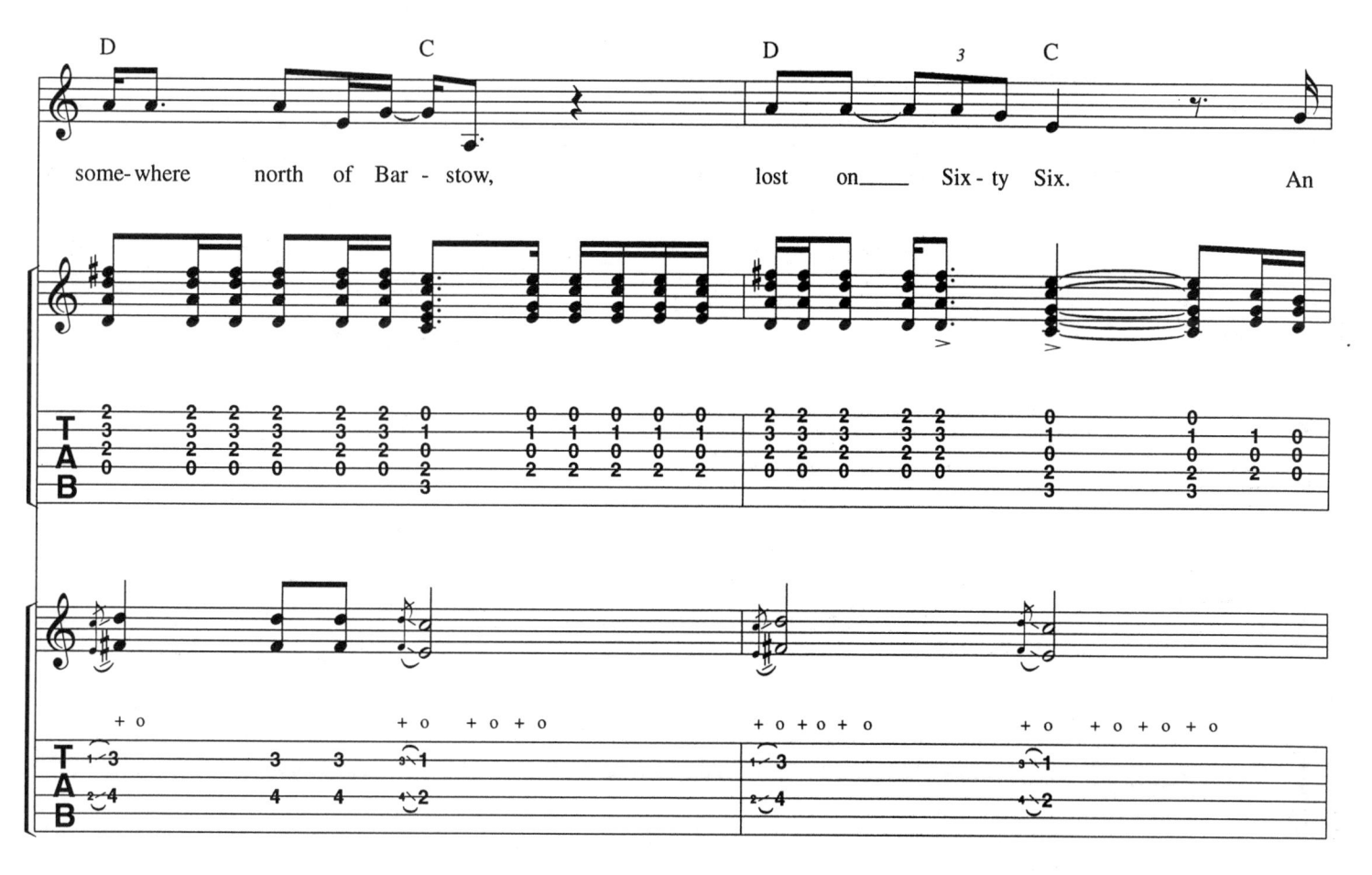

good mon-ey in it for you and me___ if we can get her back to town.___ She's some-where north of Bar-stow, lost on___ Six-ty Six. An

Trans Am - 17 - 13
PG9502

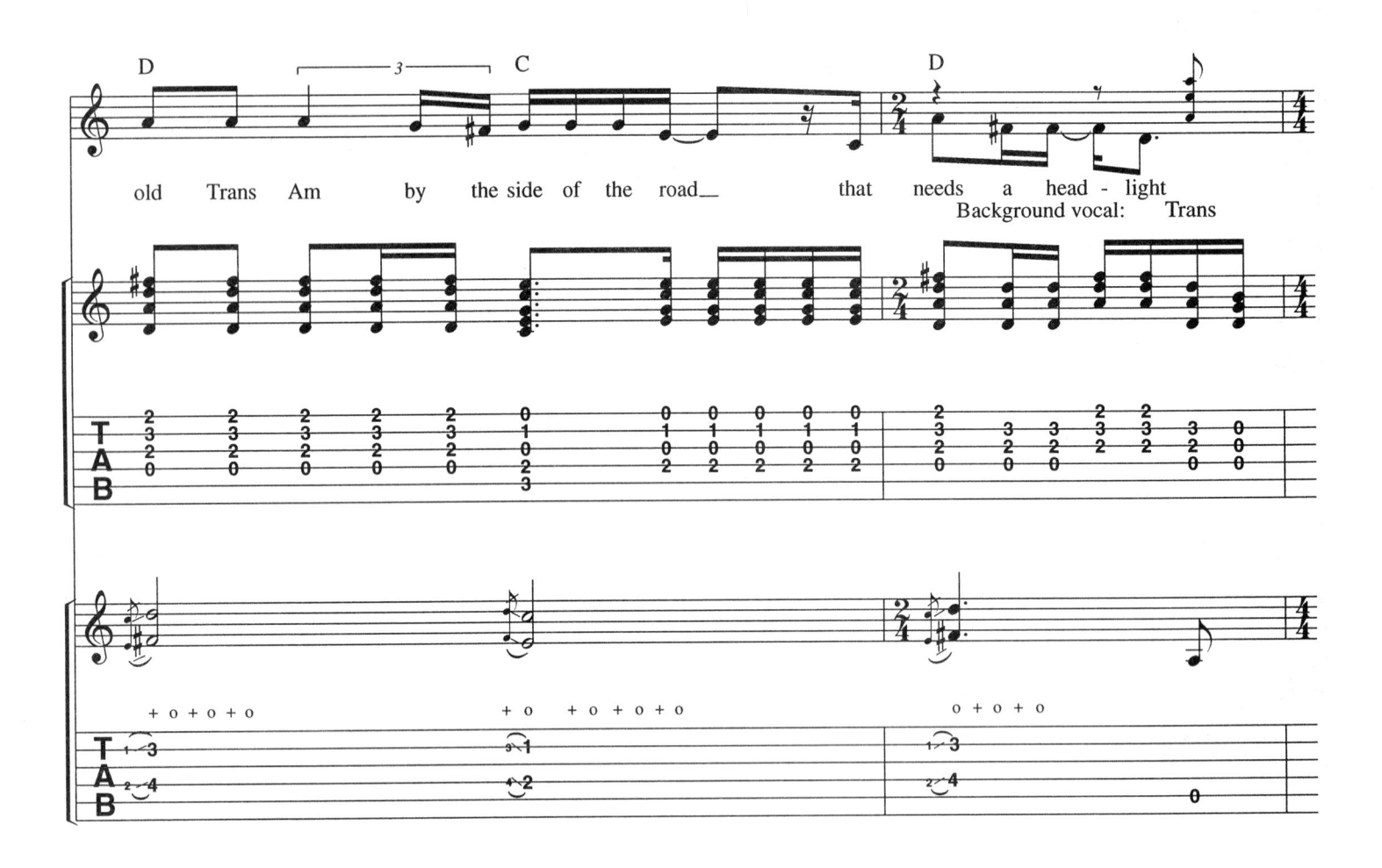

old Trans Am by the side of the road___ that needs a head-light
Background vocal: Trans

Verse: Instrumental

* Guitar 3 is downstemed, Guitar 1 is upstemed.

Trans Am - 17 - 15
PG9502

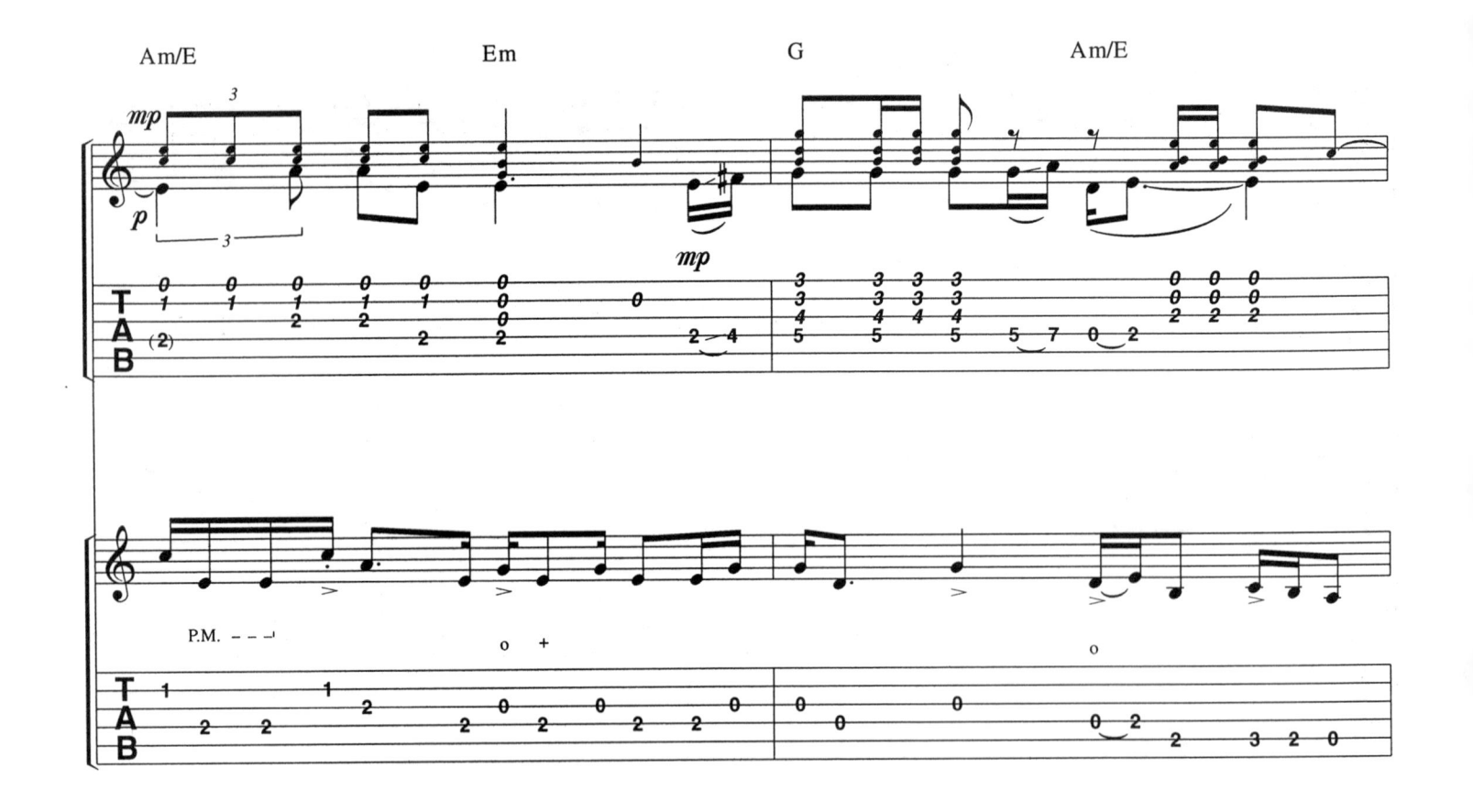

* Vibrato (volume) effect.

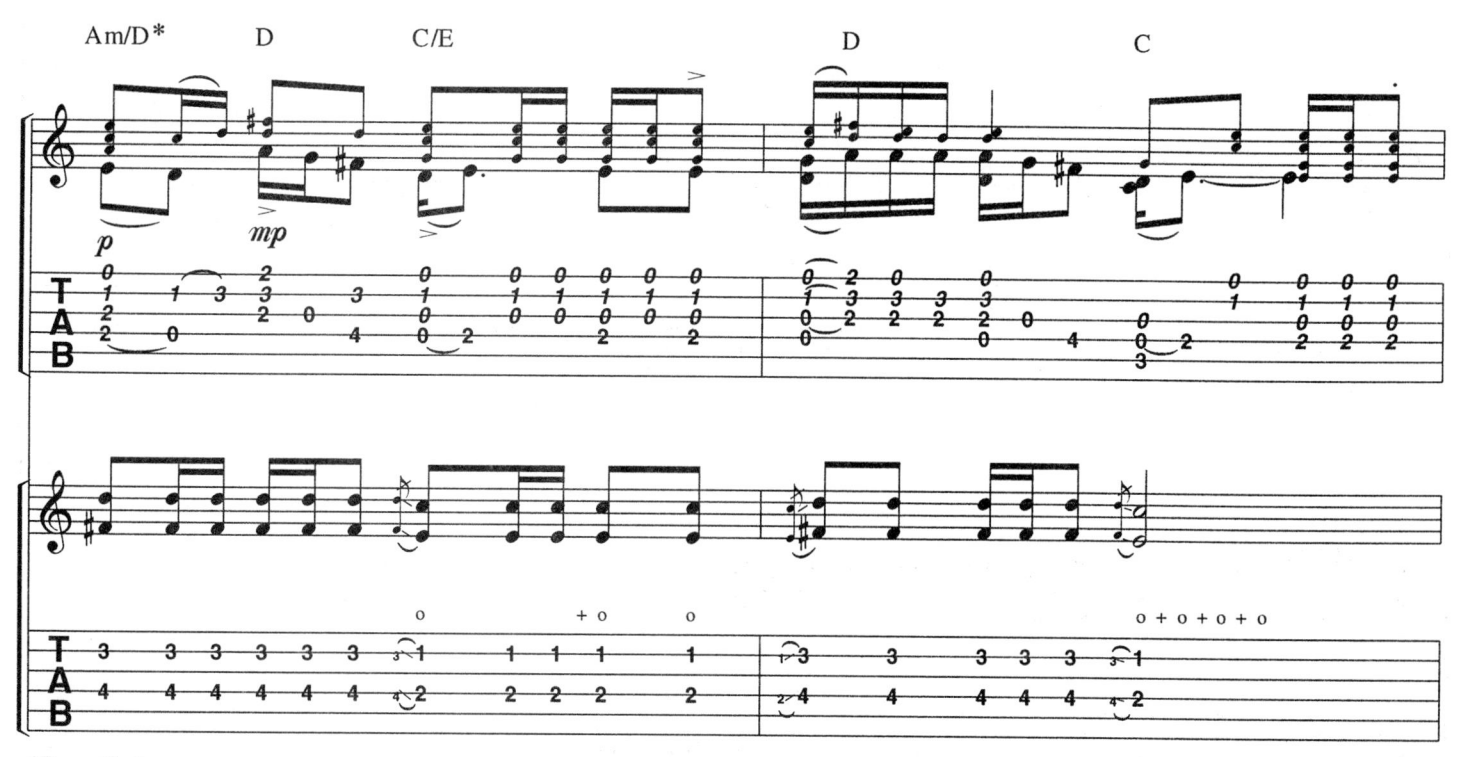

*Bass Guitar note.

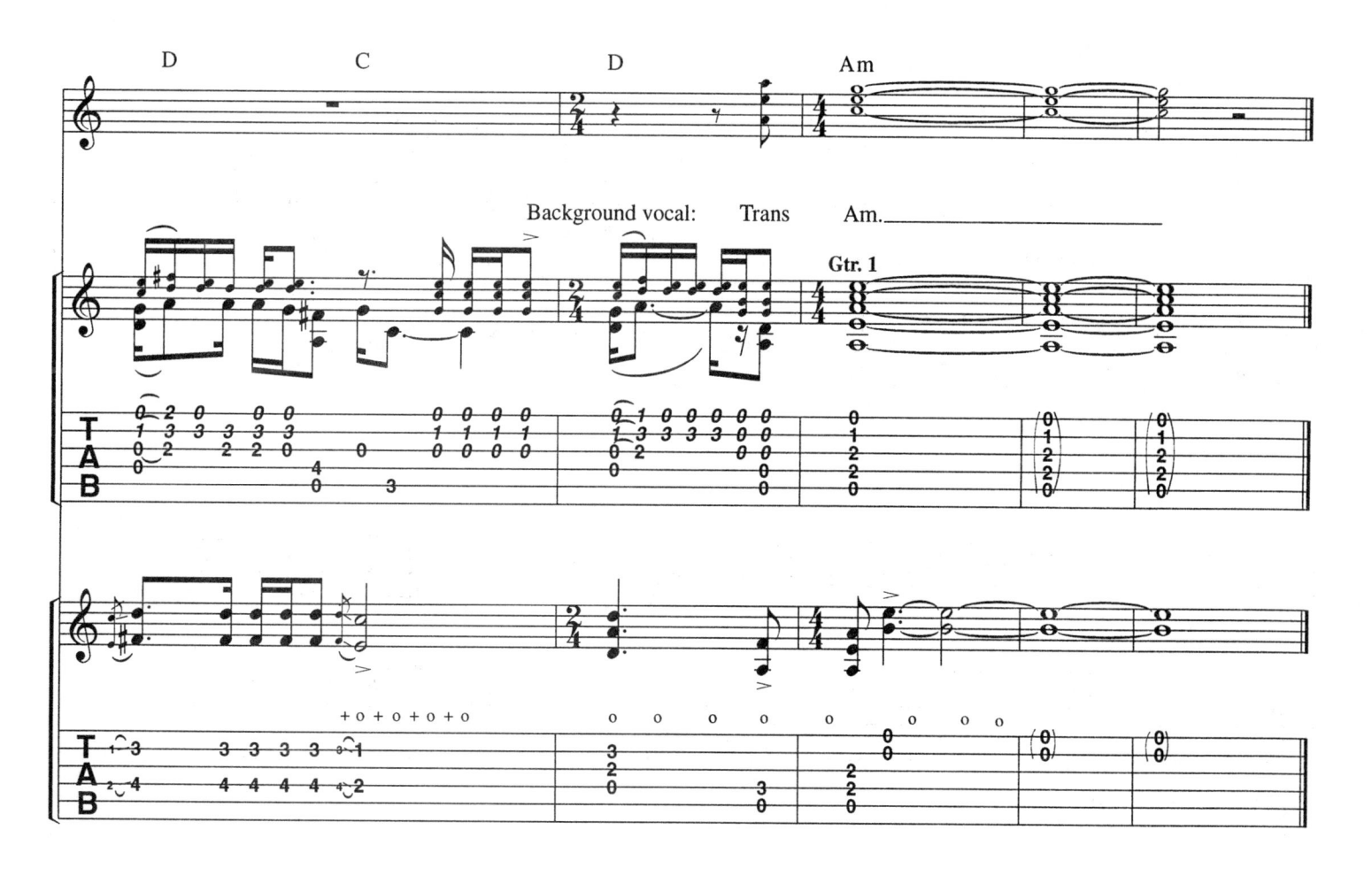

Trans Am - 17 - 17

PIECE OF CRAP

Words and Music by
NEIL YOUNG

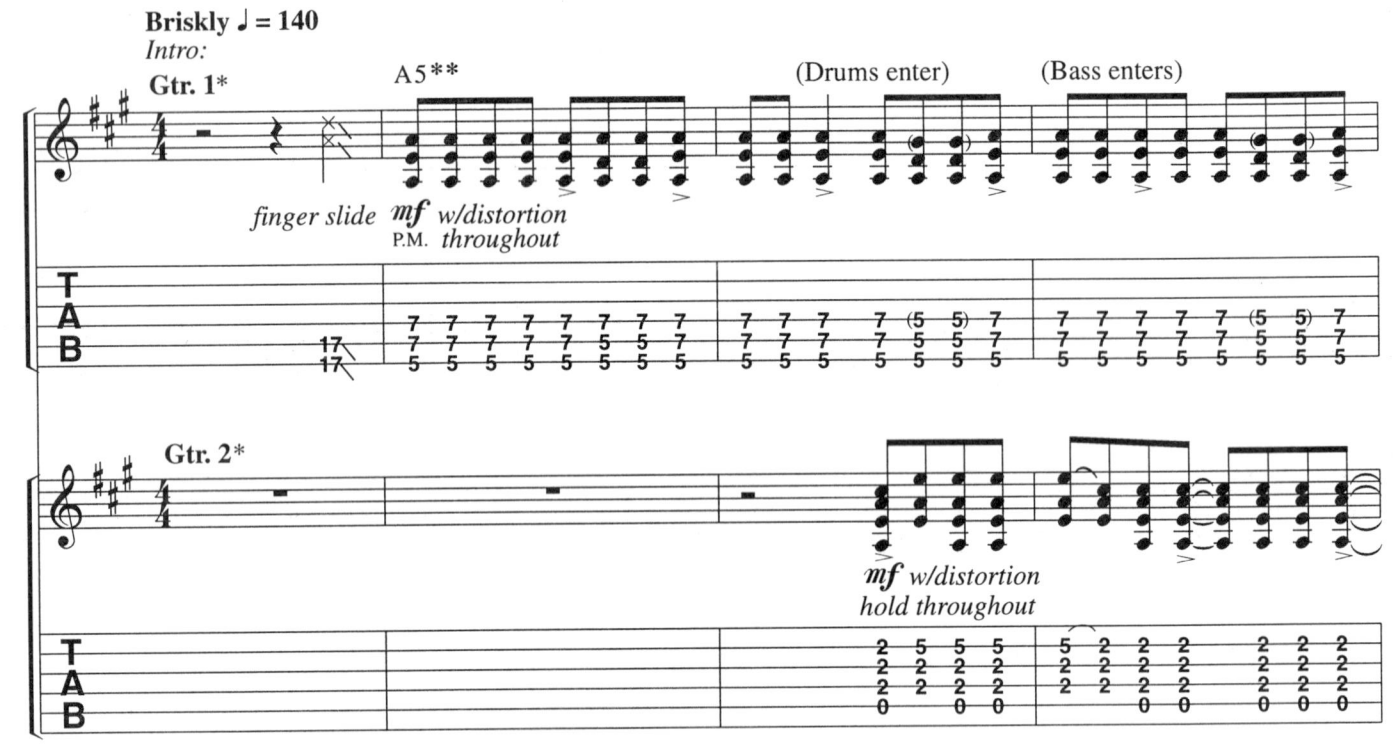

* Electric Gtrs. - Gtr. 1 (R.&L. channel), Gtr. 2 (L. Channel). Both Gtrs. Les Pauls.
** Although written as A5, an A chord is fingered. The higher notes (③ vi and ② v) are brushed by the palm throughout the strum.

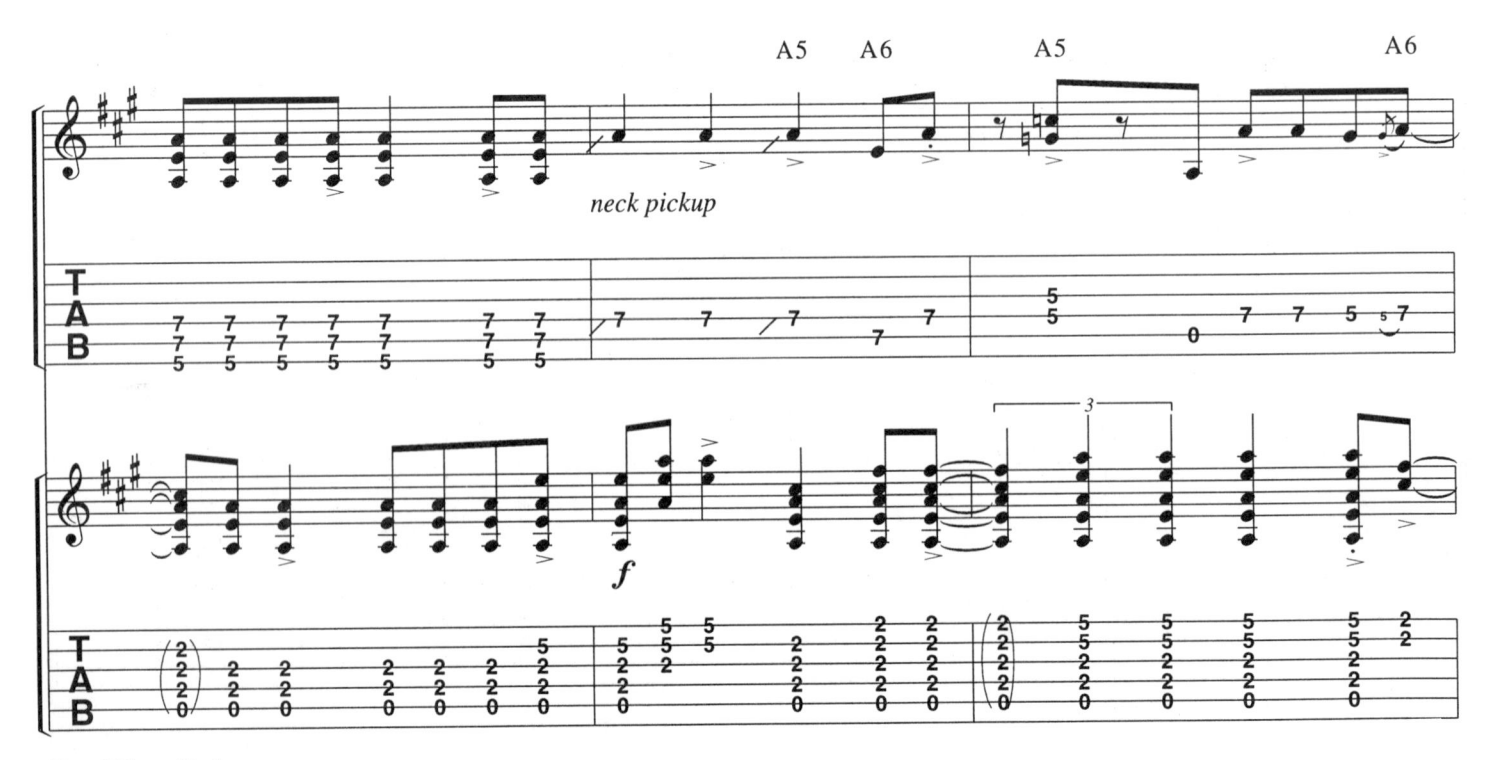

© 1994 SILVER FIDDLE MUSIC (ASCAP)
All Rights Reserved

*With slight flanging effect from this point on.

Verse:

to save the trees, bought a plas-tic bag, the bot-tom fell out, It was a piece of crap.

Background vocals: Piece of crap!
(shouted)

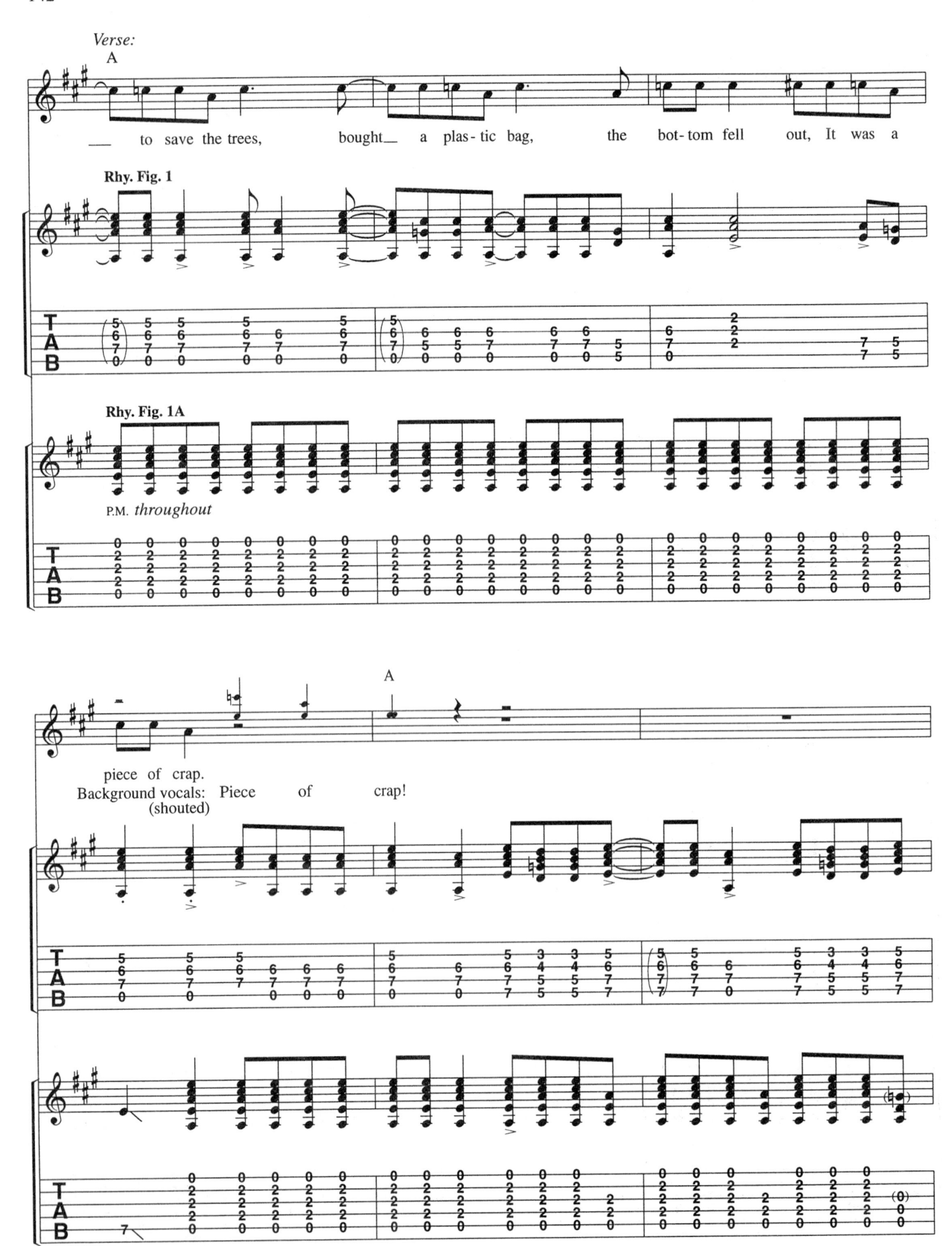

Rhy. Fig. 1

Rhy. Fig. 1A

P.M. *throughout*

Piece of Crap - 14 - 3
PG9502

Saw__ it on the tube, bought__ it on the phone, now__ your home a-lone with a piece of crap. Background vocals: Piece of (shouted)

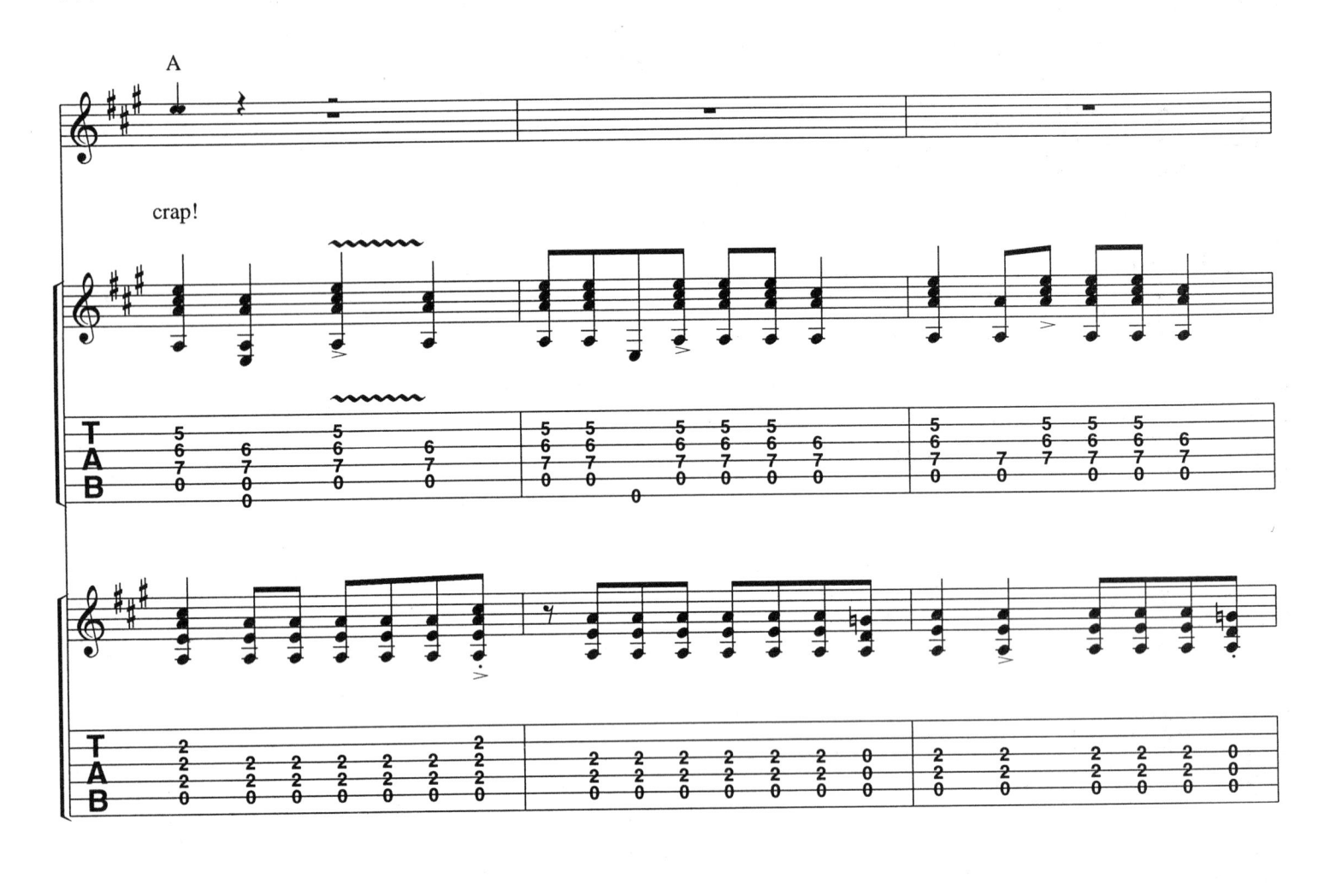

Piece of Crap - 14 - 5

145

When I got it home it was a piece of crap.
Background vocals: Piece of crap!
(shouted)

Piece of crap!

end Rhy. Fig. 2

flanger off

end Rhy. Fig. 2a

w/o P.M.

Piece of Crap - 14 - 6
PG9502

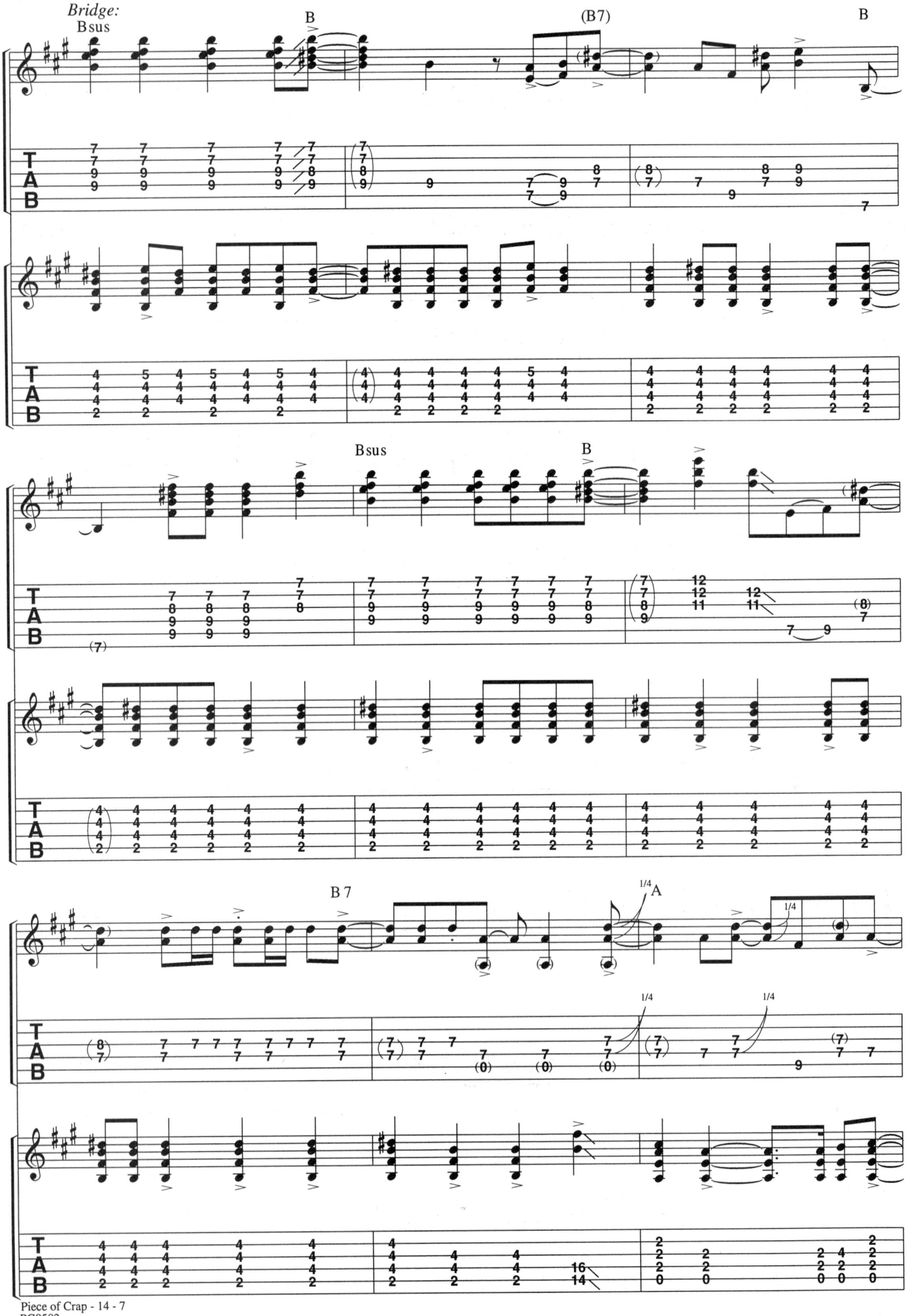
Bridge:
Bsus
B
(B7)
B
Bsus
B
B 7
A
1/4

147

Verse:
w/Rhy. Figs. 1 & 1a *simile (Gtrs. 1 & 2)*

Got it from a friend, on him (you) can depend. I found out in the end, it was a piece of crap.
Background vocals: Piece of crap! (shouted)

I'm trying to save the trees, I saw it on TV They cut the forest down, to build a piece of crap.
Background vocals: Piece of crap! (shouted)

Piece of Crap - 14 - 8
PG9502

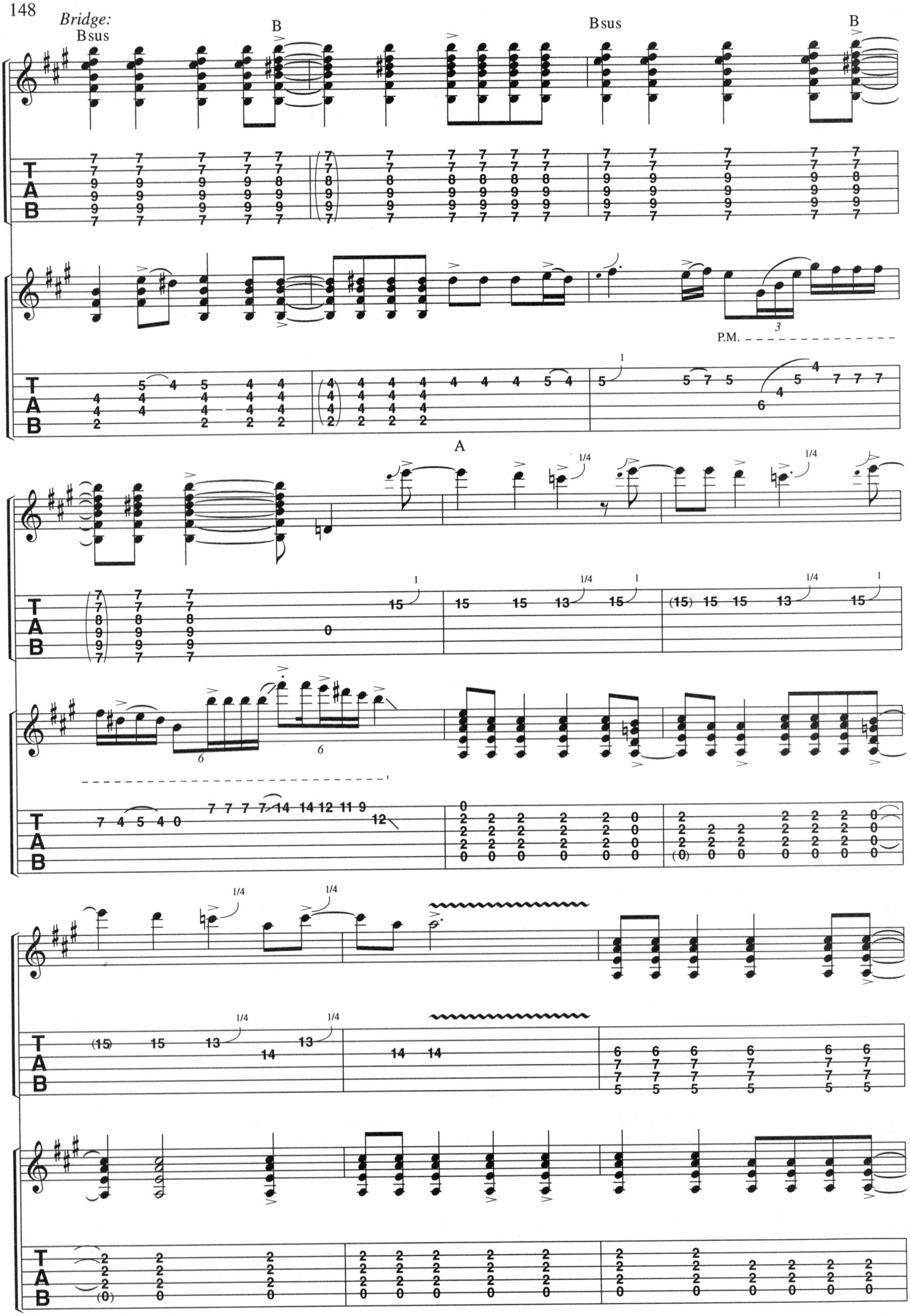
Bridge:
Bsus
B
Bsus
B
P.M.
A

149

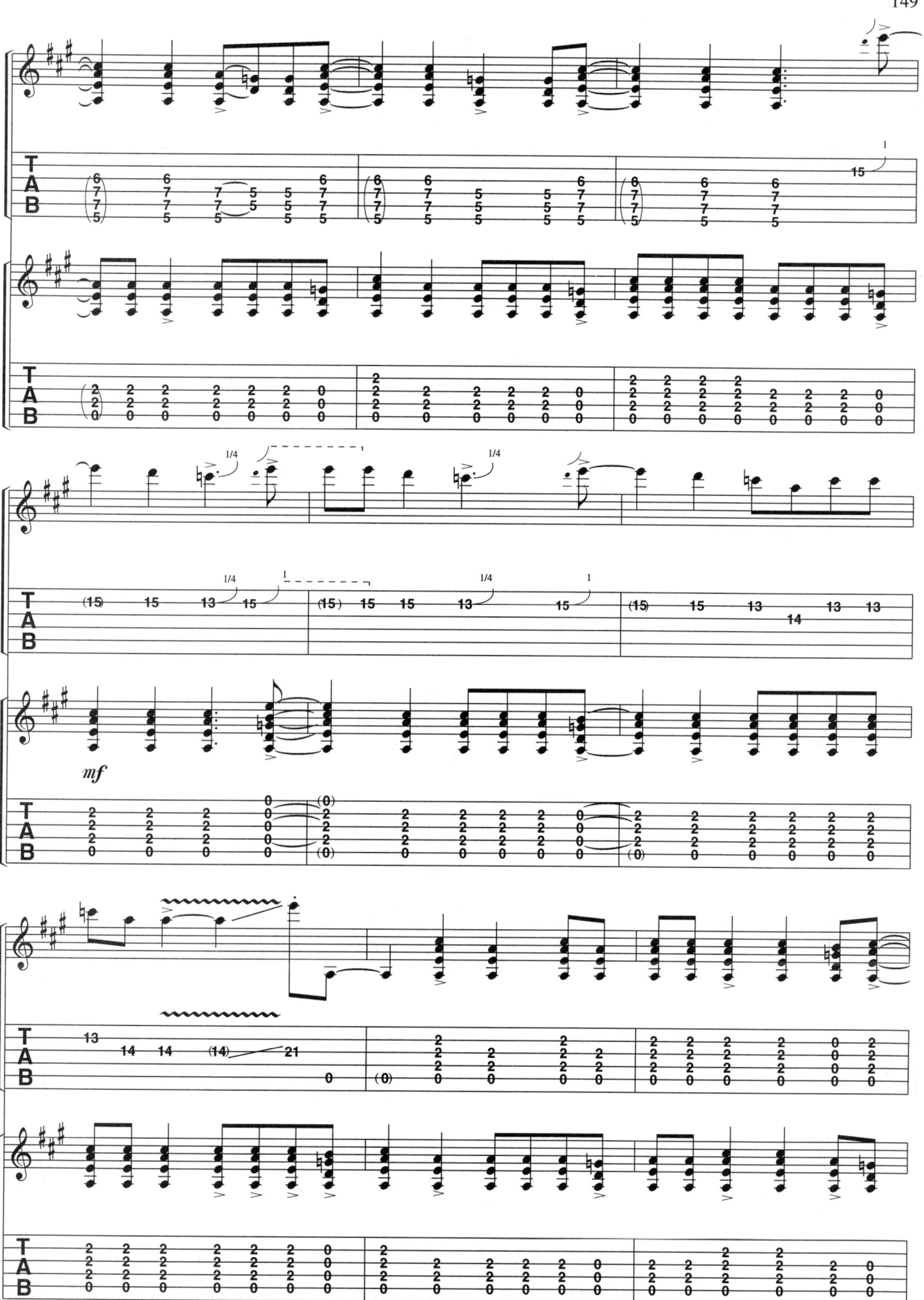

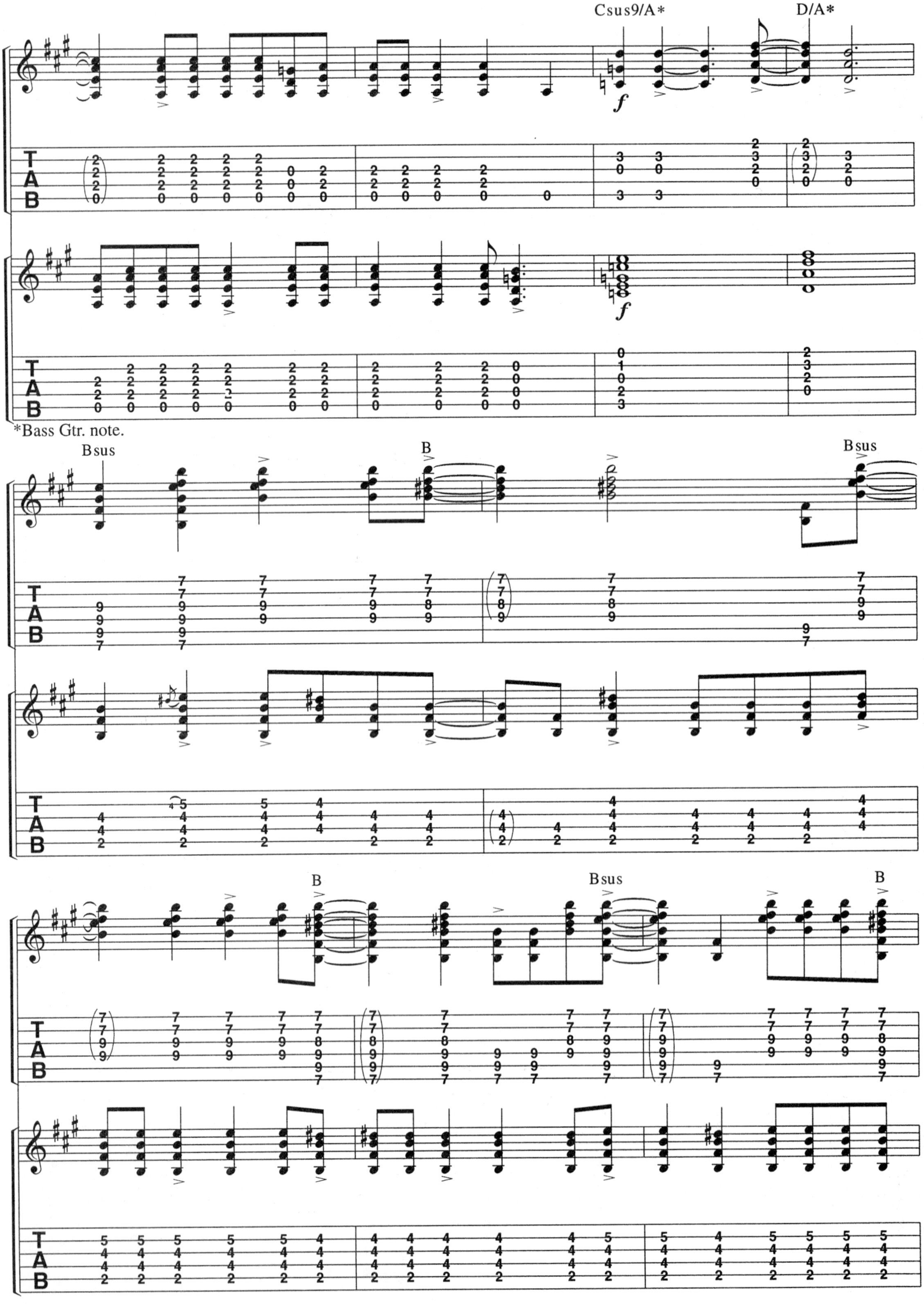
Csus9/A*
D/A*
*Bass Gtr. note.
Bsus
B
Bsus
B
Bsus
B

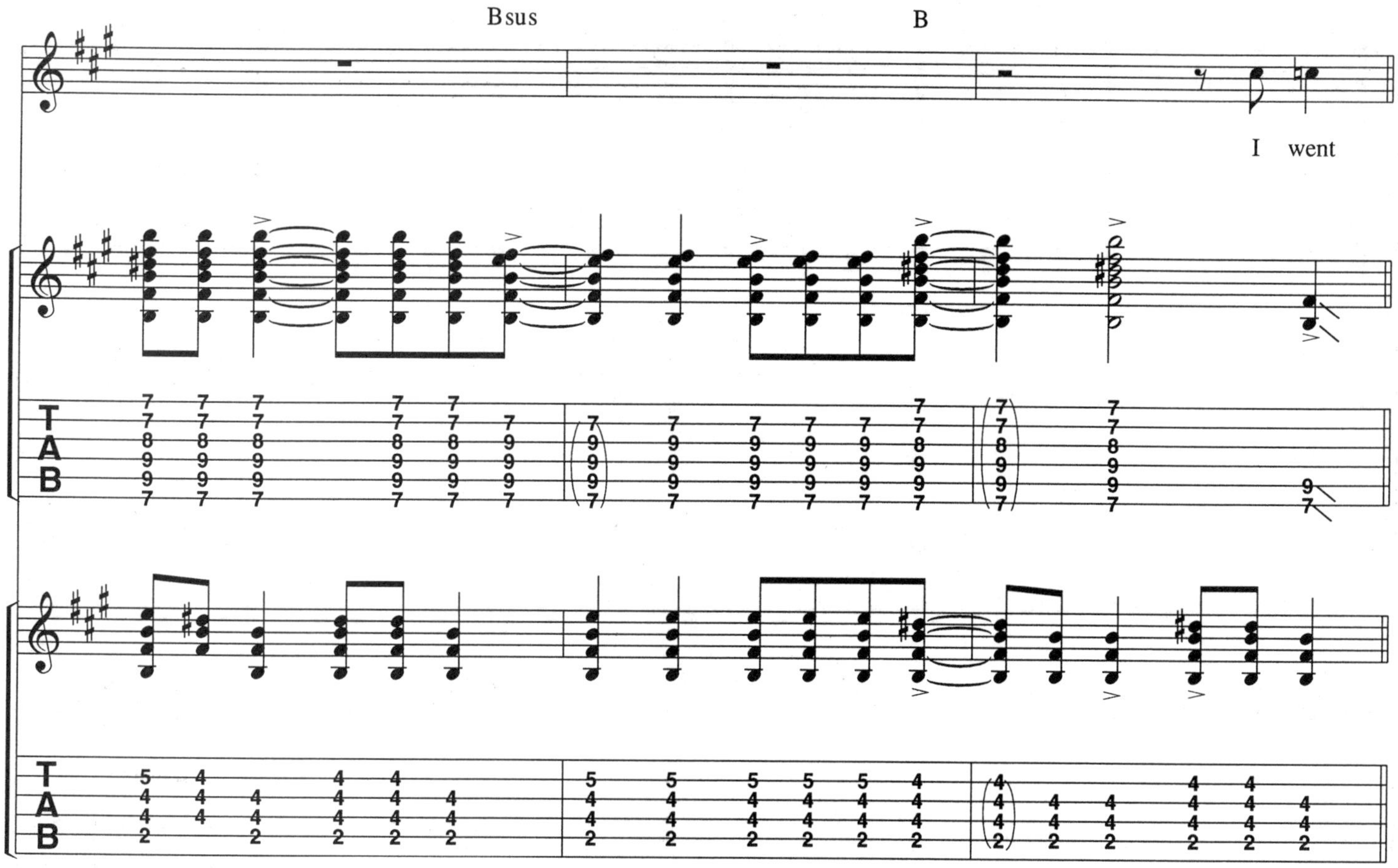
Bsus
B
I went
TAB
TAB

Verse:
A
back to the store;_ they gave___ me four more. The guy told me at the door, "It's a
mf
TAB
mf
P.M. throughout
TAB

piece of crap."
Background vocals: Piece of crap!
(shouted)

Background vocals: A piece of crap!
(shouted)

w/o P.M.

Piece of Crap - 14 - 14
PG9502

A DREAM THAT CAN LAST

Words and Music by
NEIL YOUNG

"Drop D" tuning, down 1 whole step:
- ⑥ = C   ③ = F
- ⑤ = G   ② = A
- ④ = C   ① = D

*Acoustic tack piano arranged for gtr. (sounds one whole step lower than written).

A Dream That Can Last - 5 - 1
PG9502

© 1994 SILVER FIDDLE MUSIC (ASCAP)
All Rights Reserved

Verse:

I feel like I died and went to heav-en.

The

A Dream That Can Last - 5 - 2
PG9502

Verse:

cup-boards— are bare—— but the streets are paved—— with gold.—

1. I saw a
2. And all the

To next strain | **3.** *To Coda* (Harmonica enters)

Freely (♩ = 80)

Chorus:

young girl who did-n't die. I saw a glim-mer from in her

(2.) *See additional lyrics*

D
F♯m
Bm/F♯
1. G/B
Lead vocal: I saw the dis-tance. I saw the past. And I know I won't a-wak-en, it's a
eye
A7
D.S. 𝄋 al Coda
a tempo
2. G
A7
D.S.S. 𝄋𝄋 al Coda
a tempo
dream that can last.
bet-ter life for me some - day.
Outro:
(Harmonica Solo: 8 bars, both times)
Coda
D
A
G
A
A7

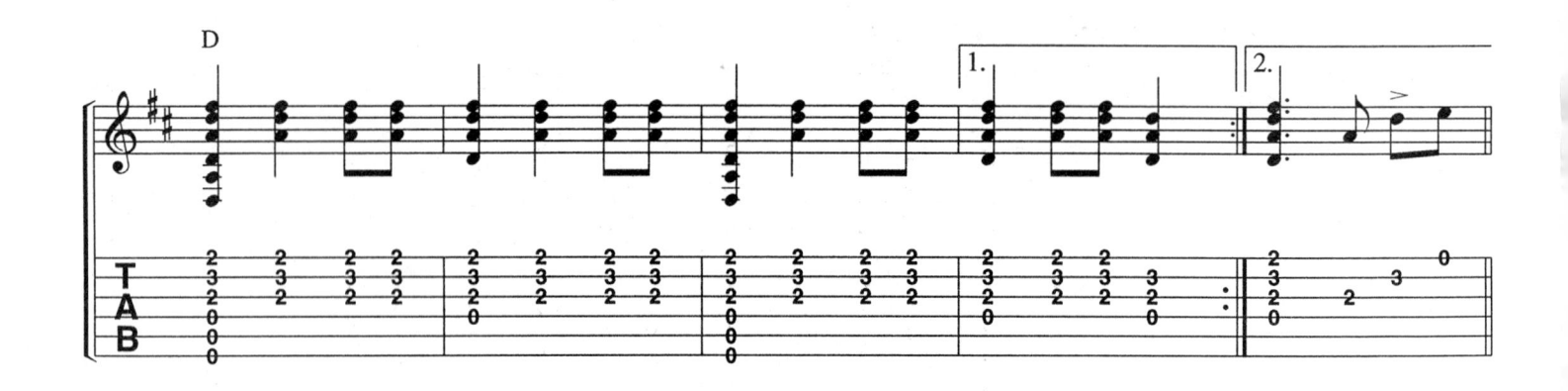

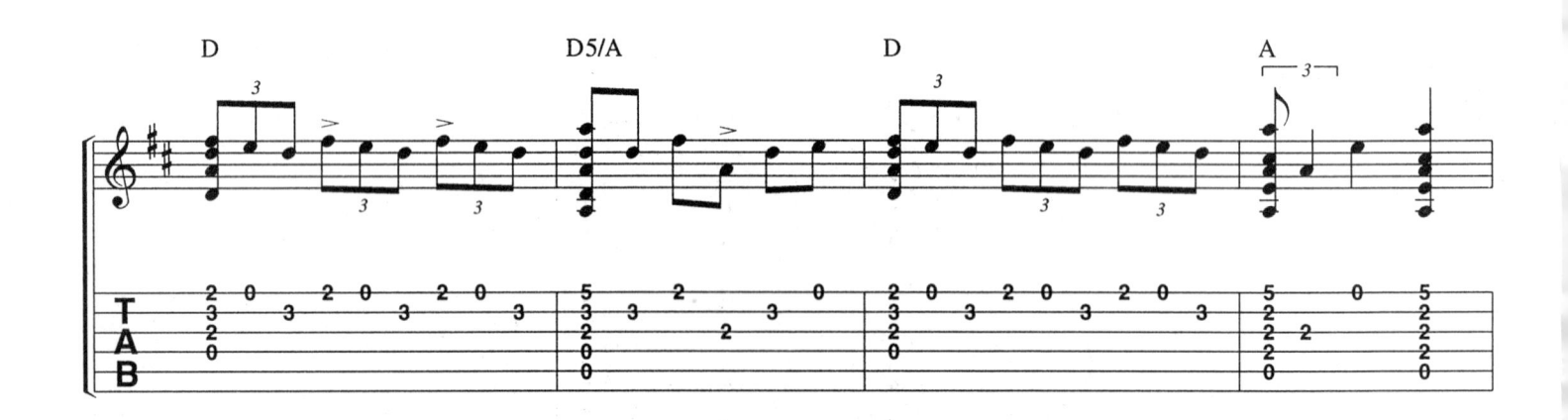

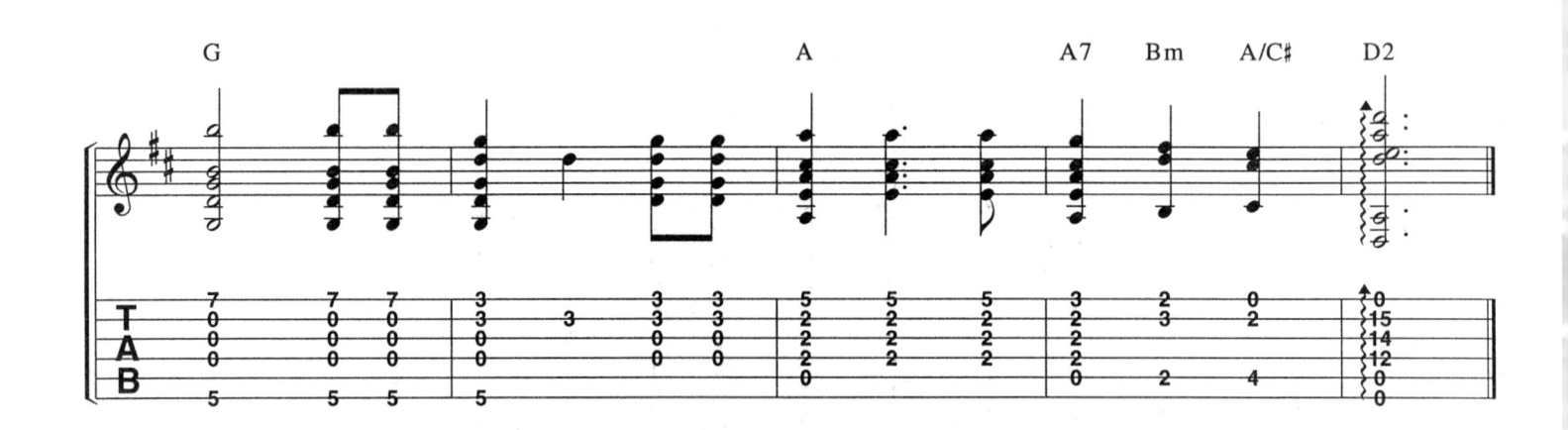

Chorus 2:
And all the lights were turned down low
And no one wondered or had to go.
Out on the corner the angels say
There is a better life for me someday.

GUITAR TAB GLOSSARY **

TABLATURE EXPLANATION

READING TABLATURE: Tablature illustrates the six strings of the guitar. Notes and chords are indicated by the placement of fret numbers on a given string(s).

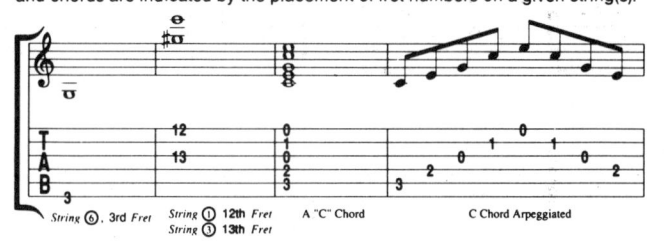

String ⑥, 3rd Fret
String ①, 12th Fret
String ①, 13th Fret
A "C" Chord
C Chord Arpeggiated

BENDING NOTES

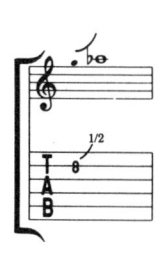

HALF STEP: Play the note and bend string one half step.*

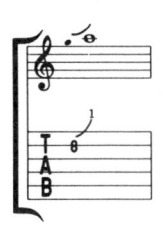

WHOLE STEP: Play the note and bend string one whole step.

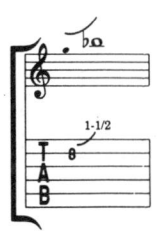

WHOLE STEP AND A HALF: Play the note and bend string a whole step and a half.

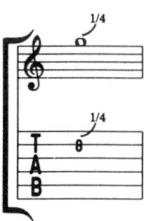

SLIGHT BEND (Microtone): Play the note and bend string slightly to the equivalent of half a fret.

PREBEND (Ghost Bend): Bend to the specified note, before the string is picked.

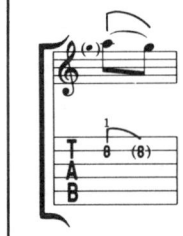

PREBEND AND RELEASE: Bend the string, play it, then release to the original note.

REVERSE BEND: Play the already-bent string, then immediately drop it down to the fretted note.

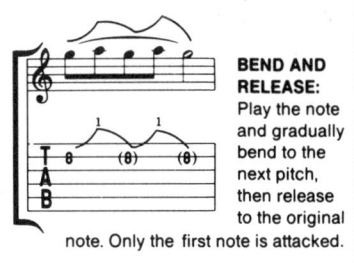

BEND AND RELEASE: Play the note and gradually bend to the next pitch, then release to the original note. Only the first note is attacked.

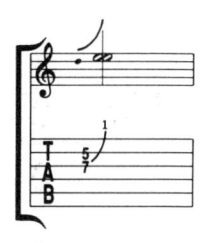

*A half step is the smallest interval in Western music; it is equal to one fret. A whole step equals two frets.

UNISON BEND: Play both notes and immediately bend the lower note to the same pitch as the higher note.

DOUBLE NOTE BEND: Play both notes and immediately bend both strings simultaneously.

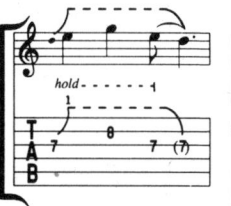

BENDS INVOLVING MORE THAN ONE STRING: Play the note and bend string while playing an additional note (or notes) on another string(s). Upon release, relieve pressure from additional note(s), causing original note to sound alone.

BENDS INVOLVING STATIONARY NOTES: Play notes and bend lower pitch, then hold until release begins (indicated at the point where line becomes solid).

TREMOLO BAR

SPECIFIED INTERVAL: The pitch of a note or chord is lowered to a specified interval and then may or may not return to the original pitch. The activity of the tremolo bar is graphically represented by peaks and valleys.

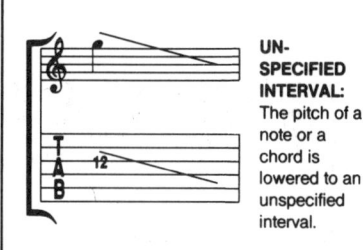

UN-SPECIFIED INTERVAL: The pitch of a note or a chord is lowered to an unspecified interval.

HARMONICS

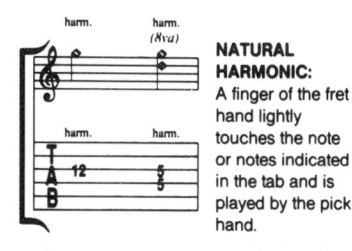

NATURAL HARMONIC: A finger of the fret hand lightly touches the note or notes indicated in the tab and is played by the pick hand.

ARTIFICIAL HARMONIC: The first tab number is fretted, then the pick hand produces the harmonic by using a finger to lightly touch the same string at the second tab number (in parenthesis) and is then picked by another finger.

ARTIFICIAL "PINCH" HARMONIC: A note is fretted as indicated by the tab, then the pick hand produces the harmonic by squeezing the pick firmly while using the tip of the index finger in the pick attack. If parenthesis are found around the fretted note, it does not sound. No parenthesis means both the fretted note and A.H. are heard simultaneously.

© 1990 Beam Me Up Music
c/o CPP/Belwin, Inc. Miami, Florida 33014
International Copyright Secured   Made in U.S.A.   All Rights Reserved

**By Kenn Chipkin and Aaron Stang

RHYTHM SLASHES

STRUM INDICATIONS: Strum with indicated rhythm. The chord voicings are found on the first page of the transcription underneath the song title.

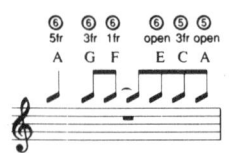

INDICATING SINGLE NOTES USING RHYTHM SLASHES: Very often single notes are incorporated into a rhythm part. The note name is indicated above the rhythm slash with a fret number and a string indication.

ARTICULATIONS

HAMMER ON: Play lower note, then "hammer on" to higher note with another finger. Only the first note is attacked.

LEFT HAND HAMMER: Hammer on the first note played on each string with the left hand.

PULL OFF: Play higher note, then "pull off" to lower note with another finger. Only the first note is attacked.

FRETBOARD TAPPING: "Tap" onto the note indicated by + with a finger of the pick hand, then pull off to the following note held by the fret hand.

TAP SLIDE: Same as fretboard tapping, but the tapped note is slid randomly up the fretboard, then pulled off to the following note.

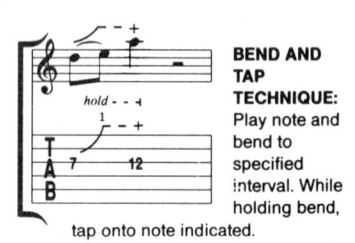

BEND AND TAP TECHNIQUE: Play note and bend to specified interval. While holding bend, tap onto note indicated.

LEGATO SLIDE: Play note and slide to the following note. (Only first note is attacked).

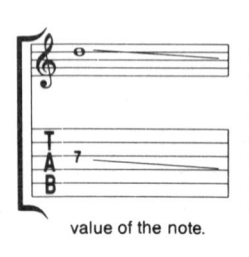

LONG GLISSANDO: Play note and slide in specified direction for the full value of the note.

SHORT GLISSANDO: Play note for its full value and slide in specified direction at the last possible moment.

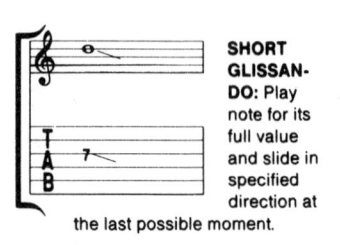

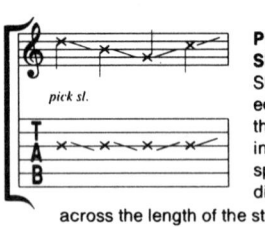

PICK SLIDE: Slide the edge of the pick in specified direction across the length of the string(s).

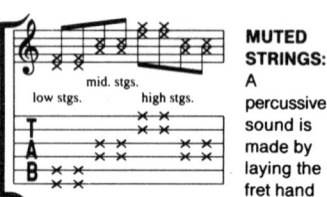

MUTED STRINGS: A percussive sound is made by laying the fret hand across all six strings while pick hand strikes specified area (low, mid, high strings).

PALM MUTE: The note or notes are muted by the palm of the pick hand by lightly touching the string(s) near the bridge.

TREMOLO PICKING: The note or notes are picked as fast as possible.

TRILL: Hammer on and pull off consecutively and as fast as possible between the original note and the grace note.

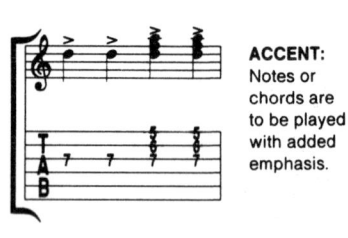

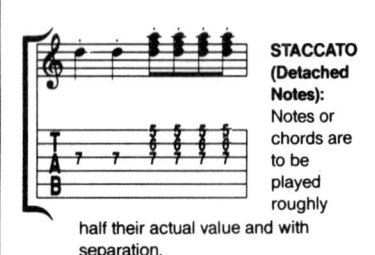

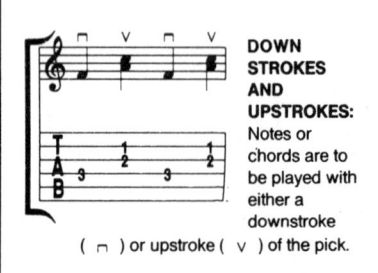

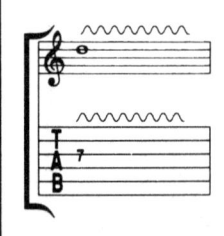

ACCENT: Notes or chords are to be played with added emphasis.

STACCATO (Detached Notes): Notes or chords are to be played roughly half their actual value and with separation.

DOWN STROKES AND UPSTROKES: Notes or chords are to be played with either a downstroke (⊓) or upstroke (v) of the pick.

VIBRATO: The pitch of a note is varied by a rapid shaking of the fret hand finger, wrist, and forearm.